SWITCHBACKS

BOOKS BY SID MARTY

NON-FICTION
Men for the Mountains (1978)
A Grand and Fabulous Notion (1984)
Leaning on the Wind (1995)
Switchbacks (1999)

POETRY
Headwaters (1973)
Nobody Danced with Miss Rodeo (1981)
Sky Humour (1999)

SWITCHBACKS

TRUE STORIES FROM
THE CANADIAN ROCKIES

SID MARTY

M&S

Canadian Cataloguing in Publication Data

Marty, Sid, 1944 –
　　Switchbacks: true stories from the Canadian Rockies

ISBN 0-7710-5669-9

1. Marty, Sid, 1944 –　– Homes and haunts – Rocky Mountains, Canadian (B.C. and Alta.).　2. Authors, Canadian (English) – 20th century – Biography.* I. Title.

PS8576.A795S94　1999　　c818'.5409　　C99-931861-6
PR9199.M39S94　1999

We acknowledge the financial support of the Government of Canada through the Book Publishing Industry Development Program for our publishing activities. Canada

We further acknowledge the support of the Canada Council for the Arts and the Ontario Arts Council for our publishing program.

Typeset in Garamond
Typesetting by Laura Brady
Printed and bound in Canada

McClelland & Stewart Inc.
The Canadian Publishers
481 University Avenue
Toronto, Ontario
M5G 2E9

2　3　4　5　　03　02　01　00

For Myrna and in memory of Keith Everts

Once you find a pace that works for you, it will work for your whole life.

– Ernest Feuz, Swiss guide

Contents

Acknowledgements

A number of mountain people helped to strengthen this book by answering innumerable questions about their experiences and by comparing their memories of events with my own. Their names appear in the text and I thank them for their help.

Among the many national-park wardens consulted, some were asked for much more of their time than others. Tim Auger brought me back to speed on many technical aspects of mountaineering and mountain rescue, and offered insights on the history of mountaineering in the Rockies. Don Mickle helped me track down a number of retired park wardens I needed to interview; Rob Watt provided information on obscure old-time wardens long since deceased.

Retired warden Lance Cooper and retired warden dispatcher Moe Vroom remembered the search for a missing warden. The late Bill Vroom told me about the rescues on Mount Babel and 3–3 ½ Couloir. Jim Davies and Monte Rose offered insights into their role in the 3–3 ½ Couloir rescue and recalled their experiences in the bear-moving business. Brian Colgan and Danny Verrall offered

insights into Neil Colgan's personality. Mountaineers Brian Green-
wood and Charlie Locke described their ambitious attempt on
Mount Babel so long ago. Mountain guides Bernie Schiesser, Don
Vockeroth, and Vitus Germann cast their thoughts back in time to
abet my own memory. Peter Fuhrmann brought the young guide
Heinz Kahl back into focus for me.

Retired parks official Jim Sime patiently answered questions
about mountain-rescue expert Walter Perren. Peter Perren recently
augmented that account. Similarly, Sid Feuz helped me to sort out
the record on the careers of Edward, Ernest, and Walter Feuz, Swiss
guides. William Cherak offered his insights and memories of the life
of amateur guide Lawrence Grassi, and this understanding was
supplemented by reference to the book by Don Beers, *Banff –
Assiniboine: A Beautiful World* and the unpublished manuscript
Mountain Climbing Guides in Canada by Alison Griffiths and Gerry
Wingenback, found in the Whyte Museum of the Canadian Rockies
Archives. Archivists Lena Goom, Mary Andrews, and Don Bourdon
speeded my researches at the Whyte Museum. Edward Feuz's story
about "the black bear and the little kid" is found in collection
S23 1-13 of the *Yoho National Park Human History Study*. Beverly
Kemsley shared her memories of her father, Wilfred Etherington,
and granted permission to quote briefly from his field notebook. Bill
Schmalz, Laszlo Retfalvi, and Jim Davies talked candidly about a
painful episode in the history of grizzly-bear management, and have
helped immeasurably in setting the record straight.

The quotations from "Tragedy on Mount Victoria" by Harry
Green, *Canadian Alpine Journal*, 1955, are used with permission of
the Alpine Club of Canada. The following stories have been previ-
ously published, in slightly different form: "The Rucksack" in *Fresh
Tracks: Writing the Western Landscape*, edited by Pamela Banting
(Polestar, 1998); "The Dude, the Warden, and the Marvel Lake Kid"
in *Calgary Magazine* (1979); and "A Horse Named Candy" in
Reader's Digest magazine (December, 1997).

Editor Jonathan Webb kept me encouraged and forging on as deadlines loomed; Lisan Jutras made the copy-editing process seem pleasant. Thank you to Rick and Eleanor of Eleanor's House and to Charles Noble for the kind hospitality in Banff.

Happy trails to all of you; may we meet and swap stories again soon on a Rocky Mountain switchback.

CHAPTER ONE

The Rucksack

My first rucksack hangs on the wall in this brooding-pen, or study. It doesn't look like much any more. It was built for abuse and got more than its share. It's been dragged up cliff faces with a climbing rope passed through its steel haul ring. It's fallen down a few couloirs, been tossed out of helicopters, gotten washed down the Panther River in Banff National Park one time and found a day later – everything inside soaked and covered in sand. It's been run over by a truck, staled on by a pack horse, and burnt by battery acid the time I rolled a Volkswagen Beetle and came within centimetres of killing myself.

The holes in that pack remind me of something I can't afford to forget.

It served as a pillow under my head more times than I'll ever remember; on the other hand (or end), I've stuck my legs, climbing boots and all, inside it and pulled the bivouac packing up as high as I could, to sit out a storm. Saw the clouds clear off and watched the moon come up on the glacier down below, keeping my feet warm inside that old pack and reflecting on the virtues of the watch and compass.

Bloodstains on the canvas remind me of the day a friend peeled off a scaly headwall on Mount Huber near Lake Louise and went tumbling down a glacier at bone-cracking speed. It served as a cushion while we splinted and bandaged his leg. It served as a pad under his bruised behind as I carried him down the mountain on my back in a makeshift rope-seat. The pack reminds me of the days when I was strong enough and bold enough to do things like that.

I've shaken fat ground squirrels full of salami sandwiches out of the old pack, scared nesting mice out of its grimy depths, rescued it from a salt-hungry porcupine, and left it as a peace offering to an aggressive black bear.

I wish I had them lined up in front of me now, the bottles of wine, brandy, and rum, the cans of beer that I've carried in that old sack from one snow cave, or tent, or alpine hut, to another. I wish I had the silver bounties of rainbow and cutthroat trout hauled in that thing from cloud-hung lakes.

Everything from bighorn sheep pellets to literary works have found temporary placement there; Leonard Cohen's *The Spice-Box of Earth* graced its weathered interior in my salad days, but harder times found it redolent with fresh elk liver carried home in an autumn snowstorm. Once it stood duty as an instrument case, when Andy Suknaski and I took our mandolins down to Deer Lodge at Lake Louise to try and impress the girls.

A pack like that just grows to fit your body. No fancy braces or webbing. Just an extra sweater or vest jammed down inside to protect your back. What mattered was that every time you strapped it on, you were going outside to do something you wanted to do. You were reminding yourself of something every wanderer knows, that everything you need to survive can be carried on your own back.

Once it had a trademark: a mountaineer with a pipe in his mouth, climbing with true Gallic arrogance and *savoir faire*. It's made of heavy duck canvas with a thick leather bottom that won't wear out in this lifetime, and leather straps of a quality that is hard to find now.

I bought the pack when I was seventeen, and a boatman-cum-dishwasher at Lake O'Hara Lodge in Yoho National Park. I chose that model because Heinz Kahl, a big, dark-haired mountain guide with a friendly grin who guided out of the lodge, had one like it. He was one of the gods then bestriding the mountains like a colossus, but he always had time to teach greenhorns a few tricks of the trade. Poor Heinz died while still a young man.

The mountains didn't kill Heinz in the prime of his life. Leukemia, that giant-slayer, did that, and whenever I look at the pack, I remember him and I see his face glowing with strength and happiness. I see the faces of so many who were young, full of confidence and quick with life.

I can't use it any longer; it's too full of holes and memories.

But I can't stand the new ones of neon-coloured nylon that smack of the look-at-me age we live in now. I'll probably wind up hiring somebody to replace the canvas and restore the poor old rag to life. It seems like the least I can do, somehow, in keeping faith with that boy back there, on the shore at Lake O'Hara, looking up at the first of his mountains with the smell of larches in his nostrils, and saying to himself, "I'm going to climb that peak at the end of the valley," thinking, in his innocence, rightly as it turned out, that if you could do that you would learn something about life and about yourself that could be found no other way.

CHAPTER TWO

The Dude, the Warden, and the Marvel Lake Kid

I found my old rucksack in the workshop this morning, hanging in the dark corner on a wooden peg under some old horse collars and a frayed lariat, covered with dust. It's been neglected for a long time. I've been using a more modern version left behind by one of Nathan's friends on a visit. Somehow the friend never bothered to pick it up on his visits since, and it has become mine by default, though I've been planning all along to take my old pack to a neighbour woman who is a skilled leather worker and have it repaired.

I throw it over one shoulder, determined to take it into the house so I won't forget it, but the smell of the autumn woods comes to me as I step out the door, luring me into the poplar forest that grows up against our west fences.

Often before the autumn equinox, when summer seems hot enough to outlast September, a cold front sweeps down through the front ranges north of the Crowsnest Pass and we wake to find ourselves propelled into the middle of December, with the aspen limbs and the honeysuckle boughs bending low under the weight of several inches of wet snow. My sudden appearance in the wet woods startles our horses, Tasha and Candy, and they take to their heels with loud snorts, knocking down a crescendo of snow from the poplar trees in their passage.

How strange it is to walk out among the aspens and see my sons' swimming trunks, wet from yesterday's summer outing in the Oldman River, hanging on the clothesline now in the frigid clasp of this instant winter. But "if you don't like the weather," an old Westernism goes, "wait for an hour and it will change." Nowhere is this more true than here in the southwest angle of Alberta at the mountainfoot. The sun soon burns a hole through the overcast, and the eavestroughs that were full of snow at 8 A.M. are running full of meltwater by noon.

I smell the sweetness of wet aspen leaves, the good, damp rot of branch and stem among the yellow brome grass and the wilted raspberry canes. And with that old familiar scent, my present life settles on my shoulders with a leaden insistence. Fingering the leather pack-straps as I did so many times on distant mountains, I gaze up where Centre Peak shines in the crystallized air. An amber glow suffuses the ridges of these home hills, and eastward the distant Porcupine Hills, seen through leagues of moist, cold air, ripple and move their backs in mirages above the tawny sweep of stubble fields.

The air is still; this is the time of year when the wind goes to sleep, and though its sleep is fitful, though it may come sleepwalking up the valley at any time, often it will not really wake up until the end of October. So I love this September snow, because it will be followed by an Indian summer, a month of warm, clear days and sparkling cool nights.

As the comedians put it – it's good to be here, folks. But then it's good to be anywhere. Yet there is nowhere on earth I would rather be – just for this enchanted month – than on horseback, among the peaks and high up somewhere in the backcountry of Banff Park or Jasper, now that the flies and the tourists are gone. Standing here at the mountainfoot in this silence, I have heard a rutting bull elk bugling from the ridge above the house, a sound that never fails to stir the hair on my neck. It takes me back to backcountry days in the warden service, patrolling on the Snake Indian River, the Panther, the Red Deer. I pause by the woodpile and stare down at the woodchips left by my splitting hammer, and I see a thousand remembered details of stream crossings, traverses over avalanche slopes, fallen logs I had to jump the horse over. Trails unwind before me, sometimes a metre at a time, so well did I learn them, so much are they a part of me, so much was I a part of those places when I was their guardian. The feel of that old pack has me yearning for the headwaters where the rivers begin, where everything is energized and urgent with the need to complete the cycle before this long curtain of white comes down on the season.

Myrna looks at me and sighs sympathetically as I enter the kitchen, seeing the pack in my hand and the old longing in my eyes. She understands the longing; she has travelled with me through most of that country and loved it as much as I did. But she is a person who lives wholly and completely wherever she is: once she gives her heart to a place she lives in it like a bear lives on her mountain, or a doe in her home grove. As for me, part of me is still riding somewhere else, part of me will always belong to the outfit, the warden service – at least the warden service of days gone by. I resigned from it in 1978; I walked back into it in 1988 for six months, and if I walked back into it tomorrow, in some ways it would be as if I had never left. The warden service is a way of life, and that way of life continues within me though I long ago tossed my badge on my supervisor's desk.

I stare out the window at these ridges, and I see the ridges over the Panther where a she-wolf dens every year. I see her tracks when I look at Mojo's track in this melting snow. And that rider, coming down the fenceline: if I didn't know who he was, I'd say he was young Neil Colgan riding again on the Panther River. The sight of that rider takes me back to 1978, to the last time I saw Neil, the last trip I made before I tried, and failed once again and for the last time, to come to terms with a political system hell-bent on the urbanization of Canada's first national park.

The rider leans down and flips open the gate latch. He is young and active, easy in his seat. Our mares Candy and Tasha whinny a greeting from the corral and come running to greet the stranger's horse. He is just riding through here, checking fence for my neighbour. He waves a greeting and I bid him good morning. I look back up the valley he rode down, and my mind is back on the Panther River, and it is September, 1978.

Horses crowded together at the hitching rail on a cold afternoon, and rustled the yellow aspen leaves with their heavy shod feet. Picking up the curry comb, I squeezed between them, enveloped at once in their animal heat, a familiar, well-known pleasure passing through my chilled skin. They pressed together slightly before giving me room.

I always think of that as a joke horses have, since they could suffocate me easily enough that way if the notion ever took them. I bent to brush the caked mud from their legs, and they bent their heads to watch me do it; their warm breath swept over the back of my neck. Already their hair had grown long, and winter still a month and a half away.

The weight of our saddles, the bags being full, had made the horses suspicious. From time to time they tugged at their halter ropes, turning their necks to stare warily at my friend Bill Banting, the dude of the outfit that day. They worried about the un-Western cut of his old ski-patrol jacket, and were offended, it seemed, by his obscene Ontario canoe hat. The sight of him caused a ripple of unrest to flow from horse to horseman and back again. They shied together at Bill's too-rapid approach. They prefer you move slowly: they want to see your hands, and see what is in them.

Sir Frederick Banting's only son, late of Cabbagetown, and of repute in the northern wilderness of Inuvik, where he had stalked the white swan with sixteen-millimetre camera on foot and by canoe, stopped to regard the horses with his intelligent but uncertain brown eyes. A canoe may have a certain air about it, but it does not have a brain, a personality, and something like a will of its own. A horse is an entity. Who says it will let you ride it? I had spoken on behalf of his nag, but Bill would have preferred assurances from the beast itself.

"Can I help?" he offered.

Squeezing upright, making a crease between two walls of horseflesh, I had to elbow the two of them in the ribs to get breathing room. Bill cleared his throat politely.

"Just watch me for now," I told him. "Do whatever I do."

That's when the brown gelding, Flurry, who was apparently a meat eater, turned to bite a neighbour's neck for the fifth time that morning, causing the victim to jump sideways and pull hard on the halter rope. A horse that develops the habit of pulling back soon starts breaking tack and generally being a bad influence.

I whacked the cannibal hard with my open hand on his shoulder. "Stop that!" Twelve hundred pounds of muscle and half-digested hay sprang to attention, eyes rolling. Glancing over Flurry's withers as I lifted his blanket up, I saw Bill's furrowed brows. "Except don't ever do that," I said, answering the question he was framing.

Bill and his partner Nancy are into bloodhounds and bassets, which they treat as if they were their natural children. But working with horses is not an owner-and-pet relationship, nor were these beasts my "companion animals" – they were my working partners. We had something to do together to earn our keep, and it was in their interests that I not let them injure each other or us humans. They knew what the rules of our contract were, and they would not trust me if I allowed them to act like spoiled pets on a hobby farm. They were proud, alert animals who thrived on work, and went to hell in a hurry if left standing around the horse pasture in Banff for too long, just like the folks that ride them. I loved and respected them too much not to punish wickedness.

The canoeist went around to his saddlebags and began stuffing them with a pound or two of pipe tobacco, which we were then both badly hooked on. The mickey of rum he had brought was on a pack horse, which was being towed by the Marvel Lake Kid and his steed, Hornet, already underway for the line shack where we would spend the night. I noted Banting's preparations with approval. He was packing his own vices and keeping the hell out of my way, which is all that you can ask of a dude.

It was late afternoon, making it an early start for government work, considering half a day had been wasted filling out forms in town to draw supplies and equipment. We were at Windy Warden Station on the Panther River in Banff National Park, and about to leave on a boundary patrol along the eastern edge of the front range. Our main purpose was to locate any local bands of elk and bighorn sheep. The hunting season had begun in the Alberta forest reserves that abut the park boundary. My job was to make sure all the head-hunters stayed on their side of the invisible line.

I had been in that country long enough to regard the high ranges on either side of the valley as rather immense fences protecting my personal demesne, but Bill, who had never penetrated so deeply into the High Lonesome before, was exhilarated by the changeable light that swept over the forested slopes, over the crags and the high meadows in the wake of fast-moving cumulus. Enchanted, he laughed aloud and remarked each new angle of repose that the golden autumn light revealed.

"Look at it Sid, would you look at it! Hell, where's that light meter . . ."

Grunting acknowledgement, I tugged on a cinch. I glanced around, but all I saw was Alberta's routine scenic splendour on every hand.

Bill chortled at me and shook his head. He fixed me in his viewfinder while I stepped cautiously astride the gelding, which was a strange horse to me. He had a hump in his back, and I turned him into me with the left rein as he tried to bog his head, spinning him into a tight circle as I found my seat. Flurry pranced and hopped in frustration for a moment.

"Cut that out now, you potlicker!"

"What's the matter with him?" asked Bill nervously.

"He's a government horse," I explained.

"Oh." Bill had dealt with the government before. I could have been more reassuring, I suppose, but I have always found that a greenhorn who stays a bit nervous is a greenhorn who pays attention.

I watched as Bill approached his mount, a lugubrious gelding named Sailor who had a talent for locating deep holes while fording otherwise shallow streams. The horse was billed as a non-swimmer, hence his cowboy-humour-type name, but I knew this to be untrue. He could swim alright, he just couldn't float – that is to say, he could keep his head out of the water, but nothing else. As to Bill's swimming ability – I was never one to pry.

After a little prompting, Bill got his foolkiller lace-up boot into the stirrup, and swung his angular frame, with amazing grace all things considered, into the saddle. Bill was in good shape for his advancing years.

I gave him a brief lesson on the use of the reins that he was holding far too casually for his own good. It was important to keep them parted Texas-style, with the middle finger. Should Sailor fall down, which he had been known to do, Bill would need to hang onto the reins, "Especially if one of those canoe boots of yours slips through the stirrups, and he takes off on you."

"Uh huh."

"Thereby converting you into a human breaking-plough."

"Hmm."

"Okay. Turn him around, neck-rein him around."

Sailor pivoted, but then came to a stop. He dropped his head down to bite at the grass. "Giddy-up," said Bill, shaking the reins.

"Kick him, Bill. With your heels."

"Uh, are you sure?"

"Put the boots to him, Billy. He's taking advantage of your kindly nature."

"I don't want to hurt him . . . Giddy-up, Sailor. Good horse . . ."

Flurry pressed against Sailor's obstinate rump, impatient to be off. Suddenly he nipped the other gelding on the buttock, which woke Sailor up with a startled snort, and Bill grabbed for leather. We were on our way.

Somewhere ahead of us, the Kid was no doubt leading our pack horse at a dead run. I congratulated myself once again at grabbing my rucksack, containing my summer sleeping bag, off the pack horse and tying it on behind the cantle – just in case. The Kid was probably completely lost by now in a maze of game trails and river fords. As far as I knew, he had no idea where the cabin was, although he might have been clever enough to check its position on the park map – if he'd remembered to bring one along. Ah yes. This would be a far cry from the show-boat circuit up Bryant Creek Valley. There, the Kid had spent most of his first summer as a seasonal park warden, patrolling on an eight-foot-wide right-of-way behind a long conga line of backpackers that stretched from the trailhead at Spray Lakes all the way to Mount Assiniboine Provincial Park in B.C. The Kid, a former flower-sniffer (park naturalist), would have his work cut out for him on boundary patrol, following game trails barely wide enough for a spiker elk to squeeze through without hanging itself in a tree. I brushed a spruce bough out of my face and felt my lips crack in a faint grin.

I liked the Kid's cockiness. In fact, I distrust any young bush ape who isn't a bit on the cocky side. Boundary patrol is no place for weenies. But the Kid had packed up in record time without asking me for advice. Thing was, he was tying basket hitches, known as squaw hitches in the trade, instead of the diamond hitch, the only knot that will keep pack horse and pack connected in rough terrain. I had done exactly the same thing years before, as a greenhorn warden at Takakkaw Falls.* It was typical of the outfit back then that he had worked all summer with horses and nobody had taught him to throw the diamond hitch. We had gone over it as night was falling, until he seemed to get the hang of it. I had first learned to tie that hitch in the dark. In fact when I think of it, I've spent quite a bit of time riding around on horseback in the dark. Government regulations and red tape long ago forced me to become a semi-nocturnal sojourner. But Neil was anxious to be off and didn't seem to share my enthusiasm for midnight gymkhanas. "I am not a bat," he observed primly.

"Well," I sniffed. "If you don't like the dark, go on ahead of us." Which he had done.

So as we rode, I scanned the trail, half hoping to see articles of food and equipment bucked off by his pack horse, a species that resents moving at any speed faster than a walk. It's not that I'm sadistic, it's just that I prefer travelling alone in the mountains, and I had been saddled with the seasonal because some VIP (Very Irritating Person) wanted to use the Bryant Creek Cabin for a fishing trip, and the Kid – whose home it then was – was in the way. I was not unsympathetic to the Kid's position. As for Bill, the fact that I had invited him along did not necessarily mean that I welcomed his presence. My personality is full of these little ambivalences: I call it the male mystique. It's what makes me such a wonderful guy, the kind of guy who thinks human beings are basically a failed species; the sort of person who looks forward with anticipation to the next Ice Age.

I always told people that I preferred to travel alone because you see more game when not distracted by the presence of another warden. This was partly true. But the real reason was somewhat more complex. Travelling alone is preferable because it's more dangerous.

---

* In the first published version of this story (1979), I wrote that I could not find anything wrong with the Kid's diamond hitch. This was meant as a joke between Neil and me. When I first met Neil he had not yet learned this knot.

Being alone makes me more alert, more conscious of every sound and scent, and more cautious. The need for caution forces me to slow down my life, and in the face of hazards, each moment of time is lived with a fullness that is its own reward. My mistakes have usually been made in the haste and distraction of other men's interests, demands, egos – which mostly have nothing to do with what I feel I am here to accomplish. I am here to be the voice of the inchoate, in a word; I am here to listen to the mountains. I need to be alone sometimes to hear what they have to tell me.

Flurry, on the other hand had his own notion of mountain metaphysics. His went: "Get to next cabin; get Fatty off back; get teeth into big pile of oats." I let him break into a trot, and I heard Bill's rapturous comments on the scenery lapse into silent exclamation marks, as his behind thumped unrhythmically on his saddle. I could sense his consternation growing.

"How fuh . . . far . . . is it?" he managed to call out after a time.

"Coupla hours."

"Oh."

I reined the horse into a walk again, to rest Bill's butt.

Imagine an alley of mountains winding ten miles through the twilight and crowded by soaring walls of crumbling limestone pushed up beyond the last stubborn larches, their autumn-yellow forms crowding the ledges below cliffs of sheerest fall. The Panther pours through it, the voice of that whole valley, fed by waterfalls on either hand. River talk dominates the senses and the alley of stone dominates the trail – forcing the track, with buttresses of stone thrusting from the mountainsides, into numerous crossings of the stream.

At times the route forsakes entirely the snarl of deadfall and rockbands that passes for a bank. Instead of a short ford, the route, marked by ancient blazes here and there, leads downstream through the riverbed itself, the horses feeling out an invisible path among slippery, submerged boulders. At one of these detours, the Kid had missed a blaze, and his horse's tracks surfaced going straight up a shaly bank on the wrong side of the river. I chuckled to myself. Ah well, the Kid had but to follow the river, assuming he was too proud to give his horse its head and let it navigate for him. I didn't know if he had realized that yet – that half the time in pathless country you just let the horse go where it wanted, because it already knew more than you did about the route. I wondered later if he had ever had a chance to learn that, if anybody ever told him, if I should have told him, or if he had just found it out for himself, like the rest of us had done many years earlier.

The blue-eyed Panther mauled at my leather chaps, sliding one icy talon into my riding boots to tickle the soles of my feet right through my thick wool socks. Now there goes that un-amphibious Sailor. Bill had tied up his lines to the saddle horn to free his hands for the camera. I would have to speak to him. A novice, and already developing the vices of an old hand. Sailor paused to muse over his reflection in the dark pool he had found. Maybe he was looking for telltale grey. Tentatively he stepped in deeper, until the water was lapping at Bill's Kodiaks, rising over the tops, cascading in . . . would he ever notice?

"Whoa! What the hell!"

"Turn his head upstream, Billy." Bill grabbed at the lines with one hand, cradling his Nikon with the other, looking a little white around the mouth as he discovered these creatures do not always work well on automatic pilot. Sailor was hypnotized by the movement of the water. Other horses have learned to keep their eye on the bank. Sailor swung slowly to port, answering the helm, and began to tack upstream, fighting the current at the proper angle until he could climb out on the trail again. He stopped and shook himself like a wet dog, making Bill cry out with alarm. Sailor turned his head to give Bill a puzzled look.

"They often do that," I told him.

"Thanks for telling me. How much farther now?" he asked plaintively as he reached down to wring the water out of his pant cuffs.

"Coupla hours."

"Whew. I don't know if I can make it. Maybe I should get off and walk for a while."

"Bill, this would not be sporting."

"I think I need a break . . ."

"Bill . . ." This called for emergency measures. Being nocturnal was one thing, spending the night under a spruce tree was quite another. I had done it often enough to know how overrated it was. What we needed was a stirrup cup for morale, but the rum was on the pack horse, and the pack horse and the Kid had quite possibly parted company by now. Wait a moment – how come this old dead spruce suddenly reminded me of the Buffalo Paddock Lounge back in Banff? Of course! Sailor had got in a wreck at this very place once before. In packing him, I had left out a bottle of elixir, and not wishing to unpack and start again, I had cached this treasure in a hollow tree for retrieval later, then promptly forgot about it.

I reined over to the tree, ungloved, and standing in the stirrups, thrust my hand deep into a squirrel hole there.

"What is it?" demanded Bill.

I ran my hand around the hollow, found pine cones and the usual litter of some beady-eyed critter who I hoped was not at home. It had been two years, and Wackerle, he of the inquisitive nostril, had patrolled here since. A hard smooth object . . . yes! I pulled it out triumphantly, a green brandy bottle, studded with squirrel shit, but intact. "Har, Billy! Have ye ever seen one of these before, laddy?"

"God bless us, one and all," cried the astounded dude. "The trees here grow booze!"

"We have a rule here, Bill . , ."

"This is a miracle . . ."

"Bill, the rule is, you have to drink on horseback."

"Rules were made to be broken."

I uncorked the brandy and sniffed the bouquet.

"Oh for Chrissake," said Bill. "Okay." And with difficulty, he hauled himself back up to Sailor's poop deck.

Bill took a good slug of the nectar and smacked his lips with approval. I took a jolt and felt it light up my life all the way down to my boots. One more snort for Bill and I filed the bottle with the squirrels for future reference. The regard Bill now held me in was embarrassing.

In a few minutes, the trail opened out into a rolling meadow of cinquefoil and willow. The tracks of the Marvel Lake Kid veered straight up the steep hillside from the river bottom, met our trail at right angles, and wheeled to the right where they were lost in a maze of fresh elk sign. The cow elk were on the Kid's heels, and moving at the canter. Colgan and his escort were moving in the right direction. "Smarter than the average seasonal," I allowed. The last animal in the menagerie, as was written in the mud, was a big-footed bull elk. Perhaps the bull planned to breed Colgan's pack horse while he was at it.

Somewhere in the distance, the bull in question bugled in defiance at the setting sun. His brassy trilling echoed from peak to peak like the cry of a soul passing over.

"Holy shit!" cried Bill. A pipe-smoke halo wreathed his hat. "I recognize the mating call of the very horny male wapiti."

"Keep a taut rein and a tight sphincter until we slip by this bull," I warned him. We pressed forward in the fading light through falling aspen and willow leaves. Bill now urged his horse so closely that Flurry was forced to tap Sailor on the chest with one hind foot to keep from being stepped on. As we rode, I told Bill how elk, second only to moose in size among the deer family, are animals that demand respect, whether in chaste or amorous moods. I have myself been rushed by the big-antlered males on several occasions, which is something like being charged by a tractor carrying a dead tree in its bucket. The bulls had been content to get my horse galloping. The females, with calves at heel, are not so easily satisfied, and I have had to flee from them on horseback a few times.

Bill's pipe made sucking sounds as he brooded over this news. The mountains to the east were now but dark shadows in the dim sky. Just before the alpenglow faded out, Venus appeared above the mountain rim. As our eyes adjusted to the dark, we could make out the trail as a thin, phosphorescent line curving through the blackness. There came a whistling bark from the darkness somewhere above us as a sharp old cow elk caught our scent. Hooves drummed the earth and branches popped as the bull herded his harem further up a dry creek bed which led to a plateau between river valleys. The horses took us down to where the Panther glowed in the starlight. We splashed across the last ford, and saw lantern light shining through the trees. So the Kid had made it after all.

The smell of frying onions drifted over the little meadow around the cabin.

We put the horses up for the night and fed them. "Come and get it, or I'll throw it away," said a voice from the shadowy porch, and we went into the warm cabin. There was hot water in the kettle to wash with, and the table was set. The kid, looking lean and fit under his shock of black hair, had everything prepared.

"How was the trip, Colgan?" I asked hopefully.

"Very enjoyable."

There is no sense at all in pissing off a volunteer cook with comments about his trail-finding ability, so I decided to shut up about it – at least until I found out if he could cook. I was expecting the usual mess of fried meat and potatoes, so I was surprised when the Kid opened by dealing three bowls of chef's salad with choice of dressing. I ate this bounty in respectful silence, while Bill, sitting on a pillow, regaled the Kid with an account of our narrow escape from death by drowning, and the miracle of the brandy tree.

The Kid listened good-naturedly to this saga, then whipped our bowls away as soon as we had finished. Opening the oven of the wood stove, he produced three steaming bowls and set them reverently down before us. It was my turn to cry holy shit, at the sight of French onion soup made from fresh onions and bouillon, and crusted with layers of molten mozzarella and croutons. The flavour of it on that sharp autumn night – I can taste it still. The main course was sirloin, baked potatoes (with sour cream, no less), string beans – and then that fakir jumped up, went over to his saddlebags, and pulled out a fat bottle of wine, while Bill and I gaped at him. "Nearly forgot," he said. With a tea towel folded over one arm for a napkin, he presented the bottle of rosy liquid. "Wine?" he asked solicitously, an ironic smile lifting the corners of his black moustache. I resisted the urge to point out the lack of proper glasses for this libation. It was clear that the kid intended to out-ride, out-cook and out-whatever me. But when he pulled out his pièce de résistance, fresh-baked raisin pie, my favourite, I could stand no more.

"Bullshit! I suppose you baked that too?"

The Kid was caught off guard, but not for long. "Well, I didn't think there'd be enough ingredients here, so I bought that at Grandma Lee's."

Cheered by this imperfection, I raised my cup and joined Bill in a toast to the chef. No sooner had we drained the cups than the Kid was up again, brandishing the coffee pot like a rapier.

The conversation that night revolved around the attributes of various professional sheep-killers who might be skulking around those parts. They were a sinister but dedicated bunch. They had been known to kill sheep right alongside the Trans-Canada Highway. They overflew the park in the latest short-take-off airplanes to find out where the big rams were to be found, and they had been known, in fable at least, to use stilts fitted with moose hooves to cross the boundary without leaving footprints. Through all this they did perhaps one-tenth as much damage to the park's sheep and elk population as the semis and trains did to it on the highways and railroads.

"The truth is, Colgan, that having both of us here is a waste of time," I said expansively, feeling the effects of Bill's hot toddies. Bill himself was now snoring peacefully in his sleeping bag.

Neil looked up from an after-supper love letter he was composing to a Calgary girl. He planned to mail it by pony express, myself being the express part. His dark eyes regarded me quizzically; he seemed always inclined to amusement.

"How so?"

I took another sip of toddy. "See, a lady-killer like you should be planted down at Sundre or Caroline, in the beer parlour, entertaining the cowgirls and picking up information. That's where all the sheep hunters go to brag about their exploits."

"Hmm," said the Kid shortly, "I like it here. It's not Bryant Creek, but it's alright."

So the Warden went outside to look at the moon, where it rested luminous and full on the top bar of the corral, and he fell into melancholy reverie about other mountains and other trails. All this would soon be no more, he believed, and with good reason, considering his poor relationship with the park administration, caused by his penchant for criticizing park panjandrums in print and on the CBC.

He wandered over to check on the ponies. He was not above talking to them, or for that matter dragging his sleeping bag out by the corral to spend the night nearer them, for the sake of their company, which he had done in days of yore out in Jasper's wild ranges. He had an almost Swiftian appreciation of their society. Taken by surprise, the Houyhnhnms snorted and stampeded to the far side of the corral, returning only warily as he spoke their names. They leaned over the corral bars and shook their heads at him in the moonlight, as if saying, don't sneak up on a guy like that.

Big galleons of cloud blockaded the full moon, and at the clearing's edge a grey owl swooped through the square of lantern light; a small mammal darted for the woodpile to hide. Silver rivulets of light ran down the ridges high above black forests as the moon floated clear, and my spirits lightened with the peaks. They had always had the power to change my moods as rapidly as the light changed their shapes. I wandered back into the cabin and rolled out my sleeping bag for the night.

We searched the valleys near the park boundary for two days, seeing nothing but one lonesome spruce grouse. On the third day we pulled out for the headwaters of a different river, the name of which I won't reveal, in case there is actually a sheep poacher left on earth who is so stupid that he doesn't know it. The way led up a timbered draw into plateau country, the domain of a small pack of five timber wolves too smart, for some reason, to take the poisoned baits set out for them in the forest reserve, where they do so much good to the ecosystem by killing cattle, the most unthreatened species in western North America. It is the home of several grizzly bears that prowl the avalanche paths along its borders under the wary gaze of a band of white-coated goats. There are no footbridges in the area; the junctions and trails have been left unmarked. Few are the hikers who venture into it, and it is truly no place for the pilgrim who can't read a topo map, or who worries too much about big hairy animals with long teeth. The river and its tributaries are today much as they were when the Creator made them. As a member of the resource conservation staff, I advised Bill that the only way to conserve this particular resource was to bloody well leave it alone.

I was personally in favour of limited hunting in the area – that is, hunting should be limited to hunting down poachers and any surveyors, engineers, timber cruisers or other such riff-raff found defiling the sacred groves with their presence.

I looked downhill to the switchback where Bill followed me as we rode, and I saw the light of mountain madness glinting behind the Easterner's spectacles. The symptoms were well-known to me: a sore neck from craning the head up at magnificent summits, dizziness from continually turning to view the panorama opening up on every hand and from hyperventilating, drawing in too much O_2 flavoured with balsam fir perfume. Bill said, moaning, that he was torn between the desire to get off his horse as soon as possible, and the wish that this journey would never end. Pain won out after a few more miles, and he dismounted to rest his sore knees, tottering along behind me, leading his horse.

We came to a stream crossing, where I got down to check some grizzly-bear tracks, those of a sow with cubs of the year.

"Is that what I think it is?" asked Bill.

"Yep. We're in the most densely populated watershed of the park – for grizzlies. A sow and two cubs made these."

"They look fresh."

We could see where one of the cub's heel prints had cut through the Kid's horse tracks, made that morning as he trotted out of camp, ahead of us, as usual. "Less than an hour old," I said. "Take a look at these claw marks, Bill. She's a big one, see . . . Bill?"

I turned in time to see Billy vault into the saddle with the geriatric grace of a poor man's Gene Autry. I wasn't crazy about hanging around there either; I could smell bear at every turn of the breeze. We rode up a draw until we reached a meadow of flame-red dwarf birch, seeing no more sign of *Ursus arctos*. About noon, we reached the summit of the pass where the Kid awaited us, and got off the horses to let them blow.

Far across the valley to the east of the pass rose a big unnamed peak whose west face was an inclined ramp of rock and heather. On it were three white dots where no snow had fallen.

"Goats," said Neil.

Through the glasses I made out two adults standing on a rock slide with a kid between them, all three looking our way. We seemed to be the only action in those parts, and there was no sign of game on the trail leading down to the east.

Above us was a low ridge, the head of a narrow valley, carved out by a creek, that ran down into a tributary of the Cascade River. According to our map, this narrow valley, or gully, was a steep but negotiable shortcut that led out on the main trail through a narrow neck at the bottom. Bill and I were heading south to another part of the district. The Kid would accompany us as far as the main trail, then swing north again to the next cabin.

We mounted up and rode onto the bench, finding ourselves looking down the gully, which was hemmed in by the mountain on one side and skirted by a border of firs on the other. And there, as if they had just been set down by an invisible hand a moment before, were the sheep we'd been looking for. Ewes and their young fanned out below us and broke for the higher ground on both sides of the creek, sending rocks clattering down its rocky bed. We counted heads, and were pleased to see several rams bedded down on the rock slides to the west. Two of them sported the full, curling horns that are the object of a trophy hunter's wet dreams.

The sky darkened in the sudden way of the mountains, and a passing shower forced us to break out our slickers. A rock outcrop to the north and above our position blocked further progress along the ridge. "Let's contour around that," said Neil.

"What for?"

"Just for the hell of it."

It was the kind of logic that always appealed to me. We worked our way up through the dwarf spruce, over the heather and the dried flowers of summer. I had to get off and lead the gelding, being far too heavy for him to carry up that angle, which God had made only for sheep and goats to walk.

We were working our way up a low point that came out in a notch on the ridge, a false pass that led nowhere but to precipices, I felt. At one point we looked up, breathing hard. There sat the stagey Kid. Horse and rider were outlined against the low, thin clouds blowing through the notch; his slicker streamed out on the breeze. The Kid was an incurable romantic. He disappeared over the edge as if the sky had swallowed him, and standing in his place was one of the biggest rams I have ever seen, its massive wide-set horns curling up in a wide arc well past the eyes – a trophy that might have fetched ten thousand dollars for the right guide leading the right hunter. I felt my hackles rise, there in the mist, at the rock surety of the creature so at home among these cold clouds, this callous, wind-blasted heath. Then, one after another, the rest of the bachelors appeared from hiding to stand watching our ascent.

The old ram watched curiously as Bill approached it to snap its picture. At the sound of the shutter it whirled, and in a few seconds the whole herd had disappeared down the cliff bands into the fir trees below.

The mists parted and the sun broke through. The rocky ridge was now a long, grassy promontory that swept west in a gentle arc. It ended abruptly in a little eroded platform of lightning-blasted limestone about four feet wide and ten feet long. On the platform stood Hornet, his head hanging warily over the edge, staring into space; on his back sat the Marvel Lake Kid.

"Hold it!" yelled Bill. He slapped a telephoto lens on his Nikon and squeezed off some shots. The Kid rode back over his airy sidewalk of heather and cloud.

"That was a dumb place to take a horse, Colgan," I told him sternly when he reined up alongside and flashed us his insolent grin. I decided the Kid would probably make a pretty good warden, if the government didn't break his spirit first. "Don't ever do that again."

"Yazzuh, Boss."

Then I rode the reluctant Flurry out to the platform and coaxed him up onto it so Bill could get my picture. When I returned he gave me his five-minute professional photographer's course, borrowed my Stetson, and rode Sailor up onto the platform so confidently that he seemed more like an old mountainman, slouching out there in the wind above the valley, than the bone-weary dude he'd looked like a few minutes before.

After that we worked our way down to the neck of the valley, forced our way through some spruce thickets, and found the main trail. We stopped by a tumbling creek in a little meadow to say goodbye. In a few weeks, the Kid would be on his motorcycle en route to Mexico. He would be returning to nuzzle at the government teat the following summer. I myself soon would be weaned permanently – or so I thought – from the soured milk of the Über-Bear. Bill would wind up babysitting a bankrupt ski lodge for the winter. "Don't run that horse all the way home now," I told the Kid.

"Oh, I'm gonna take it real easy."

We shook hands, then Bill and I watched as he rode out of sight. After a moment we heard him pop the reins on Hornet's behind.

"The Marvel Lake Kid has lots of abilities," said friend Bill, "but lying is not his long suit."

I had to agree. We filled our pipes and turned the horses for home.

CHAPTER THREE

The Old Trolls of Lake O'Hara

PART ONE: RENDEZVOUS AT ABBOT PASS

I have not been sleeping well lately. It's a product of the age I find myself at, worries about a future without pension plans, savings plans, Blue Cross plans, dental plans, vacation plans. A total absence of plans keeps me tossing and turning, while Myrna sleeps like a baby, her long hair turned to white gold in the moonlight. Thank God there is only one worrywart in this bed, or we'd never get to sleep. At night Myrna dreams she is a window blind. Catching an edge of the blankets in her hands, she spins away from me, wrapping the blankets into a cocoon around her, until I wake up shivering and pull the blind of blankets back over me. I have to hold on tight or she will spin them all away again like a recoil spring. "You pulled the blankets off me again last night," she'll say in the morning, accusingly.

My eye falls on something metallic shining by the window. Then I recall it – the steel haul ring of the old rucksack. Like an absent-minded professor, I'd carried it into the bedroom and hung it on the coat rack instead of leaving it out in the porch. It reminds me of that early version of myself who also travelled without plans, but never lost a moment's sleep over his feckless ways.

Gazing at the dull gleam of moonlit steel, my thoughts go back to that summer of 1962 in the mountains at Lake O'Hara, British Columbia, when I first stood – posed, rather – on the jetty, the brand new pack riding casually on one shoulder, a borrowed climbing rope slung over the top, with both hands on the haft of my new ice axe, staring up at the mountains and listening to Edward Feuz talk about Abbot's Hut and the Death Trap in Abbot Pass.

"Where was it the Mexicans fell?" asked the person he was talking to. It was the first mention I heard of that calamity, which was still fresh in people's memory at the time. It would be referred to frequently during the early sixties as an example of why people should stop climbing mountains.

"On the Alberta side," Feuz answered, "above Lake Louise. Right above the Death Trap." The words startled me with their dramatic import. You didn't have to strain your ears to hear Edward Feuz's loud, gravelly voice. "And right at the corner of Mount Victoria, between it and Mount Lefroy," I'd heard him say. "That's the west side of Abbot Pass. That's the couloir you climb up to get to Abbot Pass Hut."

Abbot's Hut. The first time I saw it was the first time I really understood the love affair between men and mountains. Abbot's Hut – a place to shelter climbers, a place made to be haunted by their shades. At night, the beacon of a candle flame in its window was like a lighthouse in the clouds.

The summit of the pass by night – a sickle of onyx where stars rested on dazzling spears of light – drew slowly nearer with each weary step I took, until at long last I came to the margin of the glacier. I glanced up to the west to the dark mass of Mount Victoria, where four Mexican climbers perished in 1954, and then east, up the icy ramp of Mount Lefroy to the band of rocks picked out by a fingernail moon, where Philip Abbot fell and died more than a century ago. An abode of haunts. I stepped from the living ice onto the living rock below the hut, which was itself merely another flint-edged shadow under the ridge of Mount Victoria, though one window pulsed with faint candlelight as if it were watched over by some ostiary manning a crypt. Leaning on the long-handled ice axe of that era, the haft made of seasoned hickory, I stared back down the glacier that debouches above Lake Louise. The intermittent moon slid through a portal of cloud once more and shone full upon the narrow gorge of the Death Trap, but it could not penetrate the depths I had traversed in darkness. It brightened on the jaws of ice that overhang that black maw, from Mount Lefroy in the east to Mount Victoria to the west.

I knew this vision of myself at night, as though seen from an eye in the hovering cloud, was all wrong, because there was no head-lamp on my hat. Certainly I have traversed the Death Trap (or Mousetrap, as old Lorenzo Grassi called it) of Abbot Pass often enough that I might have forgotten climbing it at night by moon-light from Lake Louise. I once descended it solo, without falling in a crevasse, though the memory of that, and its consequences had my luck been bad – a slow, lonely death deep in the ice – makes me squirm today when I consider it. Such retroactive speculations coming to you in dreams will wake you in the night, shouting. Why did I do such a foolish thing? Well, what I told myself at the time was that I was out of pipe tobacco. I couldn't obtain any back at Lake O'Hara and it was only a three-hour walk out to Lake Louise. In fact I was awash in testosterone, that frequent killer of young men.

Darkness had also dogged me on the Lake O'Hara side, where the last altitude gain of five hundred metres is sweated out on a narrow, one-kilometre ramp of sliding scree and boulders subject to rock falls from both Victoria and Lefroy. That had been during a lightning storm. I had been late getting off work, and I'd needed to get to the hut for an early start climbing on Lefroy in the morning. It had all made sense to me then.

But nevertheless, I didn't think it curious to find the old man's heavy wheelbarrow, the kind labourers use for cement work, sitting just below the hut on that rocky col at 2,922 metres, the moon picking out the polished steel on the heavy gravel bar, the silvered edges of grub hoe and shovel blade, their wooden handles eroded to the shape of Grassi's gnarled hands. Hadn't I seen him pack that thing on his back over a rock slide as steep as the southern approach to the hut? So I crossed the narrow strand at the summit, stepping, as I did so, across the actual Continental Divide and the provincial boundary between Alberta and British Columbia.

I felt the updraft of Pacific air wash over me as I stared down the scree slope into B.C., where the stars shone back up at themselves from the mirror of Lake Oesa, and I imagined I could smell the kelp at Horseshoe Bay near Vancouver, far to the west. It was like looking down a wellhead. And I saw what I had almost expected to see, the white scar of a brand new trail switchbacking down to the vanishing point. "So he got it built at last," I thought, although I knew perfectly well the old man had never spoken of building a trail up the O'Hara side. I have no doubt that he may have considered it a time or two – he used to work on the lower portion, which crosses a dangerous hardscrabble slope at the entrance to the pass. He had built many miles of trails over slopes and rock slides, singlehanded, and it seemed reasonable enough, given his ambition, that he might build a trail up a slope that some pilgrims can ascend only on all fours. If it lasted one season it would be a miracle. And just then as if in confirmation of delusion, the slope of loose rock moved all in one piece – something I had often feared while climbing it – with a noise like broken glass scraping over a blackboard in hell. But it stopped just as abruptly, leaving a gaping crack at its top edge, and my hair thrilled erect to see Grassi's creation was still there, suspended like a white ribbon unfurled into the profound darkness. What kind of pact had the old obsessive made, and with what infernal kobold, to preserve this, the most grandiose of all his wanton tread-works?

Yet it seemed reasonable. It must be something you ate, I told myself. And I was not surprised, on climbing the last steep rise up to the hut's rocky front step, to find the door open to the wind, light flickering from a single candle. "Those punks from Lake Louise have left the door open again," I muttered to myself. "I wonder if they burned the benches again while they were at it? They should have built the frigging benches out of stone, too," I told myself, a minion to an old feud. But if they had, the little frat-boy bastards would have chopped the very roof down for firewood. Strange to think there were human beings so dementedly self-centred that they would rather burn parts of this shrine to brew tea than strap a bit of wood on their packs before leaving the valley down below.

I peered into the candlelit interior and slowly entered. It seemed preordained that I would find the old Swiss guide, Edward Feuz Jr., sitting at one end of the long table as if holding court. Well, why not. He had led his last climbing party up through the Death Trap at the great age of eighty-one. He had been part of the building crew for the hut (completed in 1922), and he had spent so many nights there with his clients that the place was like a second home to him. I'm surprised the Alpine Club didn't bury him under the floor – or cremate him in the wood-burning heater.

And sitting there also, as expected, with his back to the smoke-stained panelling, was the old trail-builder and Lake O'Hara warden, Lawrence Grassi. His slouch hat was forward on his head, and he sat hunched and blinking at the candle set before him, like some species of humpback owl. Some other figures there might have been, gathered around the flickering light of the stove – but I could not make them out. Not all the dead of Abbot Pass are famous. (Indeed, there may be a few, slowly working their way through the bowels of the Lower Victoria Glacier, whose deaths have yet to be recorded.) Those two old Gorgons of my mountain youth sat together though

I had never known them to socialize in the time I worked at Lake O'Hara, which lies below and west of Lake Oesa.

Edward took his pipe out of his mouth and glared fiercely at the doorway before I could bid him good evening. His eyes looked past me – but nobody was there that I could make out. The wind moaned over the roof and the door suddenly slammed shut like a door on a vault. "Do you know how long I've been climbing dis peaks?" he demanded.

"Yes I do," I answered, since no one else spoke. "You started climbing them in 1903. Your brothers Ernest and Walter came over from Switzerland to join you – I forget the dates. Of course, your father, Edouard Sr., guided out here before that, starting in 1899."

"I come over from Interlaken in nineteen-*three*" declared Edward, in his harsh, accented English, "as a porter for my father. He was here before that, back in 1899. We guided for the CPR hotels for over fifty year. Do you know how many accident we had in that time, on dis mountains?"

"You – rather, Ernest – once dropped John Lynn, the piano player from the Chateau, into a crevasse down below here and it just about croaked him. He recovered the next day. There were the usual cuts and bruises. But you never lost a client to the mountains."

"We never had a serious accident!" cried the old man, deaf to my answers, or maybe he was addressing somebody else who I couldn't see. "We never lost a client to dis mountains. We got a perfect safety record. Look at how many die now. You have no idea."

In fact, I had a pretty good idea, although I'd given up keeping score some years ago, after the advent of guided helicopter skiing, when they started killing off the clients by platoons. Of course, Edward was talking about mountain climbing, not playing helicopter roulette with avalanches. But the old warden, Grassi, shook his head and said sombrely, "Not everybody wants to climb with guides."

"That's r-r-right! That's for sure!" cried Edward. "Nowadays, they don't hire a guide, these *kids*," he said, motioning dismissively at the mere octogenarian at his table. "That's why they get into trouble."

"I never take-a money from people, for lead a climb," insisted Lawrence, the kid, paying no heed. He was recognized by the Alpine Club of Canada in younger years for his guiding skills, but he refused to call himself a guide. At one ACC camp in Glacier National Park (B.C.) he climbed Mount Sir Donald five times in as many days, leading climbs for the club. None of his "clients" had been lost either. In fact, when Dr. R. D. Williams of Calgary broke a leg on Mount Bastion in the Tonquin Valley, back in 1926, Lawrence had carried him on his back for several miles over ice and rock, rather than leave him to the vicissitudes of high-altitude weather and go for help. And I wondered, once again, if he had not taken money because he did not feel he was entitled to it, or whether he, who had made his living mining coal beneath the mountains for so long, had grown sick of that exploitation and decided that in climbing, at least, his mountains would not be for sale.

I believe it was the latter case.

"Hah!" scoffed Edward Feuz, reacting to Grassi's claim. "Hah!" A jet of blue flame popped open the silver forester cap on his pipe bowl and some ashes flew, the ashes of his short-fused, incendiary temper. He sat glowering into space and puffing on his old Peterson bent.

"That's quite a trail, Lawrence," I said. "I can't believe you have built a trail all the way up that scree slope. A suspended trail, at that! You must have hung it up on sky-hooks. How the hell did you manage it?"

The old warden stared solemnly at his candle and growled out, haltingly, "Never let nobody tell me I work too hard, or not enough. Never let, nobody tella me, where to built a trail. Dey had told me, I would ask dem, how much dey know about trails. Mighta been enough. 'Coz most of dem donna know da first ting about it."

Then he frowned at the candle and rubbed at his eyes with one hand as if the single flame was too bright and pained him. He stretched out a gnarly old hand and pinched the candle flame out. The room swam back into the dark, then the moonlight filtered through the smoke-stained window again and shone on the empty table. The moon shone through my eastern window, overlooking the Livingstone Range. I woke thinking that a pass in the mountains leads from one world to another. What you see in the new world depends on what you noticed about the last one.

PART TWO: LEARNING HOW TO WALK

I can't claim that Lawrence Grassi and Edward Feuz had an immediate impact on the callow youth I was back in those days. My tendency towards them was the usual reaction of a rash young man to the proscriptions of his elders. Nevertheless, when I think of the Lake O'Hara days, it is those two old visages, ominous as unknown moons on an alien planet, that swim into focus, insisting that I give some accounting of what they finally meant to me.

I think more than anything, it was their style that fascinated me: their refusal to make peace with our compromised modern world; their insistence that history mattered, and therefore that they mattered and would not allow themselves to be condescended to by whippersnappers. Like old silvertip grizzlies duelling with an on-coming train, they were licked but they didn't see it that way. They stood their ground. Like all vanishing species they insisted on being themselves no matter what anybody else thought.

They were my teachers unawares. But by the time I understood the full extent of what they had taught me, and knew enough to thank them, they had vanished like wraiths of mist among the golden larches above timberline. They had melted from my life like the snows of yesteryear.

It was Mr. Austin Ford who first drew me to Lake O'Hara by offering me a summer job there. Mr. Ford owned Lake O'Hara Lodge, among other things. He was a patron of the Navy League, sponsoring organization for the Royal Canadian Sea Cadet Corps, of which I was a member; a Wednesday night sailor of the prairie ocean. It was Ford's custom to hire a senior cadet when he had an

opening at the lodge for the summer. In 1962, scrawny young Chief
Petty Officer Marty was his choice.

I came to the lodge that summer at a turning point in my life.
That fall I would be one of ten Canadian cadets to go to sea for five
months. We would cruise from the Aleutian Islands all the way to
Ceylon by way of Hawaii, Japan, Thailand, and Hong Kong on
HMCS *Assiniboine*, a destroyer escort. We would find ourselves off
the coast of Taiwan watching for Chinese MIGs in the middle of the
Cuban missile crisis that October, fully expecting the onset of World
War Three. But Khrushchev would take his finger off the nuclear
button, the world would continue on, and I would return to
O'Hara for another season.

Thumbing through an old album of pictures of those days, I
can't believe that skinny, hatchet-faced eighteen-year-old, with hair
that used to bleach blond in the summer and turn brown again in
winter, was really me. He seems more like a character I used to play,
now partly lost to memory. But I call him forth once more into this
strange twilight time at the turning of the millennium. I never want
to forget the lessons this boy learned, or the ideals he held to be
immutable, though time has reduced him to the mere state of matu-
rity I now find myself in.

The first time I stood on the shore of Lake O'Hara, I felt my old
life fall away from me in layers, like dust shaken from a young colt's
hide. My eyes had been trained for a life under prairie skies, where
mountains were mainly ragged outliers on a distant horizon. Now I
had stepped into a different heartland, unprepared for waves of
limestone, white-capped with snow, poised always to roll forward
and yet standing monumentally still, harkening to the sun. Plumes
of snow stood from the sharp summits, whose ultimate rocks were
whetted by jets of wind unfelt at lake level.

The turquoise water was dead calm. To the east, seven strands of
a silver waterfall tinselled down from hanging glaciers at the end
of the valley. The underside of heaven was an unearthly, cobalt blue.
The edges of the mountains, etched in snow, were engraved upon it.

The lake and the water-blackened cliffs of the mountains that rose from dark forests straight up into snowy summits were in a kind of communion, for the lake water held their images where snow-crowned summits met in its centre. There was the dizzying sensation that I was about to step through the looking glass into an actual Group of Seven painting into which, like brave Tom Thomson, I would disappear.

I had entered a different arrangement in the seasons. Blazing summer was underway at Calgary, but that was 970 metres lower than Lake O'Hara. By an increase in altitude, and corresponding decrease in temperature, I had journeyed back into early spring, where windrows of snow still clung to the path under the spruce trees.

Where I was raised, the price of shade runs high. The forest here was the kingdom of shadows, and I imagined whatever creatures lived within it were staring out on the lake, like spirits at the service of these gods. Humbled by beauty, I wondered what purpose a raw young mortal might serve in this mountain splendour. Then a trout, a large one, jumped where the shadows of spruce trees turned the water to pools of mercury: at the top of its liquid arc it seemed suspended between air and water. Perhaps it was the quicker eye of youth made it so, but I think Lake O'Hara imprinted itself on my brain at that moment. I have but to close my eyes and say the name, and it appears before me. Its circle of mountains comes into view, those old retainers of the absolute: Wiwaxy (Windy), Huber, Victoria, Lefroy, Ringrose, Yukness (Sharp) and Hungabee (Chieftain), the immediate familiars of my dreams.

I knew little of mountains when I signed on as boatman and maintenance worker at Lake O'Hara Lodge. My purlieus would mainly be the boat jetty and anywhere else they needed me, including pearl-diving in the kitchen once a week.

The O'Hara staff was a tight-knit bunch of young university students. We worked hard and were also expected to pick and grin for Mastah in the dining room at the Saturday night banquet, if we had musical ability, or form an impromptu chorus at the very least. They probably would have had us don blackface and tap-dance if anybody knew how. Ford paid us the minimum wage, but he treated us kindly and fed us very well. We were a healthy, hearty, suntanned bunch who thought that a bottle of muscatel or a case of beer was deeply thrilling. We partied in the staff room after hours, dancing to Roy Orbison and Del Shannon in the summers just before Beatlemania struck. To say we were largely innocent of the corruptions of this sad world would be to wildly understate the case.

The lodge guests leaned seriously towards old money and many of them had been coming to the area for two or three generations, often from the eastern United States. Although the lake is part of Yoho National Park, the older guests tended to look upon it as their private resort, a notion that was reinforced by the locked gate at the bottom of the access road near Wapta Lake. The elite attitude was summed up in the book *History of Lake O'Hara* by a long-time lodge guest, accomplished mountaineer, and heiress – aptly named Lillian Gest: "Those at Lake O'Hara who have enjoyed the quiet mountain atmosphere . . . hope that these 'Improvements' will not mean an influx of one-day tourists and souvenir stands. Lake O'Hara was made for climbers and hikers. Let's keep it that way."

I had nothing at all in common with the lodge guests, but I knew the officer corps when I saw it. They like to keep the good stuff locked away from the working man.

There were some good people in the mix though, particularly the late Dr. George K. K. Link, an American botanist. He had first come to the area in 1928 and had done an amazing amount of labour designing the trails at Lake O'Hara over the years, just for the sheer pleasure of trail-building. "Tommy" Link was glad to talk to anyone about plants and wildlife at O'Hara. He was a grand old man of the peaks whose late wife, Adeline, had been a painter and friend of Group of Seven artist J. E. H. MacDonald, the most famous celebrant of O'Hara's beauties. I loved old man Link, but I found it hard to stomach the attitude of awed reverence shown by the lodge management to its other wealthy guests, and the snooty attitude shown towards backpackers when they ventured onto the hallowed premises.

At every spare moment, I roamed the trails at Lake O'Hara, that walker's paradise, until my bones could remember every turn and switchback in the valley. The network of trails in the area, many of them originally planned by Dr. Link, others built by Lawrence Grassi and kept up in later years by volunteer workers of the Lake O'Hara Trails Club (which Link originally founded), encircle the valley and carry the sturdy walker up to alpine vantage points. It is a place of high rock gardens on the Opabin Plateau and on the trail to Lake Oesa, places where the tiny lakes and ponds are of such crystalline purity they can bring tears of pleasure to your eyes. It is an airy domain of high lookouts, like the All Souls' Point, the Odaray Plateau, and Yukness Ledges, ruled by the golden eagle, and argued over by whistling marmots sunning on the rock slides. And it is your body alone, the vehicle of your soul that carries you up – not without some aches and pains – into sublimity, the medium that mountains breathe in as we breathe in oxygen.

It soon became clear to me, however, that there was more to life than hiking. There was a warrior class at Lake O'Hara, dressed for adventure with climbing boots on their feet and ice axes in hand. I was into warriors in those days. The most notable of these were guides or guides aspirant, particularly the dark-haired German Heinz Kahl, whose whole being radiated joy and good health. The tall, fair-haired Canadian, Don Vockeroth, soon to be a guide, was another, like Heinz, who would sit with you around the fire at the Alpine Club hut of an evening and show you how to tie the bowline, the butterfly, and the prusik knot, the life-saving knots of rock and glacier travel. Also in evidence at times, tenting in the alpine meadows by the hut, were climbers like Brian Greenwood, an expatriate Brit and the most notable rock-climber of the era. He was at the cutting edge of Canadian climbing in the 1960s.

Greenwood and his cronies belonged to the Calgary Mountain

Club, a group that specialized in climbing non-standard routes and kicking sacred cows off the ledges on their fraught journeys, deeply disturbing some of the calcified spirits of the Canadian Alpine Club of those days. It was Greenwood who had led the first ascent on Grassi Ridge on Mount Wiwaxy, seconded by Vockeroth, who apparently wandered into the climb almost by accident. That alone made Greenwood famous at Lake O'Hara. At the time, his store in Calgary was about the only place where you could buy climbing equipment at reasonable prices. I hadn't climbed anything yet, but I was a North American: buy first, learn to use it later.

Greenwood's store was in the basement of his house in Elbow Park. You entered through a squall of kids and the occasional family row going on upstairs, tripped over a buckshee assortment of boots in the hallway and tumbled – at least I did – down into the basement store. "Christ, sing out 'Climbing' next time," drawled Greenwood, "And I'll belay you down."

I bought my first climbing boots there – a pair of sturdy black Lowes, and I can still remember the intoxicating fresh-leather smell of them – along with a long-handled Stubai ice axe and my beloved canvas La Fuma rucksack. The equipment was identical to that used by Heinz, who was a few years older than I. His advice to me I considered etched in stone.

In deference to Greenwood, I purchased a few pitons, a couple of carabiners, and a piton hammer. The climbing rope would have to wait another payday. Once back at O'Hara, I took to carrying the hardware and a borrowed rope around with me on my scrambles up the lesser peaks, the hardware hanging from a sling where it could be reached quickly in case I took a sudden impulse to go bounding up a sheer cliff face, and especially useful if I was confronted suddenly on the lake trail by a visiting damsel from the Chateau Lake Louise staff. The pins and 'biners made a pleasant jangling noise that promised mighty exploits, the drama of which were hinted at by the blue beret I also affected at that time. This is a mountain courting ritual known as "rattling your 'biners." I had yet to climb anything where even a rope, let alone a piton, would be needed.

That summer flew past and except for the solo scrambling, I learned little about mountaineering. It seems odd to me now, but I can't recall going to Abbot Pass Hut that first summer, for whatever reason. I would not traverse the pass until 1963. That fall I went to sea with the navy, where five months living the enlisted man's life surrounded by salty sailor men knocked a few chips off my shoulder – but not enough. Among the many epiphanies of that voyage, one stands out in particular because its memory seemed to influence my outlook on the human condition ever afterwards.

HMCS *Assiniboine* was berthed alongside the jetty in Trinco-malee, Ceylon (now Sri Lanka). I was on watch on the shadowy jetty that night, on sentry duty. Outboard from *Assiniboine*, the rest of the squadron was tied in line abreast, along with a couple of American destroyers. The American ships sprouted with armed sentries and machine guns protected behind sandbagged barricades. There was political unrest in the country at the time, but America's world-class paranoia seemed a bit overwrought to me.

But at some point it dawned on me that any terrorist wanting to attack the Americans by land had to first get past me, and my only weapon was a brass-tipped rat stick. This thought made me nervous, and a commotion on the jetty in the early hours made me jump. The authorities had overtaken a man who was trying to make his way to the foreign vessels. He was a small, middle-aged man, unarmed and running hard with several cops close behind him. He shouted something in a frightened voice – it sounded like "Canada!" – then cried out once in pain and went down under the sickening crunch of police batons being applied to his skull. I yelled a protest and started forward towards the fray without thinking about conse-quences, when "Sentry!" barked a voice of authority from the dark-ness above me. I stopped in my tracks.

"Belay that. Keep to your post."

"Sir? Shouldn't we . . ."

"Keep to your post – do you understand?"

"Aye aye, sir." The police dragged their victim away like road-kill and vanished into the shadows. I stared down at the wide pool of shining blood on the wet concrete, and saw my own face reflected there.

"There but for fortune go you and I," muttered a voice from the darkened quarterdeck overhead. But to the young man, the blood of an unasked-for sacrifice lay there in the sweltering dark. There was a cruel and fundamental injustice at work in the world, and little reason to feel smug about one's birthright: it was not a moral virtue, but a freak of good luck. The basic, decent instinct to rescue somebody in peril had been thwarted in the name of politics. Back home in Canada, I would never take democratic freedom for granted again.

One day the following summer, bestrewn with climbing hardware once again, I was jangling my way up to Lake McArthur like a travelling tinker when I overtook an old man, dressed like a garden gnome in a Tyrolean hat, ancient plus-fours and Tricuni-nailed leather boots that belonged in a museum. He also affected a Norfolk jacket and a tie. He seemed to be propelled by a steam engine, since he left a cloud of pipe smoke behind as he plodded methodically up the trail, using his ice axe as a cane – or so I suspected.

I jangled my 'biners for the passing lane: "Excuse me, sir . . ."

The old man glanced back without quitting his pace. "You are sounding very musical today," he said in heavily accented English, and he eased to one side. "Can you play a tune mit all that junk?" he wanted to know.

I came abreast of him, not responding to the teasing. "Thanks. I have to get back to work in a couple of hours," I explained.

"At the lotch?"

"Yes." I was breathing pretty hard from the exertion of the ascent and the heat of the day. "See you later."

"Yah. Probably sooner."

Whatever that means, I thought, and kept going, still trying to trot up the trail. I wanted to get up the ridge on Mount Schäffer, which was billed as an easy scramble.

The old man was out of sight when I sat down by Schäffer Creek to get a drink of water. But I had not been there long when he came steaming into view, still moving at his tortoise-like pace.

Quickly I shouldered the pack and attacked the next steep section of trail. But my lungs were still working at Calgary altitude and I had to stop several times. The old man kept coming into sight, as inevitable as God, it seemed. I thought, who is this old bugger? At last he caught me up as I was bent over, gasping, and stopped to stare at me with a mischievous light in his old eyes and round face.

"So if I'm the tortoise, you must be da hare."

"Yeah," I wheezed, grinning sheepishly. "Is that what we are doing?"

"I can tell you one thing," he said sternly, "before you schtart climbing mountains, you better learn how to walk."

I resented the comment, but kept silent. In those days we were slow to talk back to our elders. "I'm Ernest Feuz," he said, and offered his hand. I shook it, feeling a surprising strength in his grip given his age (seventy-three), and I introduced myself. His name did not mean anything to me at the time.

"Listen to me," he said. "I've been walking at this speed since I was a boy in Schvitzerland. You can walk up Mount Schäffer at this speed and you can walk up Mount Everest.

"I'll show you how ve walk in the mountains."

"Actually," I began: I was going to tell him that as a cadet gunnery instructor, I had myself taught many people to walk – or rather to march, taking a full twenty-four-inch stride – left, right, left, and so on.

"It chust takes a minute," he interrupted, waving my objection aside as if it were a fly buzzing his nose.

"First, don't take such a big schtep with those long legs and big clodhopper feet. Keep your veight forward over your feet; don't walk on your toes until you get on a cliff. Even when it gets schteep, put your foot down square on the ground. After a while the tendons vill get schtrong there. Then you breathe in nice and deep, schtep, schtep again – breathe out on the next ones – schtep, schtep. You find a pace that vorks for your body, then you just keep repeating it, hour after hour, all day long. Then you don't schtop every ten minutes to rest. You understand?"

"Sure," I said, forcing a smile. "Thanks for the tip."

"Yah." He nodded his head, as if he thought I might not be listening. "Because it's the most important thing to know, to travel in the mountains. A lot of people never learn it." And the garden gnome paced slowly off up the trail ahead of me, in a cloud of fragrant pipe smoke.

Once he was out of sight, I practised what he had taught me. A surprising thing happened: first of all, I could breathe comfortably and still keep moving forward. At the same time as my heart slowed down, time slowed down and the world came into sharper focus. Flowers took on real shape and colour; bird call and creek purling, rockfall high up in the couloirs entered conscious hearing, not distorted through the sieve of rushing blood in my ears. The mountains rose up to meet me, no longer in retreat from my aggressive approach. I learned to walk in the mountains that day, and I've walked the mountain walk he taught me ever since.

But in those early mountain days I had been watching tiny figures moving up the classic route that led across the Odaray Glacier, then up a cliff to a saddle, where it looked to be an easy walk up the summit ridge. Mount Odaray was an Alpine Club qualifying climb, the sort that would be laughed off these days. "I can do that," I thought to myself.

I don't remember now who the other babe-in-the-woods was on that climb, when I first chopped a step with an ice axe. We were impressed by all the snow that seemed to be hanging over the top of the ridge of Little Odaray (Walter Feuz Peak) right above our route.

We had no crampons. Fortunately for us, since I knew nothing about crevasses or crevasse rescue, the snow was in good condition and we had a clear, probed-out track to follow. I remember the sense of elation at being high up above the last trail; how the ice swooped away below our feet; how cold and wet the rock in the notch was under our hands; how it yielded easily to our determined strength and how we stood high on the dark summit, a parapet thrust out over the valley, brooded over by the encircling peaks. You wanted your proud, lonely soul to be recognized by these aloof, indomitable presences, and so you dared to master the abyss.

Inspired by Ernest, I had bought myself a pipe and some Swiss-guide walking fuel – Sail pipe tobacco – which Ernest seemed to favour. After the climb up Mount Odaray, I went down to the O'Hara jetty to smoke a pipe and savour my debut as a mountaineer, the rucksack slung over my shoulder with the rope coiled under the top flap. I was startled to find another garden gnome standing on the jetty in the same antique nailed boots and nineteenth-century costume as Ernest. He wore something like a marshal's badge on his lapel (it was his Swiss-guide's pin). He seemed to be an older version of Ernest, and indeed it was his brother Edward, patriarch of the clan and then seventy-seven years old. To a young man's eyes, he appeared to be at Death's door. We introduced ourselves.

Edward watched intently as I stuffed my pipe bowl. It was breezy, and I couldn't get the match to take.

"Hah!" scoffed Edward. "Call yourself a mountaineer, and you can't even light a *pipe!*"

I coloured at his words. "Well, I managed to light it on top of Odaray this afternoon," I said, coldly.

"So-oo," said Edward, still staring at me. "It vas you leading on that climb?"

"Yes."

He puffed furiously for a few seconds, considering. "I wondered who that damn fool vas, traversing underneath a goddamn cornice in the heat of the day!" he said angrily. "Vas you trying to kill yourself, or maybe your friend you vanted to kill?"

I stared at him, unnerved by the comment and at a loss for words, wondering, who does this old bastard think he is? And what the hell is a cornice? Not that I'm going to ask him.

"Yah," said Edward, nodding his head, puffing furiously on his own incinerator. "Sometimes it's good to keep quiet."

He thrust his binoculars at me. "You know Lefroy?"

"Of course. At the end of the lake, on the right."

"See that dark band of rock in the ice near the top?"

I looked up at it. "Yes."

"That's where Mr. Abbot fell in 1896. He vas from Yale University. He died there. That's when the CPR brought my father over from Schvitzerland. To keep more fools from dying. Are you from university?"

"No. Not yet."

"Guhdt. Maybe you vill live longer than he did."

I laughed nervously, but not for long. The old man bristled. "You think it's funny, Buster, going under a *cornice*, eh? Take a look at that cornice, schmart guy. See that big hole up there?"

I felt a chill, seeing a close-up of a black cavity in that white smile. So that's what he meant, that gigantic snowdrift plastered there by the wind the previous winter. "I see it," I said, feeling subdued.

"You see it, eh? That comes down after you got down to McArthur Pass. You didn't hear it?"

"Uh, I heard something. I thought it was thunder somewhere."

"Hah! That weighs many tons. You're lucky you were still alive to hear it. You don't go under a cornice if you can go around, hey? You don't lead anyone into a dangerous place if you can find a safer way. If you got to go under it, you go early in the *morning*. When it's still *frozen*. Then you go like hell underneath there."

"So you've climbed there before?" I asked, anxious to change the topic.

The old man coughed as if choking, then recovered. He seemed angrier than ever. "I have been guiding since 1903. I have climbed every peak in this valley, many times. And all the mountains from here to Jasper and many more. Nobody knows dis mountains better than me!"

It seemed like such an un-Canadian statement at the time, so much like a brag. But I found out later it was merely the truth. Among the countless peaks he had climbed, Edward Feuz had 102 first ascents to his credit and Ernest, no slouch, had 40. Edward had his admirers and his detractors. I met him first without the prejudiced opinions of younger mountaineers to sway me – " 'Keep to the ridges' he says. Ha! Why not drag a milk cow up behind you while you're at it" – and became an admirer, though I don't claim to have known him well. It was a case of, the older I got, the wiser he became.

He went on with his impromptu history lesson, like a living legend, which he was. Names came to his lips: Colonel L. S. Amery, Edward Whymper, Georgia Englehard, Kate Gardiner – people I had never heard of back then, so great was my ignorance, who had made many first ascents with him in the golden age of mountaineering.

Edward had officially retired from the CPR's employ in 1949. If I wanted to, he said, I could go to Chateau Lake Louise and I would see the log chalet that had been their headquarters in those days. The three brothers, Edward, Ernest, and Walter, all guides, were well known at O'Hara Lodge, where a number of guests had climbed with them over the years.

Finally he wound down and I asked him about Abbot Pass. "It leads over the glacier and down through the Death Trap to Lake Louise," he informed me.

"The Death Trap?" The name was startling.

"That's *right*. Never go through there during the hot part of the day. That's when the icefalls come down. You have to go through *early*, before the sun vorks on the ice. Abbot's Hut sits right on the divide. That's ninety-six-hundred *feet*. It's the highest building in *Canada*. If you stood on top of the roof ridge, you haff one foot in Alberta, and one foot in B.C. If you go in the outhouse there, you can pee in Alberta and crap in B.C. at the same time."

I grinned at the scatology. "Who built it?"

I thought the old boy was going to explode. "I did!" he shouted at me. "With my brothers and Italian schtonemasons! In nineteen-hundred-twenty-*two*!"

I blinked at him; how many of these Paul Bunyan–isms was I to believe? "Nineteen twenty-two?" I frowned at the distance between us; it was an abyss of time that seemed unbridgeable.

"That's *right*. We wanted a hut for the clients to schtay in for climbing, instead of having to come down to the Chateau every night, you see?"

"Uh huh." I didn't have a clue just then, of course, but it seemed best to play along.

"Some fools are always trying to go up there wearing running shoes instead of *boots*. Don't be that kind of fool."

I glanced down at the old man, feeling like Coleridge's wedding guest gripped by the Ancient Mariner, because he had me by the shirt-sleeve now and would shake it occasionally to emphasize points in his gnomology. That he assumed I would want to go to Abbot's Hut – which I of course did – pleased me. At the same time his assumption of my inexperience, which was correct, annoyed me greatly. What I didn't realize until later was how patient he was being with the pretentious young dolt that I was then. So forceful was his personality, this stranger, that he challenged me to prove myself better than his estimation the moment he spoke to me. He seemed to me then as the spirit of the mountains given a human shape, sent forth as their interlocutor to confront newcomers in the realm.

"Pay attention," he ordered. "That peak, all red where the sun is hitting, south of Lefroy. That is Glacier *Peak*. Then you got Ring-rose, Yukness, Hungabee. Yukness is a good scramble for a beginner to try some time. Turn around here now. To the south you got that glacier in Opabin Pass, just below Hungabee. You go through there then southeast over Wenkchemna Pass and east to Moraine Lake in Banff Park, or instead go south down to Marble *Can*yon, on the Radium *High*way. That's in Kootenay Park. Don't you try and go there, or over Abbot Pass without a real *mountaineer* with you because a *greenhorn* will fall in a crevasse and *die*. You know what is a crevasse?"

"Yes."

"Hey?" His built-in bullshit detector quivered.

"Well, no, not really. I've heard of them."

"That's *right*, you don't know. Good for you. It's a hole in the ice and often it's covered with snow, which is called a snow-bridge, so you don't see it. And if it's weak, you can fall through the *bridge*. If you don't fall to the bottom and get kilt, you get stuck partway in like a cork in a bottle and freeze to death. That's why you need the *r-r-rope*! Always admit what you don't know, except when you are a *guide*. And if you don't know how to use that goddamn *r-r-rope* – leave it at home! Otherwise you chust gonna hang yourself with it."

He paused to puff his pipe, which had gone out, while I stood there, crestfallen, and then he continued: "So above Opabin, that big wall on the west side is Mount Biddle. That ritch running north ends in Mount Schäffer, above the lotch roof there. That's Odaray that nearly kilt you today. That's okay. It's got lots of time to try again. Then you got Cathedral after that – it looks like one. But that's enough free inschtructions for now," he said, winding down, and stopped to relight his pipe with an old cylindrical lighter while I stood there, bemused, wondering what kind of a troll can hew a stone house out of the side of a mountain and set it up amongst the clouds and ice. Wondering why something in me had leapt at the suggestion *when you are a guide*, when I had yet to even climb a difficult mountain. I stood there grinning like an idjit, and Edward gave me a suspicious look.

"So why do I waste my time telling you this news, eh?" demanded Edward, squinting up at me and fixing on me the shrewd old eyes of an Oberland peasant.

"I don't know."

"That's right. You don't *know*, so you still can learn somesing. I caught you in time, you see? After you been here a month, you will think you know *everything*. But you *von't*," he added, firmly, tapping me on the chest with one knuckle for emphasis. His knuckle felt as hard as limestone. "Not next month, not next year. A lifetime; the mountains take you a lifetime. Remember that, and you will know something worth knowing."

He puffed his pipe with great satisfaction for a few seconds, then bid me good day and strolled off along the lakeshore trail leaving me scratching my head and wondering what it was about me that had triggered the combination history-and-climbing lecture. I determined, due to the contempt Edward placed on the word "greenhorn," that I'd better get through that phase as quickly as possible. One other thing I needed, I could see immediately, was a pipe lighter like his. And perhaps if I hunted around in the junk stores in Calgary I might find a pair of those high-water pants like his, too.

PART THREE: THE DEATH TRAP

Shortly after the Mount Odaray Climb, Austin Ford told me that old man Grassi – he was the older of the two wardens stationed at Lake O'Hara – wanted to see me. "Drop over in the evening," he said. "He's out working right now." I had not yet met Lorenzo "Lawrence" Grassi, who was usually out on the trails, but I had met Vitus Germann, the younger of the two wardens based at the patrol cabin, which was set on Sargent's Point at the head of Cataract Brook and across the inlet from the lodge. Sargent's Point was named for the artist John Singer Sargent, who came to the lake in 1916 and wrote to a friend

As I told you in my first or my last, it was raining and snowing, my tent flooded, mushrooms sprouting in my boots, porcupines taking shelter in my clothes, canned food always fried in a black frying pan getting on my nerves, and a fine waterfall which was the attraction to the place pounding and thundering all night. I stood it for three weeks and yesterday came away with a repulsive picture.

Grassi was a famous climber of days gone by and a noted amateur guide, according to Dr. Link. I pictured him as a distinguished-looking person wearing jacket and tie, like the Feuz boys.

It was a hot summer day. I had the afternoon off, and decided to walk up to the Opabin Meadows via Mary Lake trail. I needed to get away from the sight of Sylvie (not her real name), an auburn-haired waitress.

Sylvie was an experienced climber, who, noting my obvious interest in the sport, had taken me up on a local crag and showed me the basics of rock-climbing, belaying, and rappelling. She taught me the old *dulfersitz* method in which the rope is straddled, then passed around one hip, across the chest and over the shoulder to the braking hand. She belayed me while I gingerly leaned out, wide-eyed at the exposure, and took my first hop down a sixty-foot cliff. Naturally, I went ga-ga over this mountain woman. At first that amused her, but then it started to irritate her. Especially when I took to calling on her at all hours with my mandolin in hand, warbling Kingston Trio love tunes like a species of gawky loon.

In the kitchen, I tended to gaze pensively upon Sylvie rather than the potatoes I was peeling, which got me into trouble with Mrs. Nagle, the beloved but temperamental Danish cook. While gawking at this maiden, I cut myself on one of the chef's knives the waitresses insisted on leaving in the bottom of my sink despite my protests. I flipped it the length of the staff table, where it stuck in the bulletin board on the wall, vibrating like a tuning fork. "Do you guys get the goddamn message?" I yelled, cradling my wound. The waitresses were shocked and the cook chased me out of the place waving her rolling pin. They put a few extra knives in the sink for me after that.

So I was going up the trail, head bowed, angry at the world, thinking I'd make a suicidal climb up some precipice or other and yodel defiance to cold-hearted girls and Danish cooks, when I heard rocks cracking together. A boulder about the size of a washing machine went tearing down the talus slopes under the wall that stretched from Mount Schäffer southeast to Mount Biddle. Somebody was working over there, apparently building a trail single-handedly across a rock slide connecting between All Souls' Lookout, as we called it then, and the Opabin Meadows.

I hiked up to the meadows and found the new trail across the rocks, and followed it, amazed to note that some huge boulders that must have weighed close to five hundred pounds had been rolled out of the way, and the tread levelled out with flat stones and shale. This seemed the work of a Cyclops – or an explosives expert.

But at the end of the white scar stood a short, elderly man. The water-streaked walls of the Schäffer-Biddle ridge towered above him for several hundred metres. I had seen the old-timer before. Someone told me he worked as a trail-crew man for the national park and stayed with the wardens. The old man glanced around like a recluse looking for a cave to hide in – a typical response when you interrupted him at his work – then resigned himself to watching my approach, his hands resting on a steel gravel bar. Up to the point where he stood there was the white scar of a new trail that you could hike comfortably. Beyond him, there was no trail; just big rocks piled one on the other on the steep aspect of the slide. All he had were hand tools: a shovel, sledgehammer, two steel gravel bars, a miner's pick and some logs to use as rollers, and a beat-up wheelbarrow to carry his tools in and move loads of shale.

He took off his slouch hat to mop his forehead with an old bandanna as I drew near. "Afternoon," I greeted him.

He wore baggy work pants held up with suspenders, the brass

tabs carrying the trademark word "Police." His khaki shirt needed laundering but what was truly incongruous was his foot gear. Instead of steel-toed work boots, he wore – on this occasion at least – a tattered pair of high-topped black sneakers, the kind that were popular in the sixties and returned to teenage fashion again decades later.

"You dint sign out," said the old man in answer to my greeting. He spoke in a soft but gravelly voice, in an accent that seemed somewhat like that of the Feuz boys to my ears. But if you listened carefully, you would hear an extra syllable at times. I learned later that he was from northern Italy. I stared at him while he stared into his bandanna as if puzzled by his own sweat, until he glanced up at me with a face worked on by wind and sun, the flesh sagging with time around the eyelids and chin; a hound-dog face, but the eyes glimmered with an alert intelligence.

"Sign out?" I was puzzled. "What, to go for a walk?"

He shook his head. "To go up Mount Odaray. 'Schpose you get hurt up there – how we schposed to send you home to Momma, if we donna know where to look for you?" he enquired, politely.

I gaped at him, putting it together at last. Could this be the famous mountaineer and guide? "Are you Grassi – the warden?"

He blinked at me, then cocked one arm around and peered at his shoulder near-sightedly. "Huh," he grunted. "I forget to put on da shirt wit da badges on it." He was not tall and seemed nearly as wide as he was high. He looked positively ancient to my young eyes – he was seventy-two then – yet so strong, like a bull-pine frailed upon by the wind and only bowed a little, as if in humility, to the superior forces of time. An odour came off him, a mix of sweat, sulphur, and chewing tobacco, the sulphur released from limestone that he had been splitting with the sledge and some wooden wedges. Spalls of rock were cast here and there from this work, and a stack of flat rock, split from a block of limestone, waited laying out. Look at this, I thought. He's actually paving the goddamn rock slide! This whole valley must be a work camp for geriatric Swiss trolls. Where do they go at night? There isn't a big enough bridge around here for them all to hang underneath it.

"Dint Vitus tell you, you got to sign out for a climb, and sign back in?" he enquired.

It jogged my memory. "Hell. Yes he did, come to think of it. I guess I forgot." In fact, it hadn't seemed important at the time. We had told the entire staff exactly where we were going.

"Donna forget no more," he said, firmly. "Or else it's gone be trouble for you."

Embarrassed, I made my obeisance. Registering out for climbs was a legal requirement at that time.

"Dat's okay den," he said. He never alluded to it again.

Conversation being over, he handed me, with an absent-minded gesture, the steel gravel bar he'd been holding as if he were offering me a toothpick: it felt as heavy as an anvil to me. He picked up the other one with one hand, planted the end, and commenced prying at a quartzite block about the size of a piano. "Okay, I show you how to do this," he offered. It sounded like a protest, as if I had been hounding him to learn this trade and now he was reluctantly obliging. He pointed out where I was to place the bar. "Lift from your legs," he said. "Never your back."

I hesitated, frowning at him, but I don't think he could see that far any more. So I shrugged my shoulders in acceptance and planted the point of the bar: the boulder was as heavy as a meteorite. We grunted and strained at that thing for about ten minutes, changing our attack as he directed, looking for a balance point and finally, almost imperceptibly, it moved – perhaps an inch – onto one of his wooden rollers placed under its downhill side.

"Now we got it," he said.

"Whattaya mean, we've got it?" I said, in disbelief. I couldn't believe the effort I had put out.

"If I can move it one inch, I can move it forever," he explained.

We stopped to rest. "You was up on the ritch there," he said, gesturing above us, "with Sylvie."

"Yes."

"She's a nice girl, good climber," he ventured.

"Yeah."

My looks must have been transparent. "Whatsamatter? You are crazy for her, eh?"

"Know anything about women?" I asked glumly.

He laughed soundlessly, gazing up at the clouds over the ridge. "Women!" He shook his dewlapped jowls at the notion. "I can't tell you how to get dat gir-r-l," he growled softly. "All I canna show you is how to move mountains."

We inched away at it for another twenty minutes and then the monster suddenly shifted downhill onto the next roller with a grinding noise, tipped slowly over, surrendered to gravity and tumbled end-over-end down the rocks with a thrilling crash and clatter that made the mountains echo.

I helped him for the rest of that day and I think we moved the trail forward about two metres, max. I was glad to get back to the potato peeler, and too tired to think about how gorgeous Sylvie looked in corduroy climbing pants and a turtleneck T-shirt. A few hours of such blatant man's work had burnt off some overwrought passion.

"Vitus has to pa-trrol da Abbot Pass soon," he had said as I was taking my leave. "You should go wit' him. He'll teach you about cornices und schtuff."

So the other trolls had filled him in. But I was glad of the offer.

"Come for tea," said the old man.

Andrea Lorenzo Grassi was born in the province of Piedmont, December 20, 1890. As a young man he worked with his father, a lumberman, and learned his father's trade. He began climbing mountains in the Dolomites of the Italian Tyrol. He immigrated to Canada in 1912 – "I needed to get something to eat" was how he summed up the tough times in Italy. He worked as a lumberjack in Ontario, then moved west and worked as a section man at Hector,

B.C., just north of O'Hara, which he soon began to explore. He fell in love with the place.

In 1916 he settled at Canmore, near Banff, and went to work for Canmore Collieries Ltd. as a miner. This was the great contradiction of his life: a man who loved the mountains and the open sky spent most of his prime years labouring deep in the carboniferous heart of the mountains he loved.

He was soon known in the climbing world for his ascents on Mount Louis, near Banff, leading-edge rock-climbing in that era, like the new routes being pioneered in the European Alps. That clean obelisk must have reminded him of his native Dolomites. Many more first ascents were to come, a lot of them unrecorded, due to his modesty about his accomplishments.

He might easily have set up shop as a mountain guide, especially after being a much publicized part of a Canadian attempt on Mount Waddington in 1936. "I don't climb for money," he told his well-wishers, and people marvelled at his generosity, leading climbs for the Alpine Club of Canada and refusing all payment. Grassi worked underground shifts for over thirty years.

The Alpine Club of Canada probably influenced the national parks' decision to hire Lawrence at Lake O'Hara in 1956, when he was sixty-five years old, solely to keep track of climbing parties in the area and to dispense advice and registration slips to moun-taineers. But as Jim Sime, former Yoho chief park warden once explained it to me: "Lawrence is a man who couldn't bear to sit around with his thumb up his arse all day, so he went to work on the trails. The park was naturally not about to deny him the pleasure."

So noted was he for the miles of trails he had built on his own time, near his Canmore home and in several other places including O'Hara, that he had been cited in the House of Commons as an exemplar of a noble working man by J. S. Wordsworth, the cele-brated socialist politician. The Canadian Youth Hostel Association made him a life member to honour his work, and the Alpine Club

of Canada honoured him with a life membership at age thirty-six –
a great distinction at that time.

Grassi seemed to live only for this toil, like a monk paying
homage to the mountains he loved. His only aim was to make the
splendour of the peaks accessible to people travelling on foot. Some
people said he made the trails too accessible to the hoi polloi, but to
them he said, "I'd rather carry schtones up here than carry some
injured person home on my back."

He was a bachelor all his life. His close friend, Bill Cherak of
Canmore, maintains Lawrence never had a sweetheart, although he
had female friends. The mountains were his mistresses.

There was no light around the warden cabin on Sargent's Point
when I went to see the old man, except for the translucent glimmer
of foam in Cataract Brook breaking over a skiff of rocks into the
trout pool where the cutthroat bed, each in its own lay, and swim
against gravity all night long under the shoulder of Mount Wiwaxy.
I would learn that this absence of light was habitual with the old
man, at least until Vitus got tired of the dark and lit a lantern.

The mantle of night seemed to cling like the cobwebs under the
overhanging eaves of Grassi's cabin. Every night after supper the old
man sat in deep twilight on an easy chair, one that he had hewed
with axe and chainsaw out of a massive fir log. There he waited to
talk to whomever wandered by the cabin; waited to break the fast of
his day-long silence; waited for the darkness that would not give way
to the sun at the end of talking. On the stove he kept a tea kettle
primed and ready.

Vitus had said that Lawrence, who he liked and admired greatly,
would invite the Devil himself in for a cup of tea, so hospitable was
his nature. "He won't turn anybody away when it's wet out and they
get their tents wet," Vitus had told me. Some nights Vitus and the
old man would be tripping over prone figures in sleeping bags on
their way to their bunks.

If you had lived long in that place, you could have felt how the encircling mountains moved closer, like black clouds weaving among the stars. The mountains leaned down over the cabin door, the cave entrance of an oracle, so I thought of Lawrence's en-cabined presence back then. A match flared, and the old man's face, hooded and stubbled with whiskers and blackened by the coal tattoo of the mines, jumped out of the dark like the visage of a prophet. Logs crackled in the cast-iron heater. The match flame tapered to a cone bent to the end of the White Owl cigar he smoked of an evening (a fat corona with a real Havana wrapper in those days). It faded out, leaving only the round, fiery ember of his cigar.

The cigar end would gesture a neon question mark in the darkness, and his voice, hoarse with age and thickened by his Italian heritage, would break the cabin's gloomy spell as if a light had been turned on. He spoke softly of other days and other mountains: of a young married man who perished in a crevasse, and came out at the bottom of the glacier fifty years later, looking as young and as fresh as the day he was married, in the eyes of his wife, who was old and withered on the vine of widowhood. He spoke of St. Elmo's fire dancing on a rack of pitons, a harbinger of a lightning strike. He told me never to challenge a mountain goat for the right of passage: "He'll butt you right off the letch," he assured me.

Once I asked him about the use of crampons; should I buy a pair? He said they were like everything else, only good if you knew how and when to use them. "It was crampons kilt the Mexicans," he said. "They was told not to go out on the face. The schno was too deep that year."

Here at last was a chance to find out what happened on that day in July of 1954. "Who told them?"

He stared out where the lake water rippled on the shore, listening to that voice before continuing. "It was Walter Feuz. He was the boatman, at the Chateau, and a guide. He told dem, schtick to the east ritch, keep to the r-r-rocks. But they climbed out on the face, to the South Peak. They was going to go to the hut after, but inschtead of going down the ritch, the easy way, they try to go down the face again. That's when they fell. Four of dem went down, roped together. One man, the Mexican guide, and three women. Twenty-five hundred feet dey went, all tangled in the r-r-ropes. Then Walter looked up, with the telescope, and saw dey was gone. Just a big track in the schno. He knew dey had fallen."

"They all died?"

"No. Three women was left on the other r-r-rope."

I waited for the story to continue, but instead listened to Lawrence go through a brief coughing fit and lapse into silence, still puffing his stogie.

"So, how did they get the survivors down?"

He thought about it. "You should ask Ernest Feuz," he suggested. "He was there."

But I was not destined to see Ernest again, as it turned out. His nephew Sid Feuz would tell me in 1999 that Ernest made light of the rescue as if it was nothing special. He had taken three bellboys from the Chateau along to help him. What Ernest remembered was how well the three young amateurs did that day.

Lawrence pulled a greasy issue of the *Canadian Alpine Journal* off the shelf. He had an extensive collection of those, as well as a lot of rare old books about climbs and explorations in the Rockies. You would never have said he was bookish to hear him talk. Lawrence fooled people without trying to. He thrived on being underestimated by lesser men. "It's wr-r-ritten up in here," he said. "Keep it. I got an extra one."

I would sit in the dim cabin. In the corner, Vitus lay on his bunk, listening quietly to the old man and grinning at his yarns from time to time. Grassi startled me most with humour when I expected something portentous from his thoughtful silence.

Sylvie and I wound up at the cabin together one evening. Grassi poured us tea. The cigar made its question mark as we sipped the brew.

"Sylvie, why you want to marry dis guy?"

"What!" she protested.

In the darkness, I grimaced with embarrassment.

"Marty, he's a poet. He's a dreamer, always poor. You should marry a rich old man, a pretty girl like you."

"Uh huh." She was amused, waiting for the punch line.

"Sure. You keep house for the rich guy. You have a nice set of schteps in the house." The red eye of the cigar was Lawrence's "talking stick," sketching a zig-zag of stairs on the black palimpsest of night. "All day the old man is out making money. You stay home, polishing da schteps." The red neon circled the dark, polishing. "One day he's coming down da schteps, and he slip – or else maybe accidently you give him a little poosh – while polishing. 'Whoops! Oh chee! I'm so sorry mine darling.' Down he goes, ka-bang!"

Sylvie laughed archly, savouring the old man's scandalous humour. The red eye blazed to yellow as Lawrence inhaled. A small owl cried from the trees near the lake its song of "who cooks fo' you-all." Lawrence's eyes glinted askance in the dim light as he cocked an ear, listening, then continued his fable: "Bang – the old man is dead. It makes you sad: boo hoo." He paused to puff his cigar, leaving us hanging. "But in his will," he rasped on, "he leaves you all his money, no? Then you phone up Marty. He's in the poorhouse by then, schtill crazy for you. Schtill writing poems. Then you marry him, and have some kidts. Better you handle all the money, okay? Marty, he will only dream it all away."

The object of this satire chuckled sardonically over his mug of tea, never dreaming how accurate this sly estimation of his future prospects would turn out to be – and rueful, because I sensed any romantic twinges on Sylvie's part were fading as the summer waned.

"And what if I'm not the marrying kind?" she teased back.

"Huh!" said the old man knowingly, as if he had a basis for his presumption. "Well, I guess you chust keep on climbing mountains. Until you can climba no more. Like me," he added simply, not at all voicing the sadness that the words seemed to imply.

I recently (1998) reread Harry Green's account of the rescue on Mount Victoria that Grassi gave me so many years ago. I wondered again about what was going through Eduardo Sanvincente's head the afternoon of July 30, 1954. If he had been more experienced on northern Rockies snow and ice, he would not have elected to descend the snow-covered southeast face of Victoria on that hot July day. Was his machismo perhaps offended by the brusque warnings of the Switzers at Lake Louise? Did he have something to prove to them, or was he just totally oblivious to the fact that the south ridge of rock was the easier descent route to Abbot's Hut? One can only speculate now.

The cold, hard snow that had made his party's crampons so useful on the ascent route turned wet and sticky under the sun of noon, as they began their descent. With more experience, he might have ordered their removal. One cannot descend a steep snow-and-ice slope while wearing pontoons of balled-up snow. You must stop every few steps and balance on each leg in turn while knocking the snow off your crampons with your ice axe. On a steep face, some kind of fall can be expected in such circumstances. Each person on the rope has to be ready for such a slip. Shortly after the descent began, one of the middle women on the rope slipped and fell, and the guide and his three rope-mates were dragged off their feet before he could set his ice axe and belay them.

Ironically, it was the rope of three less-experienced climbers that survived catastrophe. They were approximately ten to eleven kilometres by boat and on foot from the Chateau, and some 1,600 metres higher in altitude.

Ernest Feuz, then sixty-five years of age, rounded up three climbers from the Chateau summer staff – Charlie Rowland, Ray Wehner, and Frank Campbell (all medical students), along with Harry Green, an Alpine Club of Canada member – and began the rescue operation. Walter Feuz took the party to the head of the lake by motorboat. They waited awhile for the Brewster company's pack-train, which had been dispatched from the Chateau to pack out bodies or survivors on horseback. Ernest, fearing the survivors might eventually panic and fall from their holds as well, decided to push on without the horses.

"We started up the Pass at 4:40 P.M." wrote Green in his account, published in the *Canadian Alpine Journal*, "and climbed quickly to where the bodies were lying. It did not need a doctor to tell us they were all dead."

Recovery of the dead would have to wait. Shaken by the carnage, the rescuers checked each body for signs of life, then pushed on as hard as they could go. They reached the hut in very good time by 6:40 P.M. As they climbed the last slope that led up to the hut, they were greeted by another kind of heartbreaking sight, as Green recalls: "Our thoughts were all about the women still on the snow face when suddenly the hut door opened and a gaily clad, smiling Mexican girl waved us in. She had been in the hut all day and had been trying to get the stove going to prepare food for the others on their return. She spoke no English; we spoke no Spanish, so we could not make her understand what had happened. It was a macabre situation, the poor girl in her bright clothes happily preparing to get a meal for four friends we knew were lying dead on the glacier."

The party had made the four-to-five-hour trip to Abbot's Hut in just two hours, but despite his sixty-five years, Ernest Feuz did not stop to rest there. Leaving three men to prepare for the arrival of the survivors, he took young Charlie Rowland and demonstrated what real mountaineers are made of. They had to gain 380 metres of altitude (my estimate) spread over a kilometre of steep ridge climbing to get to a point directly above the stranded women. They covered ground in thirty-five minutes that might normally take two hours.

Down on the shores of Lake Louise, hundreds of spectators trained binoculars on the mountain, watching the tiny figures, which looked like animated commas on white paper. Whether he realized it or not, this rescue was the very crux of Ernest's long career as far as the public was concerned. It was a public that had known

nothing of his accomplishments in mountaineering up until that
moment, nor would those many climbs and first ascents be remembered should he fail now. But to Ernest it was pretty straightforward
stuff. The essential thing, from a rescue standpoint, was for him to
set up a "bombproof" belay on the top of the mountain so he could
hold with the rope anyone who slipped.

"Ernest went out as far as possible," wrote Green, "and got a good
belay on his axe and Charlie went down on two ropes tied together,
150 feet and cutting good steps. He had a job to get the women to
move: they were nearly frozen and paralyzed with fear. However, he
got a rope tied to them and finally got them up to Ernest. It took
another two hours to get them down the simple rocks of the ridge.
So it was 9:40 P.M. before they got back to the hut."

At 10:30 P.M. Ernest led the party down the mountain. The
rescuers had only two small flashlights to guide them through the
crevasses of the Death Trap. That was fine with Ernest Feuz, who
knew the route inside-out anyway. Darkness in the Death Trap
would be kind to the living; it would hide the sight of four destroyed
human beings from the eyes of their friends. They reached the Plain
of Six Glaciers teahouse at 1 A.M. Ernest guided a larger party back
up the glacier the next day to bring the bodies down to the
teahouse. The Brewster outfit packed them down to the Chateau on
horseback. The media's verdict must have been pleasing to Edward
Feuz. The rescuers and their leader, the stalwart Swiss guide Ernest
Feuz, were portrayed as national heroes who had saved unwary
foreigners from the perils of the Canadian wilderness. Ernest probably wondered what all the fuss was about.

Vitus said I was welcome to come along on his weekly patrol
through Abbot Pass. He had a lot of building supplies to haul up to
the hut to effect repairs. I offered to carry some.

We loaded two Trapper Nelson packboards with shingles, paint,
and window shutters for the hut the night before the trip.

In the evening light we went over some of the knots we would use the next day: the bowline on a coil, prusik knot, and improvised chest harness using the climbing rope. Vitus's skill was apparent in the fluid way he handled the ropes. I told him about my wish to climb Hungabee and allowed that I was looking for a partner. Vitus knew about my lack of experience; he was noncommittal about the idea of climbing that peak with a beginner. I regaled him with an account of what Ernest had said to me, what Edward had to say about my trip under the cornice. He was quiet, fiddling with the rope. I made a crack about Grassi's running shoes. I suppose I was trying to amuse him by taking the mickey out of the old boys, trying to present myself as somehow more accomplished than the oldsters thought. Vitus just gave me a quizzical look. I mentioned that someone had told me the old man had climbed Hungabee wearing rubber boots.

"I can't imagine that. And he got to the top, too."

"Of course," said Vitus, tersely. "It's not the blooming boots that climb the mountain, you know. It's what you put inside them."

I thought about that, and was quieted.

At age thirty-two, Vitus was a tough, wiry mountaineer, brown-haired and blue-eyed and built for efficiency and speed at five foot six and 145 pounds. I thought of him as being a bit dour at times and not much for idle chat, though he would tell you he was a pretty mellow guy back then. Action was his milieu. When he got restless, he would take off on a solo climb. One August day he left the warden cabin at 5:15 A.M. (it sits at 2,018 metres) climbed Mount Wiwaxy (2,706 m.), Mount Huber (3,358 m.), and the south peak of Victoria (3,310 m.), then descended to the hut at 2,926 metres, which he reached at 3 P.M. before returning to O'Hara. I asked him about that trip, but his only comment was: "That was the longest day of my life."

We left the warden cabin in the dark before dawn, and walked down along the lakeshore, feeling the heavy loads settle in. Talk was minimal. We needed to pace ourselves and save our breath, especially me. Vitus set a blistering pace and I had to put out to keep up with him. "We have to get through the Death Trap before the sun gets too high," he explained, "and the ice starts coming down." His purpose was to check conditions in the pass, and also to spot-check for the kind of stranded greenhorns who occasionally venture into the Death Trap wearing only running shoes and hiking togs.

At that time the trail ascended next to Seven Veils Falls via some slippery switchbacks. I knew the way as far as Lake Oesa; it leads through an enchanted hanging-valley landscape of rushing water and sparkling pools, overlooked by high mountains capped with small glaciers.

Just below Victoria Falls is an amazing feature, a stone staircase that takes you up over the cliff that blocks the trail. The steps replaced an old ladder, somewhat rotted out, that was still leaning against the cliff in those days.

"It must have taken a helluva crew of men to build those," I said to Vitus.

"Yes," he said. "Ten men, all named Lawrence Grassi."

"You're kidding. Not by himself!"

"You've seen how he can work."

Some of the big, flat stones of the base would have weighed hundreds of pounds. He had levered them down from above, then piled smaller boulders on top by hand to make the steps. When I asked him about it later, all he said was, "I chust like to work with schtones. You know, the Schviss like to say – Italians built Schvitzerland."

Lake Oesa, at the foot of the Oesa Glacier, is surrounded by rock slides. Here, the trail turned into a goat path ascending over glaciated rock bands until we rounded the corner of Victoria and started up the steepest, longest rock chute I had ever seen. It was a case, as one wag puts it, of "rubble without a pause." Despite my vow of silence, a state that Vitus observed with monk-like diligence, I started peppering him with questions about the route ahead and the climbs he had done. But after about twenty steps up that slope, I slowly wheezed into silence, breathing hard under the load of window shutters and paint. The shale and boulders of the chute, resting temporarily at an angle that looks like fifty-five degrees, form a moving treadmill under your feet. In some stretches you are taking two steps for every step you gain. The pass is only about two hundred metres wide, bordered by the walls of Mount Victoria to the west and Lefroy to the east.

"Takes your breath away, doesn't it?" said Vitus dryly. His own load of shingles and stovepipes seemed almost as long as he was. "Watch for rockfall. Try to stay out in the centre."

After two hours of toil that went on for a week, I could see the sickle of blue sky that marked the summit of the pass – but there was no hut in sight. Maybe the whole thing was just an old goat's story.

A buttress depended down the pass to meet us, blocking the view. We worked our way alongside it, hanging on to its wall at times as small slides of shale and boulders threatened to carry us down the chute. Then a rattle of tin at my feet revealed signs of man's habitation – some sardine and bully-beef cans decades old. Peering around the corner of that promontory I was delighted to see the outline of a roof gable somewhere above it. Slowly the mythic structure grew to my sight, seeming to rise up before me from the very stone of the col from which it was laid up. It was called a hut, but in effect it was a stone chalet nestled at the foot of Victoria's east ridge, so close that the castellated ridge seemed melded with its back wall.

The tongue of the glacier that filled the west side of the pass lapped right up to the east wall of the hut in those days. In that wild and desolate place the hut should have looked incongruous, but built from the native stone, it looked like something far older and more at home there than its forty-one years of solitude might have conjured. Over the years, noted climbers from all over the world had sheltered here and knocked off the classic alpine ascents on Mount Lefroy and Mount Victoria and adjacent peaks.

The hut held the altitude record for a building in Canada then

(9,597 feet, or 2,926 metres), but the highest structure there by a metre or so was the infamous Abbot Pass crapper. This cracker-box boothy, built on stilts with boards nailed in place to hold its tottering shite-stalagmite in situ, perched noisomely behind the hut, quelled only by generous sprinkles of lime.

It was wired onto a gendarme of rock so it wouldn't blow away. I had heard tell that the wind coming up from Oesa in a storm was magically funnelled up through the bottom of this structure. According to legend, it was strong enough to blow one's deposits right back up one's fundamental orifice. (I found out later there was some truth in that yarn.) They said the climb up the east ridge of Victoria was far more difficult than the guide book said it was because of the slippery effluvium plastered to the rock by the wind.

At night the wind plucked a tune on the anchor cable:

and praised, with ululations,
the virtues of constipation.

When the wind got moving at Abbot Pass, everything moved. Keeping the shingles on the roof was an ongoing job for the O'Hara wardens. A place named Abbot Pass Hut (we called it Abbot's Hut) might have been an ideal spot for an anchorite-in-residence, but there was no hut custodian in those days as there is now. When people neglected to close the shutters and latch them, the wind blew them to bits, and without shutters to protect them, the windowpanes could be blasted out by flying pieces of shale.

Some young climbers seemed to take a patrician attitude to mountain huts, à la Mary Shelley: "As for living, the servants can do that for us." Vitus was involved in a feud with the student staff from Lake Louise, who were notorious for leaving the place dirty. They were careful not to leave their names in the log book, so he could not run them down easily. Vitus was a working man, a journeyman metal worker and a miner, the product of tough times in Bavaria during the war and afterwards. He came to Canada in 1951, aged twenty, poor and hungry, and worked in the mines of the West Kootenays to "feed my mouth," as he put it. He had paid his dues to earn a pro-ski instructors badge. Soon he would qualify as a mountain guide, and at age thirty-two, he resented having to clean up after spoiled college brats. "They have no respect for anything," he said. I copied down one of the frustrated notes he left in the log that September:

On routine patrol found the Hut in very dirty condition it must take a University Education to live Like pigs. found a stak [*sic*] of dirty dishes, beds unmade, shutters and doors open and garbage in just about every corner of the Hut. I have cleaned the Hut often this summer. this time I will leave it for other people to see.

I absorbed Vitus's attitude to such types along with the basic skills of glacier travel that he taught me. I think one reason for my admiration for him, Lawrence, and the Feuzes came from my own sense of deprivation in childhood days and later. They were intelligent men who had not had an easy ride. They pulled themselves up by the laces of their mountain boots. They inspired a lad who was far from sure of how to make his way in the world. And when the chips were down, they would come through, carry people out of harm's way and cheat death – at least temporarily. They walked the walk.

Lawrence had carried a climber down from a peak in the Tonquin Valley; carried an injured woman down from Castle Mountain in Banff Park; retrieved the dead bodies of avalanche victims and rock climbers. I'd asked him about those exploits, but all he would tell me was "In da mountains, we don't leave our friends behind."

We unloaded our supplies and cached them for installation next trip, then melted glacier ice in a pot on the Coleman stove and satisfied our thirst with a gallon of tea. The hut was moderately tidy on this occasion; its venerable old Hudson's Bay blankets, which

were carried partway up the ice by pack horses and on men's backs
in 1922, were folded up on the bunks in the two sleeping rooms.
There were more bunks and blankets upstairs in the loft. It was a
gloomy but not unfriendly little fortress, its windows built on the
small side for security against storms. The pot-bellied stove looked
welcoming for a cold day. We stacked the split wood we had carried
up with us behind the stove as a peace offering to the next traveller.

You didn't sit around very long when travelling with the ener-
getic Vitus. By 9:15 we were standing on the edge of the ice and
roping up for the descent. The summits of Victoria and White and
Lefroy glowed in the morning sun. I stared up at door of the hut,
picturing that gaily clad young woman waving a merry greeting to
the white-faced rescue team on a warm and welcoming afternoon.

Below was a forbidding sight. The glacier dropped away before
us towards the floor of the Death Trap Canyon, a narrow defile less
than two hundred metres wide, cloaked in perpetual shadows and
bordered by high cliffs on either side. On the west side it was
menaced by towering cliffs of ice from a hanging glacier. Massive
slabs of ice would drop off there betimes, as if cut away by an invisible blade. The floor of the Death Trap was littered with shattered
behemoths.

People refer to climbing hardware as "tools." Back then, I thought
of the ice axe and piton hammer as weapons. We girded on the
harness and clipped on ice pitons and ice screws and extra prusik
slings as if loading ourselves for battle. Vitus rattled off instructions
and I tried my best to take it all in: how to use the ice axe as a belay
post; how to chop a spot for an ice screw to tie off a fallen man. . . .
He ran through the sequence of moves in a crevasse rescue.

I fished the loop of my prusik sling, which was tied off to the
climbing rope, through my chest harness. After a fall into a crevasse,
the idea was to step into the loop, relieving the pressure of the harness
from the back and kidneys. "Don't let slack build up in the rope,"
cautioned Vitus. A fall into a crevasse would be stopped quickly if
the rope was kept snug. I tightened the loop on my ice axe and we

were off with Vitus leading the way, probing for crevasses with the steel-pointed shaft of his axe.

The ice was in good condition, covered by layers of névé snow, and I wondered if all these precautions were necessary. "Watch it now!" called Vitus soon after we left the hut. "We are coming to the 'schrund." A dark shadow made a zig-zag through the ice across the middle of the pass. In a few more steps I saw the blue ice of a major chasm, the bergschrund that forms close to where a glacier joins its headwall. This took the form of two large crevasses, one slightly higher than the other with an intact block of snow and ice in the middle. Vitus crossed it first and then I had my first look into the bowels of a glacier, a terrifying place where blue ice studded with rocks narrowed down into a black void where nothing animate could survive. It seemed like indifference had been given a physical shape.

In 1922, pack horses had carried lumber and supplies for the hut construction as far as this bergschrund. One horse perished when it fell into a crevasse. To cross the bergschrund, the guides and workers carried everything up a steel ladder on their backs, then loaded it on a sledge attached to a cable. This was winched up the ice by hand to the summit. The total cost of hut construction, to the CPR, was $30,000, a lot of money back then.

The route grew steeper as we approached the upper reaches of the Death Trap Canyon. A riff of clouds hung below us, partly obscuring the route. The main danger would be from crevasses, icefalls off Victoria, and rockfall on either hand, the "objective" hazards of mountaineering.

Vitus led the way, probing for crevasses with his ice axe as he went, though the ice was tracked by previous parties. "We don't know who made those tracks," he explained, "or if they knew anything about climbing."

I thought of the tracks I had followed blindly up Odaray: who had made those? This glacier travel was more complicated than I had imagined. If my partner had fallen in a hole, I would have been powerless to help him out.

I concentrated on minding the rope. "That's where the Mexicans fell," said Vitus, pointing out the upper slopes of Victoria near South Peak.

So this was the place, I thought: whistling past the graveyard. I was staring up at the cliffs, overhung with towering ice walls, in fearful fascination, imagining that terrible slide. The dead still keep their names, and their secrets: Eduardo Sanvincente, 43, Beatriz Diaz, 24, Lucia Ocaranza, 26, and Maria Luisa Fabila, 35, slid and tumbled for over six hundred metres down the face of Victoria, entangled in the climbing rope in a mill of flailing crampon points, first over ice broken by rock outcrops, then over bare rock. Death, or at least unconsciousness, probably from striking projecting rocks, would have occurred shortly after the fall began. They would have fallen free over the precipice above me, landed there on the ice – dispatching anyone still living – and narrowly missed being swallowed by a large crevasse, before gradually sliding to a stop.

I was still staring up at the cliffs when one leg suddenly went through the snow up to my hip and I fell on my side. I thought my heart would jump out of my throat. There wasn't time to yell a warning, but my hands lighted close to the edge of the hidden crevasse, where the snow was firm, and it held me up. Feeling the rope come tight, Vitus stopped, turned quickly, and slipped the coil in his hand around his shoulder to make a standing belay just in case the bridge collapsed. I stared down through the hole and saw a tube of darkness into the depths and I scrambled over the weak spot, trembling a little. "You should probe with your ice axe, too" Vitus warned. "Don't just follow blindly. Use your head."

The sun was getting higher and we picked up the pace at the bottom of the canyon. As if in warning, there was a cannonade of rocks falling down a gully on Lefroy. They clattered on the big scree terrace above the cliffs, then there was a fluttering sound for a few seconds, then a hollow "boom" as the biggest one struck the ice a few hundred metres up in front of us and shattered into flying fragments. "It's the one you don't hear coming that kills you," commented Vitus.

"Now we're gonna move fast," he added, "before some of that comes down," and he gestured to the ice that overhung the precipice to the west. My eyes were big: this whole place was a shooting gallery, and we were the targets.

The mice were entering the Mousetrap, as Grassi called the Death Trap Canyon. Once he had guided a party of cooks from the Chateau up this canyon. They had wanted to go to the hut for a celebration. A chunk of ice the size of a small ship had toppled down in front of them with a tremendous rumble and crash, right in their path. Ice was the strike bar of the Mousetrap for Grassi, I guess. The cooks took off running back to Lake Louise, jumping over crevasses like hurdlers in a race, discarding their packs as they went. "For a long time," he recalled, "coming up da pass after, out from da schno would melt us a bottle of rum, schnapps, or a frozen roast chicken. It was good."

It was in the canyon that Edward Feuz had his closest brush with disaster. An avalanche of snow and ice had caught two parties in the Death Trap. The wind blast from such a slide is severe. It knocked the second party off their feet and sent them tumbling across the ice. Some were injured when they struck the cliff of Mount Lefroy. In the first party, people, including Edward, were buried in the snow. He wound up with just his fingertips above the snow, like a man signalling for "time out" in a game called Death. One of the Chateau cooks saw his fingers, and dug him out with his bare hands, crying with cold and pain as he did so. Once freed up, Edward spotted a hat under a slab of ice. There was a head under it and it was still connected to a live body "kneeling like a priest in the snow," and Edward dug him out. Nobody died that day, though several were badly hurt.

Vitus and I hugged the cliffs of Mount Lefroy, moving fast, beetle-like things in the scale of that trap, until we came out where the pass opened up and the going was flatter. I breathed a sigh of relief. But here was a different obstacle: the ice was scored with water runnels and small crevasses. The outlet stream was rumbling through a cavern somewhere under our feet. We played hopscotch with these man-traps until we came to the lateral moraine above Lake Louise. Ahead of us was the Plain of Six Glaciers teahouse, succour for a raging thirst, where a young man could lounge picturesquely among the sudden influx of tourists, a traveller from forbidden realms.

After a few pots of tea, we trotted down the trail to the Chateau, which has always reminded me of a naval barracks plunked down in paradise. We were headed for the O'Hara bus, but Vitus detoured towards the big doors of the hotel. Our boots were muddy and I hesitated about entering those posh corridors. "Your boots are not that bad," said Vitus. "Besides, they never worry about leaving a mess for me to clean up."

The sudden crush of humanity was overwhelming after those hours of solitude on our journey from Shangri-La back into syphilization. A hotel worker saw us enter and rushed forward officiously to intercept us. Grubby-looking mountaineers had no business wandering through a mountain hotel. He stopped short, seeing Vitus's national park uniform and the chiselled set of his jaw. I left a fine set of tracks on the polished floor out to the north doors and the bus. It was silly, but very satisfying to bring a bit of the outdoors into that urban outpost.

I had been thinking about Hungabee – for the wrong reasons. I imagined that climbing Hungabee would be an act so desperate (given my lack of experience) that it would actually impress the unimpressable Sylvie.

Its presence was a heavy hand in my dreams. It rose from a rough couch of ice and rock above the Opabin Glacier to lean against the sky that fell from its overhanging eastern arêtes. Where the other peaks gazed into the lake, that one stared only upwards from its angled western face, giving back the sun's fierce glare by day with its gleaming snowfields, and cupping the moon in its cols by night.

Lawrence's voice grew quieter at the mention of the peak, as if wary of rousing its attention.

"I climb it, a couple of times," he said, but declined to elaborate, except to add, "Near da top, da rock gets black, like coal."

"Um. Did you use many pins?"

"What's dat?"

"Pins – pitons. There's supposed to be some steep pitches," I continued. "Thought maybe you might have used a pin – to anchor a belay stance or . . ." my voice trailed off. The dark silence the old man sat in was intimidating.

The cigar puffed yellow again. "No," Lawrence answered.

"Oh."

There were often long silences between sentences when Lawrence spoke, as if he needed to catch his breath. I had the feeling that even in darkness he could see what I was thinking though I couldn't see him. I used to feel uncomfortable with these silences. "I only use one piton," he offered, sympathetically, offering me a crumb of hope after a long moment went by.

"So, you only used one piton on Hungabee?"

"Only use one piton in my life," corrected Lawrence.

"Oh." I gaped at his shadowy form. It seemed incomprehensible that a man could scale as many mountains as he had, including first ascents and tough rock climbs, and never use a piton to anchor a belay position, or for the leader's direct aid or protection when making a new route up an unclimbed pitch.

"You know dose slab on Sawback?" asked Lawrence.

"Those steep buggers near Banff?"

The cigar end nodded. "One time I use a piton there," confessed Lawrence. "To make a rappel. Only make a fifty foot rappel. I din't really need it," he added apologetically. "I was in a hurry, dat's why. Had to get back to da mine, to go on shift."

"I see." I was beginning to get an inkling. "So, you don't like using pitons?"

The old man cleared his throat as if he might want to spit but thought better of it. I suspect he had a trace of black lung from the pits; there was always something rasping in his chest. "It's okay for them," he offered, meaning the climbers of the new generation, "if they like to build a ladder up a face. I won't like it."

He paused for a moment, then went on. "I like to go up da mountain da easy way. I follow da ridges. Like to take time to look around. Like to look at the scenery. But you can't see nothing climbing a face like dat. You got to watch where you put the pitons. You too busy hang-ging on to look at the view. I know I won't enchoy it a-tall."

I ventured the opinion that pitons could be a very useful tool to have along, even on the standard routes. Local climbers had told me to take some pins along, should I attempt Hungabee.

Lawrence replied with more silence. "You know Greenwood?" he finally demanded.

"Brian Greenwood? I bought my gear from his store down in Calgary."

"Greenwood knows about Hungabee," said Lawrence.

"Greenwood is an amazing climber," I interjected.

"Usc a lot of iron, dese new kidts," said Lawrence, gruffly, and it seemed politic to button up. That Greenwood might be thought a kid had not occurred to me. The new technology, relying on hardware to climb what was once pronounced unclimbable, was anathema to many of the Old Guard who felt that faces that could not be climbed without hardware should be left alone, and who predicted dire consequences for the iron-mongers of the peaks. Edward Feuz called such heretics "blacksmiths."

"When you get caught, high up on da peak, in a lightning schtorm, you have to get down fast," said the old man, who was now a dim outline in the room. "Sometime you got to take all dat iron off and put it away from you, if you can't get down fast. You see fire on da schteel . . ."

"Fire?"

"St. Elmo fire. Everything metal, like it's on fire, shooting off sparks. On your hair, too. 'Lectricity in the air. Get down fast. All that metal, you are like a damned lightning rod, eh? Dat's what happened to Greenwood," he confided, his voice like a harsh whisper now, cigar end leaning forward in the dark. "On Hungabee. Near the top, on that black rock. Hit by lightning. It blew his boot sole right off his boot."

The hair rose on the back of my neck. It sounded like Hungabee had struck Greenwood down for profaning the mountains with pitons. Lawrence leaned back again, puffing his cigar. "He comes here with his friend, Lofthouse. One o'clock in the morning. Lofthouse has to rope him down the mountain. Lofthouse has some cord along; he ties Greenwood's boot together so he can walk. Greenwood is in very bad shape. Took him a long time to get better."

I marvelled that a man might be hit by lightning and survive.

"Mountains are big," said Lawrence. "Men are small. The clouds come in very fast. They hide behind da big peak, and before you know it, they are on you. You got to keep your eyes peeled."

I wanted to climb the mountain, but it didn't seem like the right time to mention that. I would not climb it until 1967, climbing second behind Tim Auger, who I would later work with in the warden service.

This boy I was thought of the peak they called "The Chieftain" as waiting for his attempt upon it back then, not because his ego was so towering that mountains waited for him, but because everything a young man does seems charged with import to him, in the absence of knowing the history of a place. If you had said – as a better climber said it years later – "We may love the mountains, but the mountains don't love us," he would have said it was a true statement, but in his heart he would have doubted it.

But after that I would think about the lightning, always, when I was climbing, and I would watch for the clouds that had nearly rubbed out Brian Greenwood, who was, like Heinz Kahl, a true son of the mountains. If it could happen to Greenwood, it could happen to me.

Like Sylvie, Hungabee started to recede a bit for me. It wasn't going anywhere. There was world enough and time for Hungabee and me.

I started looking for mountains that were within my reach and settled on Lefroy one September day. I hiked up Abbot Pass from Oesa September fourth, on a night of wind, rain, and serious lightning, "all alone and loney." Things were rattling down the mountain from the thunder wading among the peaks. And rounding the pillar near the summit after this desperate clutch and stagger, I looked up and saw a light in the dark sky, which was the window of the hut. Bursting in out of the storm I found one Arnold Shives boiling tea over the flame of a Coleman lantern. We climbed Mount Lefroy in the morning in perfect conditions, kicking steps in the snow for one and a half hours to the top, and descending in long, wild glissades back down to the hut in thirty minutes. That time I led the way down through the Death Trap to Lake Louise, and the Death Trap was the entry to the other world called The Rest of Your Life. When Lawrence told me we were lucky to have such good conditions on Mount Lefroy, I was too young to know what the conditions might have been in the past, but interested enough to sit down and hear his explanation. In the end, that was the most important lesson the old trolls taught me – how to listen.

I'm still trying to get that one right.

CHAPTER FOUR

Grub-Hoe Days

The Twice As Much Kid was starting to get on my
nerves. One day the Kid, who was destined to be a ski
resort mogul in Banff Park and elsewhere, would get on
other people's nerves also, at least on those of park
lovers who think of themselves as conservationists. Not that in his
more mature version he is not seen by his admirers as a conservationist also – but hold on: this is Alberta, land of Orwellian double-
speak, where the term "minister of the environment" actually means
"minister of industrial development." Or maybe there is just a
fundamental difference in aesthetic perception between conservationists who can admire the beauty of ski lifts, ski lodges, clear-cut
ski runs, hotels, parking lots and heavy vehicle traffic in a national
park, and conservationists who can't. Or perhaps Albertans don't
really have a clue any more about what the word conservation
means. For my money, a conservationist is someone who understands that when Mother Nature says no, the lady means no.

Anyway, we were building a new hiking trail (which also would
not be met with approval by many conservationists of today); I

believe it led to Hector Fire Lookout. I was twenty-two, and beginning my career in the national parks service at the very bottom rung
– by swinging a grub hoe on the warden trail crew.

This is an hoary and forgotten path of entry into the mountain
outfit. Your nineties-style park warden, adjusting his cycling or
paddling gloves during a well-earned day off, will typically have
degrees, sometimes at the Master's level, in resource management,
biology, or environmental design. This is the age of the credential,
worshipped by personnel managers everywhere. The name of the
game is to make things that work in practice, work in theory – a
Herculean task. Hard to believe that only thirty years ago the words
"environment" and "ecology" seldom crossed a newspaperman's lips.
Nowadays, thanks to the environmental movement and people like
me glamourizing the warden occupation in print, there are hundreds
of applicants for every position. Few of us showed up with university degrees prior to the 1970s. The low-paying job of a practical-
conservationist cum cowboy cum maintenance-man cum tree-fuzz
had little cachet in the 1960s. Chief wardens were not looking for
the computer literate so much as the merely literate high-school
graduates, the ones with horse sense, the ones with bush smarts
rather than "communication skills." Slinging the bullshit – the
homelier term – was as popular then as it is now. In the sixties it was
seen as a vice, not an attribute you tarted up with euphemisms for
your resumé. But then the only resumé we knew about in the olden
days was as in "resume working."

Today's new recruit typically starts off with a pencil and a notebook – if not lap-top computer. In the 1960s, we started out with
work gloves and hardhats, degree or no degree. "You buggers don't
look smart enough to handle an axe yet," said Zony, the trail crew
foreman, during those first halcyon days spent on the federal teat.
"Stick to the grub hoe for now. If you don't kill each other with that,
you'll graduate to the polaski. That's the hoe with the axe blade on
one side. And like I told ya before – keep your heads up when you
hear the chainsaw stop. Could mean a tree's comin' down."

"Aren't you supposed to yell 'Timber'?"

Zony stared bleakly at the insouciant young Jerry Walsh. He it was who had enquired about the idea of trading grub hoes for axes.

"You in college too, like Slim here?"

"Yeah."

Zony spat out a stream of smokeless tobacco, a.k.a. "snoose." "You guys read too many books. It'll wear your brains out before your time."

Jerry smiled thinly at me as Zony moved up the trail. "I guess that means they don't yell 'Timber.'"

I glanced up the line of blue seismic-ribbon marking the new eight-foot right-of-way where Brown, the ancient chainsaw man, bent among the stumps of his victims, touching up his chain with a file. He suddenly hacked convulsively and spat something out. He did not look well. "Looks like he has to save his breath," I muttered.

I had only worked a few weeks on the trail crew but it seemed like a year. I was paying my dues, trimming off the urban fat and getting ready for the much coveted acting-warden job at Lake O'Hara, and I was already on the boss's shit list – literally. Fred Dixon was the warden in charge, and he'd overheard me not only bitching about horseshit on the trails, but expounding on how horses wrecked the trails and had no place in the national parks. Trouble was, the warden service was (and still is) a cavalry outfit. The shit came from Fred's favourite saddle horse, and he was sitting on his horse at the time, right behind me. After that, whenever I buttonholed Fred and wanted to know when I would be going to Lake O'Hara, he'd get a faraway look in his eye and mutter something about it being a little hot out for snowshoeing and sort of change the subject. "There's still a lot of snow up at Lake O'Hara," was about the only concrete fact he would offer.

In fact it was fiery hot and as dry as a popcorn fart on the steep slopes where we worked, and snow seemed like a pleasant fantasy. Lake O'Hara gets fifteen feet of snow some winters. But there was nothing for me to do up there, as Zony kept reminding me, until the snow went out and the tourists went in. At the end of each sweltering day, he would shift his wad of snoose, maybe pick another wood tick off his neck and hold it up to admire it for a moment before flicking it back into the bush and saying "Well Slim, another day, another inch of snow melted. Only about sixty inches more to go. Now if you figger no cloudy days this summer, which you can't, you should be into O'Hara about September first. Just before the first winter snowfall." Then he would slap his leg and wheeze out his Woody Woodpecker laugh.

I swung the blade down, cut through the duff, through roots, pulled the dirt and tree roots towards me, raked them to the edge of the eighteen-inch-wide tread of the long, narrow wound. Carried over streams on log bridges, sometimes following and sometimes bisecting game trails and old Indian travel routes, park hiking trails will ford muskeg on corduroy of felled logs, and switchback up the mountainside over rock and scree slopes to make a grade of ten percent per mile – when possible. Trails carry hikers, mountaineers, and equestrians from the highway up into the old slow world of foot travel, the backcountry, the country at the back of our minds where the wilderness begins in wild surmise and stretches at the beck of our muscles to be discovered.

"Hey Sisyphus," I called to young Jerry, that inveterate reader of many texts, but especially Jack Kerouac. He would soon be ensconced atop this mountain as a lookout man. His girlfriend, known on the park radio net by the code name "The Blue Elk," was probably packing her rucksack back in Calgary right then, judging by the faraway look in his eye. "Gimme a hand rolling this boulder up the mountain. Is it not fit for rip-rap, forsooth?"

"Or more likely back-crack, in truth," replied Jerry. Grunting, we pushed it over the edge of the trail, where it would rest against a tree and make a bulwark to hold the dirt in place. Young Charlie Locke, another labourer on the crew, frowned at our parley and struck bitter blows at the wounded earth, like a man bent upon the Lord's work.

Zony's crew consisted of a faller (chainsaw man), axe men, and the rest of us, mere grunts with primitive tools – the grub hoe, the shovel, the pry bar.

Charlie had caused Zony to frown, due to his work habits. He liked to work hard; no doubt he still does. Some inner fire was driving him to excel, and one day he would achieve much in the world of business. In these fraught times ending the millennium, when capitalists talk and talk and the rest of us are expected to listen like famous Nipper, the RCA Victor dog, Locke has been somewhat in the public eye. In an interview, he recalled thinking at the far-off time I write of: "This is so boring, my challenge is to do twice as much as anybody else. So if one labourer wheeled one wheelbarrow full of dirt, I'd do two. So it was interesting. It was my first experience with the wardens."

I don't quite agree with Locke's take on the situation back then. He is critical of park wardens these days and I think his point, looking back, was that the rest of us were a bunch of loafers. So every morning he would shoulder his pack, grab whatever object needed hauling, and take off up the trail at the trot, leaving the rest of us hiking up at the approved government pace, which was, I admit, not a trot. On the other hand, we were carrying odds and ends such as chainsaws and jerry cans of gas on our backs, so it wasn't exactly a nature walk with the Brownies. As I recall, our chainsaw man was sixty-five years old, known to cough up blood occasionally, and his running days were over. Frenchy, the axe man, though lean as a greyhound, was likewise too old for the pentathlon.

Anyway, the Twice As Much Kid would usually reach the end of the construction, a kilometre or two up the trail, before the rest of us and would have already grubbed out several metres of new tread before we arrived on the scene. He would greet us with his usual fierce grin, the effect made more sinister by the steam covering the thick lenses of his spectacles on cold mornings. I think it was just to annoy Locke at this point that Zony would order a coffee break before we had done a lick of work.

I stared at the rocks below my feet while resting, thinking of Lake O'Hara. I was to spend the summer there working with one Bernie Schiesser who I had yet to meet. Don Vockeroth, the last incumbent, had broken his leg while skiing the previous winter. There were some projects at O'Hara that needed doing, and the park had decided to hire two people instead of one.

"Bernie's a good woodsman," said Zony as we hiked up the trail together one morning. "He's a lumberjack, like me. Runs the other trail crew in the summer, same as me." Zony gave me a friendly slap on the back – which was like being petted by a black bear. It sent me staggering. "He says to tell you, stop pesterin' Fred Dixon about when you go to O'Hara. The more you ask him, the longer he will leave you on the trail crew. Bernie knows Fred. So don't cross Bernie," he advised, and he spat out a bead of tobacco juice, which dissolved a nearby anemone as if hit with battery acid. "I've never known young Bernie to lose a scrap. Ha! Ha ha ha!"

Never lost a scrap: I pondered that. The last scrap I had been in had turned out badly – for me. I never knew when to keep my mouth shut, especially when people insulted me. I blame my parents, especially my feisty Geordie mother, for inculcating this prideful attitude. Three toughs in Montreal had jumped my room-mate Barry McKinnon and me on Côte des Neiges the previous fall after making obscene suggestions about our relationship that were untrue. (After that incident, Barry and I vowed never to be seen in public together again while wearing identical corduroy sports jackets.) Barry, who treated the incident as he would a grizzly-bear encounter in our native mountains, came out of it okay, the shrewd little swine. He had set down his bag of groceries as a peace offering, then backed away slowly, talking soothingly as it were, then dropped to the sidewalk and assumed a fetal position with his hands protecting the back of his neck and requested, in his quiet way, "Please don't hit me, sir."

"I wish I had done the same." That's what I had told the intern up at the Royal Victoria Hospital afterwards.

"Oh bullshit," he had replied. "You macho assholes are all the same." I hear his hard words now as if it were yesterday. "Do you mind if I sew your ear up without anaesthetic? There's not many nerves in that part."

"Oh please, be my guest," I had said bitterly.

I had broken my wrist alongside the head of one of them. I should have known better than to use a fist on a knothead. In fact, I had just pried the cast off my arm, using a serrated kitchen knife, a month or so before reporting for work. Now I was going to have to share the tiny Lake O'Hara cabin with this scrapmeister, Bernie Schiesser. Don't cross him! Hell, I would have to cross his path every morning, unless I remained motionless. The prospect of playing Xs and Os with a bull goose of the woods had me worried. For a while, I took up chewing tobacco just to get toughened up to deal with Schiesser – until I swallowed a chaw by accident and shat fire for three days. I decided, better the old peace pipe and the philosophical approach for me. In the meantime, I resolved to stay mum around Warden Dixon.

One morning as we sipped our coffee, a spruce grouse stalked slowly out of the shadows of the old-growth forest, froze with one foot in the air, regarded each of us in turn with tiny jerks of his head, then turned around and ran back into the shadows. Frenchy sat down on the fallen log next to me and gave the Kid a sidelong glance. "Dis Charlie guy," he hissed at my ear, "What is he on?"

"Testosterone," I answered. "Same as everybody else on this crew."

Frenchy thought my entire generation were depraved drug abusers. He called me the hippie, and he used to tell me to get my hair cut about every twenty minutes.

There was no doubting that Charlie Locke had *cojónes*. He came to our lowly trail crew as one of the new *wunderkind* of the Alberta climbing scene. He and his longtime friend Don Gardiner had astounded the old fogies of the peaks just a year earlier, completing a traverse of twenty-three peaks from Moraine Lake to Lake Louise in just six days, a feat which has yet to be repeated as I write this. His climb on the ice-swept north face of Mount Temple, led by Brian Greenwood, would briefly set a brand new standard in North American climbing. He would quit the trail crew that July in order to second Greenwood on the Mount Temple climb.

Locke knew that my climbing experience did not match his own, and I believe it rankled him that I should have been given the assistant warden job at Lake O'Hara, which was much coveted. The warden at O'Hara was known as the "climbing warden," because he (there were no women in the warden service then) was expected to climb all the standard routes so as to be able to offer mountaineers current information on route conditions. Aside from professional guiding and Lake O'Hara, there were no other jobs where you actually got paid for climbing mountains. There had been many applicants for the job. The subject came up one morning as we talked climbing with Jerry Walsh, also an aspiring mountaineer. Locke, along with Walsh and mountaineer Chick Scott, would make the first ascent of the north ridge of Mount Stephen that very July. "How come they gave *you* that job?" he finally demanded.

I explained that it would not have occurred to me to even try for the job if Vockeroth hadn't written me in Montreal, where I was at university, and urged me to apply. In fact he had recommended me to the chief warden. To my amazement I got the job, which saved me from a second summer of tire-warehouse hell in Calgary, humping truck tires and dodging fork lifts. Trying to mollify Locke's outrage over life's basic unfairness, I told him that they'd given me the job because of my wonderful personality. Locke did not seem to find my jest amusing. Nowadays I'm sure he has, like me, mellowed gracefully and become a model of charm.

But despite my elation and bluff exterior, I was intimidated as hell, not sure if I could measure up to those mountain-guide predecessors I regarded with awe: Vockeroth, Vitus Germann, and Lawrence Grassi, who had all done things in the mountains I would never match. This was on my mind as *das wunderkind* fixed his fierce grin on me every morning before rushing off into the timber to work off some steam with his singing blade.

The rescue of the Mexicans in 1954, led by Ernest Feuz, had demonstrated, once again, how essential the guides were to national-park rescue operations. In November 1954, J. A. Hutchison, director of national parks, was informed that the CPR intended to discontinue the Swiss-guides service at Lake Louise. In light of the above event and other serious climbing accidents in the mid 1950s, the parks administration began staffing the Lake O'Hara area with experienced climbers.

Hutchison was one of several park officials who realized that the national-park warden service must be trained to meet the mountain rescue demands of a new era. In fact, Warden Noel Gardner, a good all-round mountaineer, had begun training his colleagues in ski touring and winter search-and-rescue operations in 1951, as the department responded to the public's increased interest in ski-touring in avalanche terrain. By 1953, Gardner had trained two four-man warden teams to conduct winter operations in the mountain national parks.

Training on summer rock and ice, however, had not kept pace with winter ski-mountaineering. Director Hutchison, formerly superintendent of Banff Park, believed that a "supervisor of mountaineering activities" must be appointed to train the park wardens for rescue work, and to update the mountaineering equipment then in use. His first choice for the job was Noel Gardner; however, Gardner had resigned from the service before the official offer was made. According to former Chief Warden Jim Sime, after a meeting with himself and Edward Feuz at Golden, B.C. in the fall of 1954, Hutchison elected to hire Walter Perren, age thirty-five and youngest of the Swiss guides imported by the CPR. Perren loved the Rockies and had decided to spend the rest of his life among them, but he planned to marry and needed a secure position. Since he had also apprenticed as a stonemason, he had decided he would follow that trade if he could not guide for a living. Hutchison went to Banff

Park, the logical place for such an office, and put his case simply before Superintendent B. I. M. Strong: Perren would be put on the payroll immediately. But the only position open at the time was that of janitor. So Perren, soon to be known as Canada's foremost mountain-rescue expert, started out his career as a janitor teaching wardens how to climb. When the budget allowed, he ascended directly to the loftier title of "chief warden for mountaineering services." By the time I was hired, Walter Perren was already a legendary figure who had led a number of difficult rescues.

In the warden service and among the professional guides, he was thought of not only as a superior climber and leader, but as an all-round good person. One guy who revered him was a friend of mine, Andrew Suknaski, who, thanks to Perren saving his life, would go on to eventually become a well-known Canadian poet. Suknaski, a Saskatchewan farm kid who worked many summers at Deer Lodge near Lake Louise, had been part of an ill-fated trip across the Waputik Icefield that went badly astray. He and his friends were found by Perren, half starved and clinging to some wet rock a few hundred metres above Hector Lake and the icefield highway. They were roped down the cliffs by Perren's team of wardens. I must have said something critical about Suknaski's navigational skills (he has no such skills, so far as I could tell), because he decided to kill me. He wrote a work of fiction based on the event and partly modelled the main character, a ranger hombre named Buzz, after me. Buzz gets bitten by a rabid dog (his own), becomes maddened by the sound of water running in a creek, then jumps into a crevasse and perishes before the rescue team arrives.

I mentioned this rescue of Suknaski at lunch break one day, thinking the crew might be interested in the story.

A rufous hummingbird spitfired out of the woods and came to a loud hover a few inches in front of my nose, attracted by my yellow hardhat. I stared, hypnotized by the shimmering iridescences along its throat. Each tiny eye was presented in turn to solemnly regard me and in a blur it was gone again, leaving me blinking, but blessed. Zony claimed the hummingbird migrated down to Florida every winter clutching the down under the wing of a Canada goose. I wondered why this childish yarn intrigued me so.

"Walter Perren is a has-been," said the Kid, dismissively.

I turned, still dazed from the visitation, and looked at him where he sat, a little apart from the rest, not sure I had heard him right. He gave me his usual fierce grin and continued chewing on a sandwich. This was my introduction to Locke's sense of humour.

"Walter Perren is probably the best mountaineer in Canada," I spluttered. Charlie grinned even wider in reply, and I realized he was just baiting me since I so obviously admired Perren. But his words echoed in my head. There was something ominous about this kind of jest: it seemed like bad karma. I thought, forget it, you've been reading too much Kerouac.

Yet the comment had an odd effect on me. From then on, when Locke left the truck to trot up the trail, I trotted right behind him. I wouldn't allow his boot heels to get more than a metre ahead of me all the way to the job site. My determination to match Locke in every move he made probably just inspired him to work even harder. If I wanted to match Twice As Much, then he'd be Thrice As Much. We were trying to work each other to death, as far as I was concerned, and were driving the foreman and the old-timers on the crew crazy in the bargain.

In that early summer of 1966, grinning furiously at each other as we swung the grub hoes into the mountain earth – seeing how close we could come to each other's feet before one of us flinched – we were blissfully unaware of potential disaster lurking for both of us just a few miles over the mountain ridge. Sweat poured down from under my helmet like rain.

"Hey boys," called Zony. "Friday today. Short day today, boys."

"I hope I'm not going too fast for you, Charlie," I enquired with fake concern, grubbing a bunch of stones and dirt over his boot toes.

"That'll be the day," said the Twice As Much Kid, whispering his hoe past my shin and thunking it into the earth.

"Hey boys!" yelled Zony. "I said it's quitting time. We quit half an hour early today. We ain't paying you by piecework on this job, you crazy buggers." Charlie and I stopped and glared at each other, still grinning that rictus grin of two guys who might either punch each other silly or burst out laughing with equal arbitrariness.

The moment ended. I stopped to strap the chainsaw on my packboard as the others trooped off down the trail. A horse whinnied up the trail behind me, and in a minute Fred Dixon rode out of the timber in his green uniform, a well-worn Biltmore hat tilted back to reveal his greying hair. He reined in and regarded me with no-comment green eyes.

"Marty," he said, "I guess you better pack up your stuff tonight. Looks like we can't use you here any more."

My mouth opened, speechlessly for once, and I swallowed hard as he searched his pocket for tobacco and papers, then began to roll a cigarette. I wondered frantically what to say, cursing myself for not keeping quiet about Lake O'Hara and horseshit on the trail to the promised land. Obviously the man had taken a real dislike to me. I saw the whole summer of sunlit lake and mountains floating away like a mirage, and an ugly asphalt parking lot capped by a tire warehouse, shaped like a gigantic coking oven, coming sharply into focus. A horrifying vision replaced it: I pictured Charlie Locke walking along the lakeshore in front of the cabin in a warden uniform, climbing rope slung jauntily over his shoulder, and several young lovelies trailing fondly behind. Fred twisted the paper and looked up enquiringly. I gaped stupidly at him, realized what he was waiting for, and fished in my pocket for a match. Maybe it was not too late to try and change the man's mind. It flared in his cupped hands there in the shade, his sharp features focussed on the flame.

"You move up to O'Hara tomorrow," he said quietly.

I burst out with words of relief and gratitude. I think I ran all the way down that trail, I was so eager to get packed.

As for Locke, I would not see him again for thirty years, though I would hear much about him. I believe the trajectories of our lives were already determined long before we met on the Yoho Park trail crew. When at last we met again, at a party for Brian Greenwood in 1995, we lived in worlds so different and so changed from the world of 1966 that I doubted we held so much as a memory in common.

CHAPTER FIVE

Porters of the Great Signs

I should not have told Warden Dixon that horses made a mess of the trails, and that I didn't see any use for pack horses in the mountain parks in the days of helicopters. Fred was a horseman, one of the best horsemen in the park warden service. He was also the kind of guy who thinks ahead, always a year or so ahead of the greenhorn patrolman, who tends to ponder only short-term plans: how to get the next case of beer, climb the next mountain, or get laid.

I can almost hear Fred thinking aloud back in 1966 – though he departed this vale of sorrow some years since – "Now what can a fellah do to get this college kid educated about the value of a mountain horse for transport and freight hauling? So as to disabuse him of his loyalty to the bunion derby mode of travel . . ."

And then Fred thought about the Signs, the Great Signs. And his weathered face broke into a grin. He shook his head slowly with the sheer poetic justice of the thing, as he got out his makings and started rolling a smoke. "Now why didn't I think of them god-awful monstrosities before?" he asked himself. It made his day, maybe his whole week – I don't doubt it.

It was a summer afternoon in late June as I stood by the gate of the Lake O'Hara road, smoking a pipe and proudly wearing my khaki warden-patrolman shirt and trousers for the first time, blissfully ignorant of the tortures Fred and the demonic carpenters of Yoho Park had planned for me. At my feet was a pile of duffel and my old Harmony guitar leaning against the gate post. I felt it was a shame there were no damsels within miles to admire the cut of the cloth. It didn't occur to me at the time that in this plebeian uniform I looked more like the local breadman than the nouveau Mark Trail. In fact, I was listed on the warden payroll not as a warden but as an "alpine technician." There was a name to conjure with. It was a good title – for a ski repairman.

I was anxious to get up to Lake O'Hara and was waiting to meet my partner, who had gone into Banff to buy groceries for our first shift. I knew Bernie Schiesser was a bushman, but most of that ilk had little skill or interest in climbing above timberline. He was the lead hand on this job, but who would do the leading if we had to carry out a mountain rescue? I feared that the responsibility might fall on my young shoulders, and frankly, I didn't have the training for that load. But as I said, my boss was way ahead of me when it came to preparing me for carrying a heavy load.

I heard a vehicle coming and stared down the road, expecting to see a battered half-ton pull up, driven by a bearded guy with a tiny head and no neck, clad in a wool mackinaw. I thought Bernie would look like Bluto in the Popeye comics. But instead of a truck, a silver Alpine sports car, top down, came streaking out of the woods from the direction of Lake Louise. The driver geared down and braked to a stop at the last moment a few inches from my climbing boots. He wore a brand new khaki uniform and national-park shoulder badges like mine. "It can't be him," I thought.

Bernie Schiesser was a tall, lean twenty-nine-year-old whose aquiline face usually featured a happy grin. The grin, I would learn, could be disarmingly goofy; some women were charmed by it, but the guy behind the grin would prove to be nobody's fool. He vaulted out of his car like a man dismounting from a horse. I was startled to notice the well-worn grey kletter shoes on his feet, which were de rigueur with rock climbers in that era. That augured well. Actually, the only sign of lumberjack about Bernie was the telltale edge of the long underwear he habitually wore winter and summer (no matter how hot the weather) visible at his throat and shirt-sleeves. He also had the sloping shoulders and long-armed reach of a boxer. I could feel the power in those arms when we shook hands in that first greeting, sizing each other up.

With my gear tied onto the luggage rack behind us, we fairly flew up the road to Lake O'Hara, shouting a bit of small talk over the engine's roar and making the gravel fly. "Hold on," shouted Bernie as the Lake O'Hara bus suddenly loomed on a tight corner. We swerved sharply to the right, slid on a drift of gravel, straightened out, and I caught a glimpse of the driver's startled face as we squeaked by. Cars were few on that jealously guarded right-of-way and sports cars were rarer still. Many a minion in the parks department wished to drive it; very few were permitted the privilege.

"Whoops," said Bernie, glancing back. "I bet we hear about that one from old man Ford."

Grinning crazily as we pulled up at Grassi's cabin, I got out, pleased with this first meeting. If Bernie was a lumberjack, he was the coolest jack I'd ever met. And how I coveted that car – though it seemed to lack a clutch. It was Walter Perren who had suggested the "alpine technician" title for our jobs. I always wondered if the title was Perren's sly joke about Bernie's vehicle needing full-time repairmen. It would have fitted with Walter's dry sense of humour.

As I stared at the circle of mountains again from the porch of Grassi's cabin, I felt the old joy of greeting combined with a powerful rush of unrestrained animal spirits. To not only be back at O'Hara, but to be paid to climb mountains, to have the passkey to the little cabin; to have the best job in Yoho National Park – hell, the best job in the whole country! I couldn't believe my luck. And to think they were paying me, too – the princely sum of $1.88 an hour – not to mention the extra five cents per hour for possessing a first-aid certificate. I stared over at the lodge, where I had once toiled on behalf of free enterprise. Those days were over, and now a different outlook was required. Bernie and I shared the roles of game warden, forest ranger, trail crew, and initial rescue team for the entire valley.

"Oh oh," I heard Bernie say just then, in a tone that ended my reverie.

I set down my plunder on the porch and went around the side of the cabin to join him. Hands on hips, he stood surveying a huge pile of signs that were stacked several metres high on some wooden blocks in a patch of late-season snow. I felt my grin growing strained. They were highway signs, each sign board some eight centimetres thick, some of awesome breadth, all of them mounted on varnished poles some twenty-five centimetres in diameter and more than three metres long. Big letters were deeply routed into the varnished cedar and then painted bright yellow to catch a motorist's eye. They were beautiful signs, meant to be hauled on the back of a three-ton truck equipped with a crane to lift them and a power auger to bore post holes. What the hell were they doing up here in the roadless alpine zone, where a few inches of soil soon gave way to solid rock?

I read off the names to myself: "Odaray Grandview," "Opabin Pass," "Lake Oesa" and so on. There was a sign for every destination point and every trail junction in the valley, complete with mileages.

"Now we know why they hired two of us," said Bernie.

I caught his meaning at once. "No way," I protested, leaning down to grab one of them and try its weight. "Shit! Must be around two hundred pounds." I let it fall with an unceremonious crash. "We can't pack these babies. They obviously plan to lift these out there by helicopter."

"Helicopter?" Bernie grinned. "That's a novel idea." Indeed, in 1966 it was just about unheard of in those parts. But I couldn't see any other explanation.

"No way we can dig a hole for those posts out here," I said reassuringly. "Probably gonna fly Zony out here with the portable rock drill. They drop the signs off where needed, Zony drills the holes, slaps 'em in – and we go climb some peaks, right?"

"It's good to look on the bright side," said Bernie, frowning down at the signs, "especially on the government payroll." Looking up at the surrounding mountains he added, "Somehow, I don't think we'll be climbing too much in the next while. Probably just as well. Too much snow up there."

He left me there scratching my head, and staring up at the summits around us. He was right about the snow. There was plenty of it on the higher peaks. Mount Hungabee had put on its seasonal war-paint. Streaks of water-blackened rock on its west face, shining through the snow, marked the tracks of recent avalanches.

Bernie was rummaging around in the toolshed. He came out with an old Pioneer chainsaw, set it on the chopping block, and commenced sharpening the chain with a round file. Feminine voices distracted us for a moment. Two young lovelies from the lodge staff, college women, no doubt, wearing waitress uniforms, were taking a stroll along the lakeshore before starting work. They called out a friendly greeting as they passed.

There was a skookum pile of firewood already split and stacked. I saw no need for extra chainsawing, especially by me. The sight of the women reminded me that I needed all my fingers to play the guitar with. The chainsaw is not a courting instrument.

"How do you know it's dull?" I wanted to know.

"It's a government saw," he explained.

"Well," I said uncertainly, "maybe I'll make supper then?"

"Go right ahead, you smooth-talker."

I entered the cabin, feeling a bit like an interloper. The place smelled of cold ashes, oakum, and wool blankets needing an airing. Coiled climbing ropes, slings and racks of pitons and carabiners

hung from wooden pegs on the varnished log walls. Grassi's old
carved easy chair looked strange without him sitting in it, but there
was kindling in the wood box as a note of welcome from Don
Vockeroth's tenure the previous year. Bernie had already tossed his
pack on Grassi's homemade bed, staking his claim. I had the worn-
out lower bunk in the opposite corner. It looked more like a
hammock than a bed, but I wasn't complaining.

I laid the fire and started making like a cook, while the first
plume of woodsmoke drifted over the clearing and announced our
arrival for the summer. Cooking, unlike chainsawing, was something I knew about. My mother insisted I learn the basics at a young
age. "Who knows," she had said hopefully, "maybe you could even
teach your father."

But where to begin this first evening? "When in doubt," she'd
always said, "fry some onions. The smell will inspire your stomach;
you'll figure out what to cook next."

We were expecting Fred Dixon to show up that night to talk over
the season's work. He was the district warden, stationed at Hector,
near Wapta Lake on the Trans-Canada Highway, where he lived with
his wife, Ann, and their two young daughters. No doubt he would
explain the sign business.

There were several things to remember about staying out of trouble with our boss, as Bernie explained to me over a meal of steak and
potatoes (smothered in onions), but number one was to have a pot
of coffee just about ready to boil when he pulled up in the yard. Fred
Dixon was an old-time warden from the days when wardens lived in
the backcountry year round. Bush survival skills, horsemanship, and
the ability to shoot straight were important attributes for getting
hired back then. As far as mountain rescue went, old-time wardens
felt it was a crazy notion to go anywhere a horse couldn't carry them.
Veteran warden Mac Elder once told me he could "probably get just
about any crazy bastard down off a mountain – with a .270" – that
being a rifle renowned for its long range. Fred Dixon had a highway
district, which was supposed to be an improvement to his lot, but

like all wardens he was on call twenty-four hours a day to deal with any emergency, from forest fires through bear problems to stranded climbers. He assisted the local RCMP with highway accidents and other human vs. human mayhem when they were short-handed. Fred worked long hours in the summer with no overtime pay, and in lieu of cash, coffee plus nicotine helped to keep him motivated. He drove up to the cabin later that night. Entering the room, he greeted us, then sat down and took out a pouch of Export tobacco and some papers. A cigarette soon materialized from between his calloused fingers. I added coffee grounds to the pot on the stove. We made coffee mainly on the cowboy plan in the old enamel pot: fill with cold water, add coffee to taste, bring to a full boil, then serve.

For a guy who looked more like an Alberta cowboy than a bureaucrat, Fred had brought a startling amount of paperwork along with him. It seemed as if we would have to fill out a form every time we saw a squirrel or sold a fishing licence. "I guess we're lucky we don't have to report when we go to the outhouse," drawled Bernie.

"Somebody's probably lyin' awake figurin' on that one right now," said Fred, grimly.

The talk came around to the lodge and its place in the scheme of things. It seems the cultlike mystique of Lake O'Hara Lodge and its wealthy devotees had failed to captivate Warden Dixon. I had heard a story about a conversation between Fred and Austin Ford that summed up his attitude. The two had hiked up on the Odaray Plateau to get acquainted – or feel each other out. Mr. Ford was sometimes in need of co-operation from the park officials to speed through the red tape so he could complete his annual projects on time. They had stared down at the panorama below, where the red roofs of the lodge cabins dotting the shore of the lake were visible. "Look at that, Fred," said Ford. "Isn't that the most beautiful scene you've ever laid eyes on?"

"Uh huh. There's only one thing wrong with it though, Mr. Ford," drawled Fred.

"Wrong with it!" exclaimed Ford in disbelief. "What on earth could be wrong with it?"

Fred gestured down at the scene below. "That goddamn motel sitting right on the lakeshore is what's wrong with it," he'd answered, mildly. Needless to say, the comment had not endeared him to Austin Ford, although Ford later painted his roofs green to make them less obtrusive. That was Fred's point, I believe, or one of them. Ford and Dixon both loved the mountains, each in his own way.

Fred advised us not to get overly chummy with the lodge management. "If you hang around the lodge too much, they start thinking of you as part of their operation," warned Fred. "Same goes for the Alpine Club. You work for the park, not Mr. Ford, not the Alpine Club.

"If you catch people fishing over the limit, you'll have to pinch them. If you catch them running dogs off a leash, or littering, you'll have to warn them. Most important, keep an eye on their garbage storage because if they get sloppy over there, we will have a bear problem to deal with. Same goes for the Alpine Club and the campers. If we get a bear problem up here, you two will have a Fred Dixon problem. The list goes on. Better both read up on the regulations. There's a copy right here." He pointed out a massive black tome that looked as heavy as an anvil.

And then there were the signs. They were a mistake, Fred agreed, but he didn't seem that perturbed by it. The usual failure to communicate between section heads down at Field, B.C. "Better get used to it," he advised.

"Of course," I put in confidently, "we could get them up pretty easily with a helicopter."

"No doubt about it," agreed Fred. "If the chief warden had money in his budget to pay for it. Which he don't."

I caught a warning look from Bernie. He shook his head, but I went on anyway, convinced that logic must win the day. "I mean, the thing is, Fred, those signs are a bit much for us to carry up a mountain."

"So you don't feel up to the demands of this job?" asked Fred, mildly.

That stopped me for a second. "I'm not saying that. Hell, we can do it somehow."

"I'm glad to hear that," said Fred.

We sipped our coffee for a moment; then it came to me.

"What about pack horses?"

Fred gazed thoughtfully up at the ceiling, as if there were something written there that he was pondering.

"Pack horses?" he mused. "So you think horses might be useful, do you?"

"Well, under the circumstances. It seems justified."

"Now you see," said Fred, "That's kinda the way the chief warden looks at it. We have a horse herd to carry stuff we can't carry on our backs. So we don't need helicopters, do we?"

"Yes," I agreed. "I can see your point."

We sipped our coffee. I was relieved that a solution had been found. But why the warning look from Bernie and the shake of his head?

There seemed to be a lot of silence in conversations with Fred. But Fred's silences were like the space in a snare loop, or the vacuum in your mouth just before you put your foot in it.

"So," I continued. "I take it we can use pack horses then?"

Fred shook his head. "I'm afraid not."

"Hey? Why not?" This was exasperating.

Fred cocked his hat up above his greying temples. "Horses aren't allowed up here any more. We got too many complaints about horses mucking up the trails and horseshit on people's climbing boots. This habitat is too sensitive and high-strung for horses."

Fred warmed to his theme. Horses had trampled the thin soils, shat on Grassi's flagstone walkways, and scoffed down the exquisite alpine flowers after their insouciant fashion. Also, the clanging of their bells, when pastured at night, disturbed the campers on the meadow, whose tents were likewise killing the flowers as they slept.

However, the superintendent had no intention of spending more money to replace the signs.

"The word is 'be cre-ative,'" drawled Fred, in conclusion. "'Tell your men up at O'Hara to be cre-ative. And get those signs up.'" Fred sipped his coffee and added, "I'm sure a college man such as yourself will find a way, Marty." His poker face gave nothing away.

"I know little of physics."

"That would make two of us," said Fred.

"Somebody said you were studying engineering," said Bernie hopefully, no doubt thinking of fulcrums and hauling tackles.

"Nope. The other E-word – English Lit."

"Oh. That should be a real help," he observed.

"I might get a Master's degree in creative writing after that," I blurted. There was a beat of silence while the silliness of this admission sank in.

"There's that C-word again," drawled Fred.

The signs proved to be our first priority. After breakfast the next morning, I was wondering how we'd do it, but felt energized enough to take on anything. This was the result of Bernie's pancakes, especially the pancake syrup recipe, a concoction of Mapeline extract, brown sugar, and a stiff jolt of Coruba overproof rum. As I was cleaning up after the meal, I heard the chainsaw popping. I finished up and hurried outside.

Bernie tuned the high-speed jet with a small screwdriver and revved the saw to an angry roar, cocking an ear attentively to the chattering racket with the studious frown of a surgeon listening for a heart murmur. He made one more minute adjustment, smiled his approval, then let it idle back down till the eighteen-inch blade was barely turning. He glanced up and saw my puzzled grin.

"I'm feeling creative!" he shouted. Apparently those long sign posts had brought out the hidden artist in him. He revved the saw up again, and without further parley began cutting lengths of post from each sign, making the sawdust fly. The sharp chain zipped through the wood like a knife through butter. These leftovers we would buck up and split for firewood. "Unless those potlickers down in Field have some other use for them," he shouted.

The trim job lightened the signs enough to change the task of backpacking them up the mountainsides from impossible to merely unbearable. To carry the signs, we placed them on the cabin porch and lashed them, upside down, to the ancient Trapper Nelson packboards we had been issued. (These old packs were made of canvas with a wood frame. The government had not yet entered the era of aluminum and nylon.) Standing up under that load was the hardest part; it could not be done without a prop such as the cabin porch or a large boulder. After that, we moved at a coolie shuffle in a kind of crouch. The thin canvas pack-straps raised welts on my shoulders and chest, despite the pads I put under them. The weight overhead tried to push us on our faces when going downhill, and dragged us backwards going up, despite improvised tumplines around our foreheads. Our way led mostly up. I felt like I was dragging a stone boat behind me by means of two meat hooks imbedded in my chest.

"Now I know how Jesus felt going up Calvary," I whined to Bernie as we crept painfully up the switchbacks by the Seven Veils Falls in blazing heat one afternoon. Bernie offered a few woodsy epithets in reply, mostly modifiers of the term "potlicker."

Since we seldom found enough soil to dig a hole for our posts, we had to erect monumental stone cairns around the signs to keep them standing. Big spikes nailed in the posts at right angles kept the signs from revolving like propellers in a gale, but up at McArthur Pass, migrating grizzly bears would bat them off-kilter anyway as they ambled by, causing unwary newcomers to go wildly astray. They were quite the eyesore, though they were embraced by porcupines who would chew on them by the hour, savouring their toxic glues and chemicals. We spent many a miserable day at that task, until I came to see myself not as an alpine technician but as a mountain mule.

By way of a diversion, we would take a day off from sign-hauling and spend our time cutting deadfalls off the trails, repairing Grassi's old stone culverts damaged by washouts, or grubbing and pick-axing new portions of trails through spring landslides. If I felt more like martyr than Marty, it was also due to those climbers and lodge guests who cared not a whit for our suffering, as we cluttered up O'Hara's sublime natural rock-gardens with our stupid signs.

"Another goddamn billboard!" exclaimed one crusty alpinist, glowering down at me as I laboured up Grassi's monumental stone steps one morning, blinded by my own sweat: "What's next? Pavement and dotted lines? Traffic lights?"

"You wouldn't be related to Lawrence Grassi by any chance?" enquired another, suspiciously. She didn't mean it as a compliment. Some outdoor purists are not in favour of stone stairways on hiking trails.

Warden Dixon was notably unsympathetic when I mentioned how sore my back was. "Eat more oatmeal," he advised. "I'll get the barn boss to send you up a sack if you want."

The trail-crew labour and sign-humping did have one salubrious effect on me; the work built muscles in places I never thought muscles belonged before. I was no longer the undernourished scholar I had been at term end; for one thing, I had money now to purchase groceries. The changes were pointed out to me, approvingly, by my girlfriend, Myrna Jamison (now my wife of many years), on her weekend visits from Calgary. The memory of her Sunday caresses helped me shoulder Monday's burdens.

The mountains went unclimbed while we toiled like ants over their rocky flanks. The mountain artillery boomed out its dire warnings in the sound of late-season snow slides and rockfalls. At night, I twanged away on the guitar, playing Wade Hemsworth tunes, Woody Guthrie tunes, Bob Dylan tunes – songs of the working man, songs of protest, while Bernie reclined on Grassi's comfortable bed, deeply engrossed in a science-fiction novel, by the look of it. It was entitled *Atlas Shrugged*. If I thought Bernie would have a natural affinity for tunes like "I'm Sticking to the Union," he soon disabused me of the notion. For him, the song might have been better entitled "When the Union Sticks It to Ya." It had never occurred to me that loggers, who tend to be piece workers, might see themselves as entrepreneurs for whom unions could be anathema.

I discovered I was bunking with a backwoods philosopher who disagreed with almost every tenet of fuzzy liberalism I thought admirable. The author of his novel was Ayn Rand. My partner saw himself as an individualist and thinker – "somewhat of an intellectual, I suppose," as he modestly put it. At that point in his life, Ayn Rand was his icon, and her philosophy of Objectivism, his Book of Revelations. Bernie urged me to read Rand's *Atlas Shrugged* and *The Fountainhead*. I made a manly effort at the former, but too much time spent reading the classics spoiled me for *Atlas Shrugged*. I came away concluding that Atlas shrugged trying to get the Objectivists off his back. I told Bernie that Rand's cast of privileged but unloved industrialists–cum–demi-gods reminded me of the signs we were packing around: they were heavy, wooden, easy to read, and they gave me a pain in the neck.

Bernie patiently suggested I was missing the point. The novel itself was not the point; what was important were the lessons it contained about how rational, talented individuals must be allowed to realize their own destinies without interference from the state – or words to that effect.

I wondered aloud why all these heroic characters of Rand's seemed to be capitalists bent on destroying the earth to satisfy their own gigantic egos. They were just as anthropocentric in their view of nature as the Christians and other "collectivists" that Rand despised. Bernie suggested the real problem was the brainwashing I'd undergone from those pinko professors down east.

Those old arguments around the stove at Lake O'Hara were very heated, and in the end, I had to back away from the contest. I see now that I couldn't best Bernie in the debate because I could not offer an alternative to a creed which was central to his life at the time. I had read philosophy as a mental exercise without committing to any particular ideal. It was a kind of "bead game," as in the novel by Herman Hesse. I had thought my attitude was that of the skeptic, in accord with my goal, which was to become a professor of literature and a poet. In fact, I was a cynic, which is the typical lazy pose of a young academic dabbler. If Bernie was not as well-read as I, he had nevertheless found an exemplar that worked for him. At the time, I did admire his determination to excel at whatever he turned his hand to. In the lumber camps, he had once excelled at falling trees, drinking people under the table, and beating them in fist-fights. Objectivism had convinced him to excel at being productive and fulfilled in ways that were easier on his body and his soul. Bernie, whose parents loved the outdoors, climbed his first mountain at age ten. He loved the mountains, and liked the people he met while climbing and skiing, and so he aspired to be a well-rounded mountaineer. He noted that ski instructors were often the best skiers, so he qualified as a Level Three instructor and taught skiing in the winter. He had also worked as a ski patroller and avalanche-control man in the States. Now he was preparing to qualify as a mountain guide the following year.

It's just too politically correct these days, for my taste, to dismiss Ayn Rand out of hand. Her essay on racism in *The Virtue of Selfishness* is one of several essays that are worth thinking about today. But for my part, it seems bizarre that Rand, who maintains in that book that "one must never attempt to fake reality in any manner (which is the virtue of Honesty)" and says, further, that above all "one must never seek to get away with contradictions" would so obviously contradict her own principles by creating fake realities, meaning her novels, which she then refers us to in the above book in order to illustrate those same philosophical principles!

Young Bernie was not a typical disciple of Objectivism. For one thing, he had a sense of humour. For another, I don't think he has a selfish bone in his body. What impressed me ultimately about the Bernie of those days was not just his belief that ideas were important, that ideas could shape your life; it was this contemplative side combined with his good-natured manliness and general physical competence that impressed. That and his generosity, his willingness to teach what he knew. Like Walter Perren, he was (and still is) a leader who taught by doing. Some of the things he taught me are things I would later use at work every day as a backcountry warden and that I still use now around the ranchette: how to swing an axe so you take the biggest bite out of a log with every swing; how to whittle squaw sticks for kindling; how to sharpen an axe with a bastard file, its handle crooked under one leg for an improvised vice; how to correctly notch the angles in the teeth of a chainsaw; how to read the clouds and predict the onset of thunderstorms when you are high up in the mountains. How to make wicked pancake syrup that stays with you all day.

These lessons came slowly, day after day, through pleasant, easy-going suggestions. The only time he got really bugged at me was when I used his favourite axe without permission and put a nick in the edge.

As the snows melted from the peaks, visitation at Lake O'Hara picked up considerably. Every day one of us was on hand to meet the Lake O'Hara bus. We greeted hikers and climbers, sold maps and fishing licences, and registered parties out for overnight trips and mountain climbs. Our most important function was probably to provide newcomers to the area with current information on the routes. Our most potent public-safety weapon on many a rainy afternoon, following Grassi's practice, was a full teapot. Over a cup of tea, the standard mountain drink, some trust was established. People volunteered information on their previous climbs, abilities, and equipment. Sometimes their experience much exceeded our own. More typically, the less-experienced would ask us our opinion on a climb or hike they might enjoy. Thus we could help steer them clear of trying Victoria without crampons and ice axes, or attempting the Opabin Glacier wearing running shoes. Of course there was no legal requirement whatsoever for anybody to follow our advice, which is as it should be. Too many rules sully the mountains. But people who criticized the registration system simply did not understand that wardens have to deal with the general public, and therefore with the lowest common denominator. A typical "rescue" at O'Hara might involve coming to the aid of someone suffering from sunstroke because the silly bugger refused to wear a hat, or climbing up to rope a stranded novice down from the cliffs on Mount Schäffer or Strawberry Cliff at the end of the lake. We also ran a first-aid outpost at the cabin, where campers came for treatment who'd burned themselves with exploding camp stoves, cut themselves with knives or hatchets, or just wanted us to remove slivers and wood ticks.

A guy named Peter Poole suffered the worst injury I saw during my stint as O'Hara warden. He was climbing Cathedral Mountain with a trail-crew alumnus name of Rick Kunelius, who later became a park warden. Poole apparently tripped over his own crampons – a not uncommon event – and took a header down a couloir "for about the length of a football field" according to Kunelius. He was saved from death when he struck a very large protruding rock and did an unintentional wraparound on it. He looked like he'd been wrestling with a roll of barbed wire by the time he and Rick staggered down to the road and flagged down the bus. The nearest doctor was at Chateau Lake Louise. I had purchased my first car by then, a red Volkswagen beetle, from Myrna's brother. Poole's face was about the same colour as the car. We bundled Poole in the back seat of Hitler's Revenge and headed for Lake Louise. When he staggered in the big front doors of the grand hotel between Rick and I, swathed in gauze bandages with his clothing ripped and tattered, a piano recital was in progress. The pianist stopped playing and the guests looked up from their knitting to gape at the bloody spectacle. Poole managed to give them a sweeping bow of greeting, before warning the musician, "I was the last piano player."

That first summer, I soon discovered that dealing with the public requires patience. Some climbers, who had to get started early to climb peaks like Victoria, preferred rousting us out of bed at 3 A.M. to registering out the night before. Then there were the Snitch Sisters, as I called them, two elderly lodge guests who took it upon themselves to make sure our morals were up to Victorian standards. They liked to peer through the windows just before dawn, to see if there were any female guests staying with us. I woke one Sunday morning with the beam of a flashlight in my eyes, and jumped up as it focussed on Myrna, who had the top bunk. "They've got a hussy in there again," I heard one of the old hags cackle. "The superintendent will hear about this."

And to my amazement, I found myself on the carpet before Chief Warden Dawson. "That's a government office, as well as your residence," warned Dawson. "It's not a hotel."

I frankly resented paying rent for my employer's office, but decided to keep that thought dark. This curb on our social activities caused Bernie to complain of a morning, "I sure have big antlers today." I wondered how we could get rid of the Snitch Sisters so that our female guests could resume their visits.

Bernie had worked a long time in the bush, where thick clothes protect you from thorns and brush and where long johns become like a second skin. In the heat of summer, he believed that long johns did for him what flowing robes did for the Bedouin: they helped evaporate sweat and kept him cool. As a result, Bernie in his birthday suit was a remarkable sight. His face, neck, and hands were deeply tanned, but the rest of his finely tuned body was a phosphorescent, mushroom white. The next time the Snitch Sisters visited, Bernie was up early and had stripped down temporarily, perhaps for a quick sponge bath. That's when the flashlight beam caught him

"Have a good look this time!" yelled Bernie. From outside, he would have appeared as a headless white torso sans hands and sans fig leaf, a ghostly Michelangelo's *David* in the mountains. There was a shriek of fear – tinged with a coo of naughty appreciation – outside the window. The Snitch Sisters fled the scene, cackling like scandalized spruce hens, never to return, or to complain, again.

Day after day, I went on doggedly hauling my freight uphill, like the beleaguered Dagny Taggart in *Atlas Shrugged* despite all Commie nay-sayers. Perhaps the unkindest cut of all came from that "subjectivist" professor of botany, Dr. George K. K. Link, known to some of us as the Old Man of the Mountains.

Though his venerable feet were battered and ruined, he still bestrode the high-line trails at O'Hara with goatlike grace, having cut the toes out of his favourite walking shoes to cool his suffering dogs. Ratcheting my way up to All Souls' Lookout one day through swirling mists, dreaming of cool water, with a mighty highway sign tapping the back of my head at every step, I was suddenly confronted by ten antique human toes protruding over the edge of a boulder. I staggered backwards with a yelp of alarm, scrabbling for a hand-hold. Craning my neck up like a turtle from beneath my wooden carapace, I beheld Dr. Link, his usual carved walking staff in hand, glowering down at me. His white beard seemed all a-frizz as if galvanized with static electricity or inner angst, and his glasses were partly steamed over. He seemed the very archetype of the demented mystic that Ayn Rand would have loathed. Perhaps he had been communing with the spirit of his beloved wife, Adeline, whose ashes he had scattered nearby many winters previous. Wearing his trademark French beret, he lifted his staff and shook it in righteous admonition, like some maddened old boulevardier transplanted from the Left Bank, and beamed down from the clouds. Humbled, I crouched there under my varnished gibbet, its crosspiece inscribed with the gnomic legend "All Souls Look Out," the aptness of which was lost on me at the time, as I awaited Dr. Link's angry words of judgement.

Instead of thunder and lightning, he merely sighed deeply, took off his glasses, and gave them a swipe on his bandanna. He put them back, peered sadly down at me, and delivered his verdict: "I am very disappointed, Marty," he said.

He stepped past me, strode down the mountainside, and soon vanished into the mist.

I was sorely wounded by this verbal spear thrust from Lake O'Hara's archetypal defender, and in need of existential comfort. What would old Grassi, the immortal trail builder of O'Hara, do in a situation like this? I asked myself as I crept upward again. Ha! The stubborn old paisano! He would have done the exact opposite, *con impeto*, of whatever Tommy Link wanted done, that was certain. He would not only carry this cursed crucifix up to All Souls', he would do it without one murmur of complaint. He would have taken along a crown of thorns for a bandanna. He would have punched a hole for the post through solid rock using only a mason's hammer and cold chisel for tools. And what would the Twice As Much Kid have done? Why, he would have carried two signs on his back and run all the way up. He would have called Tommy a has-been and blown him off the trail as he rushed by. He would have sharpened a point on the post with an axe and then pounded the sign into the virgin limestone with the back of it. Then he would have run all the way over to Opabin Pass, pounded one in over there and climbed Mount Hungabee before supper. "Hell. You've got it easy," I told myself, and was consoled.

The great sign-portering of 1966 finished like many another bureaucratic initiative, in ignominy. Like the $12,000 Trail to Nowhere, built by Banff Park staff in the Bryant Creek district, and abandoned hastily when a park visitor threatened to write it up for the papers. Or consider how the park created a brand new avalanche path along the Trans-Canada Highway, a swath of snow and destroyed trees created by a certain erstwhile employee during an avalanche-control operation – using high explosives thrown from a helicopter, he missed the path he was aiming for. Like these and other ill-conceived enterprises, it would have been forgotten if aficionados of folly like me didn't insist on recording it in print. The mighty highway signs were long ago replaced by tiny plastic or aluminum placards mounted on thin steel posts. The big bruisers, hugged, clawed, and feathered by the teeth of several generations of porcupines, were eventually collected by helicopter and whisked off to the nearest landfill for internment.

Atlas shrugged, and the signs vanished into oblivion. But by my aching back they will long be remembered.

CHAPTER SIX

Accident on Mount Babel

"Well, another mountain conquered, again with no equipment and alone . . . I seem to recognize the names of a few other diehards. Take care of yourselves and we'll see you on the summit of EVEREST"

— Entry in the summit register for
Mount Lefroy (3,436 metres)

I n the Canadian Rocky Mountains at the tag end of the millennium, where the words "heritage tourism" are heard rolling from the lips of hoteliers and their public-relations flak catchers, the term "legendary" has been applied to every old-timer who ever plugged a grizzly bear or donned a set of crampons.

Among the legions of the legendary, most are legends, if not just in their own minds, then in the minds of very few. Yet the word, clichéd as it is and crying out for burial, still fits some mountain people whose exploits are remembered – and embroidered on around a candle lantern in a snow cave late at night – though they themselves have long since melted into eternity, *comme les neiges d'antan*. Among mountaineers still living, Brian Greenwood, who pioneered so many new routes in the Canadian Rockies, is such a real-life legend. In the warden service and among professional mountain guides, the late Walter Perren remains such a figure.

One of Perren's contemporaries, Chief Warden Hal Shepherd, summed it up for many when he said that hiring Perren "was the best move the warden service ever made. . . . He was a gentleman personified in every way. He had a quality of leadership, and an ability to instill confidence into us that you very seldom find in a man. Only the greatest leaders have that, and Walter had it." Shepherd, who spent part of World War Two as a prisoner of the Japanese, knew leadership when he saw it.

Walter died young, which is too often a trait of the legendary. But to the wardens of the previous generation, he was a friend and a teacher, and a supporter of their integrity. He took a bunch of cowboys, most of whom were flat-landers from the prairie provinces, and turned them into a competent group of mountaineers and rescue hands. Many people thought it could not be done, including E. Rex Gibson, former president of the Alpine Club of Canada, who in 1954 wrote the minister responsible for national parks, recommending that European guides be hired to do rescue work. "Needless to say" he wrote, "this type of work is outside the experience and beyond the scope of the average Park Warden, and the Wardens should not be called upon to undertake this sort of work." Gibson's letter was more than impolitic, since he himself had to call out a rescue team, supervised by a chief park warden, after losing a companion in an avalanche on Mount Schäffer – this after failing to register out at park headquarters in Field. At any rate, Director Hutchison ignored his advice, and Perren was hired to train the wardens.

Walter Perren was from Zermatt. His family was one of the twelve families that founded the canton in the 1500s, according to his son, Peter. He was a small man, only five and half feet tall, but he was a natural athlete. The wardens had a flagpole at Lake Louise, and apparently one of Perren's favourite tricks was to climb the pole and then balance on the top of it. He took to climbing at an early age. He climbed the Matterhorn as a boy of twelve; he would go on to climb it as a porter and guide 144 times. After obtaining his guide's pin, he climbed in summer and taught skiing at Crans-Montana in the winter, where the view of the Alps stretches from the Matterhorn all the way to Mont Blanc. According to Peter's Swiss godfather, Walter was selected for the Swiss Everest team of the late thirties, but plans for the attempt were aborted due to the advent of World War Two.

Walter Perren was a lifelong Catholic and a deeply religious man who seemed to have been destined to be a leader of rescue teams. When he was fourteen years old, and working as an apprentice guide or porter, something happened that shaped his outlook on mountaineering forever. He was caught in a storm near the summit of the Matterhorn with a guide and his client. The storm hammered at the little party, which was unable to descend, and forced it to bivouac without shelter from the freezing wind. According to Perren's friend Jim Sime, the client and the guide suffered from severe frost-bite. The client would eventually lose both his feet, the guide one foot and both hands, but the young apprentice would come through physically unscathed.

Some days went by, and the party was given up for dead. It was the custom at that time to hold a funeral ceremony in a chapel part-way up the mountain when people failed to return from the peak. At last the storm broke, and the guide led his exhausted party down the mountain. But it was too late; the ceremony was underway when the chapel door flew open, and Perren, with his guide and client tottering on frozen feet, staggered in out of the snow.

Perren had walked into his own funeral.

That close call did not diminish Perren's love for the mountains and mountaineering; instead, it forged in him a determination that the mountains would never find him unprepared again. In his career as a guide and instructor, it is said that he never had a serious-injury accident in the mountains.

Perren was a keen judge of character and a man who led by example during training climbs and rescues. When your knees began to tremble and your toes were numb and ready to slip, he would appear at your side with encouraging advice and some dry Swiss humour to break the spell of gravity. During training climbs, the most common question Perren heard was "Walter, how much further?" His answer, which became a motto, was always the same: "It's chust a little more up." And when somebody choked up on a climb, about the strongest admonition they heard were two heavily accented words that somehow conveyed a world of disappointment: "Chee whiz!"

On the ridge of Mount Victoria, there is a sickle of ice, part of the Continental Divide that has to be negotiated in traversing the mountain. From this knife edge that splits both earth and sky, an ice slope drops away several thousand feet into Abbot Pass. On the other side, a steep couloir funnels the air above Lake O'Hara. The spot is not far from where the Mexican party came to grief. Many novice climbers are psyched out by this blade of ice. On one training climb, two novices who were roped together as a team insisted on straddling it on their buttocks, shinnying nervously along it as if the Great Divide were a bucking bronco. Walter stood watching, doodling around on the edge of the precipice with his hands in his pockets as usual. "Chee whiz!" he finally exclaimed. "You can stand up now, boys. You won't hit your heads."

With nervous giggles, the two candidates rose gingerly to their feet, letting their crampons bite into the ice, and driving in the ferrules of their axes for balance. They stared nervously to either side. "By the way," said Walter, "what do you do if one of you falls on a ridge like this?"

"I'd have to move pretty fast," offered the first climber.

"Yes, but where to?" asked Walter, dryly.

The novice and his partner glanced around again before answering.

"Guess I'd have to jump to one side or the other, to make a belay," said one of them, uncertainly.

"Good idea," said Walter. "Chust make sure you don't both jump down the same side."

Perren enjoyed a practical joke. On another climb of Victoria, he carried a small bag of dry horse dung in his rucksack. He slipped away from the other climbers and scattered this rustic eluvium along the sickle before they got there. Perhaps he thought his cowboys would feel it was safe to walk upright where a horse could cross. He was often heard to say to a novice questioning the difficulty of a climb, "It's not so bad. I could lead my Swiss milk cow up that peak."

Perren had defined our rescue function at Lake O'Hara. We were to be the first to respond in case of climbing accidents or other public-safety issues – anything from lost kids to bear maulings. We had a bag of candy on hand for the kids and a government-issued rifle on hand for the bears. (We never had occasion to use the rifle.) One or both of us, depending on the situation, would make contact with the survivors or witnesses to begin operations. As for climbing accidents, we would lead, or assist the rescue if it could be done safely by one or two men. Otherwise, we were to assess the kind of help that was needed, then radio the information back to park headquarters. This might save Perren from committing a full rescue effort unnecessarily in the busy summer season. Like firemen, rescue teams don't appreciate coming out for false alarms.

Although he was usually miles away, an *éminence grise* who we heard directing distant operations on the park radio network, you never knew when Perren might show up. He had showed up before dawn one morning the previous year, after an all-night party Vockeroth was hosting at O'Hara. Vockeroth wasn't feeling too swift as he tried to reach the door, stumbling over the prostrate forms of climbers sleeping it off on his cabin floor.

There stood the boss, nattily attired in clean climbing togs. "Donnie," he said. "Get your pants on and let's go. There is a rescue on over at Glacier Park, and they need assistance."

As they drove off, Perren filled him in on the details. Two ropes of New York climbers had got off-route climbing the east ridge on Sir Donald, and wandered into steep, smooth rock on the north face. There had been two falls that immobilized the party. One leader had attempted to descend for help and had also wound up stranded; a second had managed to descend and get to park head-quarters. Alpine specialist Fred Schleiss had taken a team of wardens in and pulled off a daring rescue, traversing steep terrain with one casualty on a stretcher. They had gotten everybody out on the ridge above the Sir Donald–Uto col. Then, in descending, Warden Bert Pittaway, who was belaying the stretcher party, had tied into the New Yorker's piton to rappel down and join the party below. The pin pulled; Pittaway survived the ensuing fall but slashed open an artery in his wrist and lost a lot of blood. The Americans, who were not as seriously hurt, had to bivouac in six inches of fresh snow, helped by a warden who stayed behind while Schleiss evacuated Pittaway. Now he had to return to get the Americans off. It was their second night on the mountain, and a storm was brewing.

Vockeroth's memory, influenced by that old hangover, is a little muddled as to the details of the operation, which involved an early use of a helicopter. They drove to Golden where they got into a heli-copter (pilot and machine type have so far eluded the record) and bounced around through miserable weather up to Roger's Pass where they picked up Fred Schleiss. They flew up the Beaver River to the Sir Donald–Uto col. In fact, as Schleiss could inform them, Warden Bill Laurilla had already tried a helicopter landing on that col two days earlier. "The helicopter nearly crashed into the moun-tain," Schleiss recalled for me in 1999. "The wind was blowing so hard through the col, it pushed the helicopter over to the wall of Mount Uto. They could see sparks flying out from the end of the rotors – that's how close they came! So after that the pilot and machine left the area – no landing that day." Schleiss and company had gone up on foot instead.

On this second attempt, a storm was blowing in and visibility was poor due to the driving snow. The pilot had his hands full dealing with wind and up-drafts on one side of the mountain that switched to down-drafts on the other. His passengers were craning their necks to see how close Mount Uto was getting in the narrow col. Below them was some slabby looking rock, covered with verglas ice, where he could not land, though he could touch against it with one skid. They needed crampons to step down onto that ice safely, but they could not put them on in the helicopter, for fear of damaging the hull.

The rescuers exchanged looks; Vockeroth remembers the twinkle in Perren's eye, even on that dangerous occasion. "You go first, Don," he shouted over the engine noise. "You young guys are much better." With Perren gripping the belt on Vockeroth's climbing pants to steady him in the wind and driving sleet, Vockeroth stepped out onto the left landing skid, where he balanced on one booted foot while strapping a crampon on the other. This is quite a feat in itself. He then stepped down onto the rock. The first thing he did was drive a big angled pin into the first likely crack with quick blows of his piton hammer. He then clipped a sling from his harness into the pin and breathed a sigh of relief. Perren handed the ropes and packs out to Vockeroth, then he and Fred Schleiss stepped down to join him. The helicopter slipped away, leaving them in the sudden quiet of a precarious perch. After roping up and getting their crampons on securely, the three men climbed up two or three rope lengths, where they met the stranded climbers. Then they helped belay and lower the injured people down the mountain to reach the waiting ambulance.

It all sounded very cool to me: a daring use of the helicopter which was not often seen in the mountains back then, and I couldn't help envying Vockeroth the cachet of having assisted Perren and Fred Schleiss, though I wasn't sure I envied him the actual experience itself.

For a while, it looked like we were going to get through the entire summer without a serious incident. Being young and foolish,

I had mixed feelings about that, not yet having learned the true meaning of the ancient Chinese curse, "May you live in interesting times."

On the evening of August 21, as Bernie prepared to leave the district on days off, I turned on the radio for our nightly radio check. We were surprised to hear Perren's voice as he talked to District Warden Wally McPhee at Lake Louise. There was a major operation slated the next morning for Mount Babel (3,101 metres), a peak in the Moraine Lake group. Two climbers had gotten stuck on a tiny ledge seventy-six metres from the top of Babel's great eastern wall. Perren was organizing men and equipment for a rescue operation. Bernie radioed in and offered his services, and asked if I would be needed as well.

Perren accepted Bernie's offer at once, but informed of the number of climbers we had in our area, he ordered me to stay put. I felt like the kid who wants to play ball but doesn't get picked for the team.

Bernie signed off. "The east face of Babel!" I exclaimed in disbelief. "What crazy bugger would be fooling about up there?"

"Probably somebody we know," he replied with a wry look. "See ya later." He grabbed his pack and headed for his car.

I left the radio on a while longer, and heard the name "Greenwood" through the static. I jumped up, startled at the news. I couldn't believe that Greenwood was stuck on a ledge. And his partner, it turned out, was none other than Charlie Locke of trail-crew days. One of the two was injured and unable to move up or down. We would not know which one until the next day.

The east face of Mount Babel is the subject of a beautiful painting by famed Canadian artist A. C. Leighton. He has captured the essence of the mountain as a jagged bronze lance head, fractured by ice and time, polished by the weather. It was a peak that Brian Greenwood had come to know well, as Phil Dowling reveals in his book *The Mountaineers* (1979). In 1961 Greenwood made the first ascent of its north ridge with Calgarian Glen Boles, and he climbed the left side of its forbidding east face with fellow guide Leo Grillmair. But it was a more direct line, an elegant *direttissima* up its east face, that he most coveted, and during the climb with Grillmair he had a chance to look for a line that would "go." The east face, which rises above Consolation Valley, is a terrific precipice some 1,000 metres high, footed by tottering quartzite columns, scarred with cracks and chimneys, and garnished with overhangs near its summit.

Although big-wall climbing was not a new concept to the climbing world of 1966, no one in North America had tried to scale a limestone monster like this one. It was cutting-edge mountaineering then, and even now the east face of Babel is seldom visited. In the old days, climbers would likely grade Greenwood's route, under the system then used, as being a Grade Six, meaning it was a vertical – and even overhanging – rock climb that might take several days and the use of direct aid. Such a pioneering climb would have some pitches that very few people had the skills to handle back then, requiring the use of pitons or bolts for protection and étriers (stirrups) that support the leader where no natural holds are available. Greenwood had attacked it twice before the August 1966 attempt, but had to back off on both occasions. In those days, as Greenwood pointed out to me recently (1999), there were so many things unclimbed that it didn't really matter if you didn't feel up to it on a particular day. "It wasn't as if a lot of people were out there trying to knock it off before you," he reflected. "You could always do it later."

"Later" in his case turned out to be a sunny day in late summer. Early on the morning of August 20, Locke and Greenwood hiked quickly up the trail from Moraine Lake to Consolation Lakes, then ascended the last of the talus slopes above the second lake and reached the base of Babel's great wall. They scrambled up the easier ground, then stopped to rope up. Looming above them was steep and unknown terrain, the kind of wall where snow doesn't stick in the winter, and where rotten slabs of limestone, undisturbed by human intrusion, might be poised to collapse under unwary feet.

Looking back, Greenwood recalls, modestly, that until they got stuck, "it went very well. It was a good rock climb with some good pitches of limestone. There were some quartzite pitches lower down, and some of those quartzite tower things that you see on the Tower of Babel" (a nearby feature). "Just up toward the top there was a lot of loose rock, but you get used to that in the Rockies."

But as Dowling points out, there was also a difficult crack part-way up that Greenwood called a "thrutch" – a term, according to Dowling, "which represents a feeling of panic combined with desperate physical action."

Greenwood, then thirty-two, led confidently, putting together a line of cracks and chimneys, slowly fashioning the route in his head and then trying its virtues hold by hold, as Locke paid out the rope from below. Young Charlie Locke was in good spirits and enjoying the climb. "This was just like the books," he recalled. "This was tiny little pitons, pendulum traverses. I mean, this was cool, right? And after a couple of days you tend to relax when you get on these faces." It was a slow process, however, and as the shadows of the day lengthened, the two climbers found themselves obliged to bivouac for the night partway up the face. Staring into the gloom, Greenwood knew it was quite likely they would have to spend another night somewhere above where the face looked to be the steepest.

The great wall was a lonely place, a vertical world ruled by cloud and wind. The silences there, broken suddenly by the sound of rocks clattering down its gullies, now echoed occasionally with human voices, the jangle of climbing hardware, and the singing note of a piton being driven into the rock. It was evening and the face was hard to make out as Greenwood belayed Locke up to the last ledge of the day, a wedge-shaped thing about a metre wide by three metres long, tapering away to nothing on their right. Above them on that ledge was an ugly sight: an overhanging wall pushing out perhaps five degrees past the vertical, overhung itself by a roof at its top. It was scored by a fissure of variable width and depth, angling off to the right and upwards, but that looked improbable at the time, given the kind of primitive hardware Greenwood had to rely on.

The ascent line above their bivouac ledge led over a drop of at least a hundred metres of free fall to the next ledge – not that it mattered, with so much space beyond that between them and the valley floor. They would have to overcome the roof and hope the angle would change to merely vertical above it. The final pitch should take them to a natural aperture in the line of the east ridge, marking the end of the route, though they could not see it from their ledge. The two climbers anchored themselves to the rock with pitons for the night, and after a cold meal of sausage, cheese, and chocolate, they zipped up their down jackets and tried to find enough room to lie down on the cramped ledge. They stared up at the glittering stars, trying to sleep and to not worry about the morning's challenges, particularly the fact that they were nearly out of water and food.

Morning found them awake with the sun. After fortifying himself with a breakfast cigarette, Greenwood tackled the wall.

According to Greenwood, he had registered out at the Lake Louise warden office allowing for several days on the face. But at Lake Louise, District Warden Wally McPhee believed Greenwood was overdue on August 22. It is fair to say that the Locke-Greenwood team made the warden service nervous. Their famous first ascent of the north face of Mount Temple earlier that season had Perren's troops wondering about their outfit's ability to pull off a rescue on that massive wall of rock and ice, if anything went wrong. Greenwood's talents were definitely upping the ante for all concerned. McPhee sent his assistant wardens – Paul Peyto and Jay Morton – out to see if they could spot the mad Englishman and his partner, and duly received word by radio that the climbers were on the face, near the top of the route and moving upward apparently in good form. McPhee noted the information, and turned his thoughts to other tasks.

In fact, Greenwood was having trouble making headway on the crux pitch of the mountain, and could not find a way through the overhanging roof. He suggested the younger man might give it a try. The two changed places and Greenwood belayed from the ledge and had another smoke. "So I went up, and I knew how to do that, right?" cracked Locke during a recent interview, "'cause I'd seen it all in the books and all these slings and tiny little pitons and whatever." He moved up to the roof, "about thirty to thirty-five feet" by his account, where he banged in one short-bladed piton after another in the sloping cracks until he was moving along below the roof, standing in stirrups and fighting against gravity to move up over the obstacle, which kept trying to push him into thin air. At last he got a look over the overhang at the wall rising above it. Then it happened: "One of the aids I was using pulled out and I fell backwards," recalled Locke. "All the pitons I'd used for protection went – ping, ping, ping – until I finally hit the rock about ten or fifteen feet below where Brian was."

On hearing of Locke's account, Greenwood's dry response was, "One of the pins must have held." He meant that he might have been pulled off the ledge by the force of Locke's fall if not for the mechanical advantage of the rope passing through some protection.

As the rock came up to meet him, Locke reached out to ward off the impact, crashed into the rock, and dislocated his left wrist. He remembers scrambling back up to the ledge, half stunned by the fall, using his good arm to help, with Greenwood hauling on the rope. Locke, his wrist bent into a painful right angle, was now unable to climb or to belay Greenwood. He lay on the ledge half in a faint from the pain and bruising body-shock of the fall. It was 11:30 A.M. and the climb on Mount Babel was at an end, only seventy-six metres short of the top. The climbers were out of food and water and tired out after two bivouacs on the face. Greenwood was now faced with either awaiting possible rescue, going for help, or lowering his partner, a rope length at a time, all the way to the bottom of the mountain, which would have required Greenwood to rappel himself perhaps twenty to twenty-five times. We can assume that a helping hand, coming from the ridge which was not far above them, would have definitely been safer.

Looking back at it from 1999, he feels that he could have pulled off the lowers if he'd had to, but circumstance decreed otherwise. A friend of Locke's had hiked up to Consolation Valley to see if he could spot the two on the face, and was himself spotted. "It was embarrassing," Greenwood recalls, "but there we were shouting, Help! Help!"

Fortunately, the cries were heard, and the friend ran back down to Moraine Lake Lodge where there was a radio-telephone. Wally McPhee was notified at 2 P.M. He sent Jay Morton back to the scene on horseback and alerted Chief Warden Walter Perren in Banff. Perren drove to Lake Louise, where McPhee had a government saddle horse trailered for hauling to the trailhead. Around 4 P.M., Perren trotted his mount up the last part of the trail and joined Jay Morton at the foot of the face.

Walter Perren got out his binoculars and took a hard look at the east face and the position of the two men. He knew Greenwood's abilities; it was he who had tested Greenwood for his guide's licence. "One of them is injured," he told Morton as he studied the two minute figures, one standing and one slumped against the wall that rose behind them. The standing figure could be Greenwood, but it was hard to be sure at that distance. At least their position close to the summit ridge, on such a formidable route, would prove to be a kind of blessing for the rescue team. "Ve go from da top," he said decisively, eyeing a small saddle in the ridge that seemed to offer a good line toward the climbers. "Ve have to use da cable gear."

Morton stared up at the mountain, thinking that it would take forever to haul the gear up that steep ridge on men's backs. It was too bad these old guys were so out of date and stingy about paying for helicopter time.

But Perren, the old twinkle in his eye, had read his thoughts. "Yah, Jay. Ve use da chopper," he said, to Morton's surprise. Perhaps he was remembering that hasty trip to Mount Sir Donald with Vockeroth.

I'll have to call the superintendent for permission, thought Perren. And if he says no, I will hear yes. He glanced around and thanked God for the fair weather. He prayed that it would last for a while longer. A sudden storm could delay the operation. Rain in the valley would turn to snow above; cold, wet weather would weaken the climbers on their tiny ledge with only bivouac sacks to cover them – if they had brought bivouac sacks along. He stared up at the ledge, fearing what could happen if Greenwood tried to come down, willing Greenwood to hear his thoughts: Stay put, Brian, please. Do not try to descend.

He turned to the younger man. "Jay, it's very important Greenwood knows ve are coming. I want him to stay put. Let's go fast down to the lodge. You get some rolls of toilet paper, come back up here right away, and you make a sign so they read it."

The bemused Morton agreed. They mounted up and hurried down the mountain.

The objects of all this concern were hungry and thirsty. More seriously from Greenwood's point of view, he was getting dangerously low on cigarettes, which his body had learned to use as alternative fuel when food was unavailable – or so it seemed to his friends. Their cries for help had been heard – but were they truly understood as distress calls? Should he leave Charlie tied off here, descend the face and go for help? He doubted that was possible before night fell. What were those silly sods up to down there? The answer came when they read a sign on the meadow far below, which Warden Jay Morton had created with humble rolls of butt wad in letters several metres high. It read:

WAIT
HELP
COMING TOP
A M

The message cheered them though they were in for a third night's bivouac and their second night on the cramped and dangerous ledge. Greenwood eyed the sky; at least the weather was cooperating. As the night went on, Locke, his brain foggy from pain and his young body crying out for food and water, worried that they might be trapped on the ledge for keeps. "I remember staring at Brian's leg," joked Locke as he recalled that night for me, "wondering what it would taste like."

Walter Perren had anticipated a rescue call on a big-face route when he'd imported the first Austrian-made cable rescue gear a few years earlier. The equipment, depending on a thin steel cable with a breaking strength of 4,000 pounds (1,814 kilos), had been tested in the European Alps on a number of occasions, most notably on the Eiger in 1957. On that occasion, a multi-national team of climbers and guides lowered Alfred Hellepart more than three hundred metres down the infamous north face to pluck the injured Claudio Corti from a tiny ledge, an event that occupied the international media at the time. Perren watched the event from Canada, where a minor revolution in climbing was then underway. Climbers like Hans Gmoser, Heinz Kahl, Leo Grillmair, Brian Greenwood, and Dick Lofthouse left the ridges to the old guard and set new standards doing high-angle rock climbs on mountains like Mount Yamnuska east of Canmore, Alberta. Yamnuska was merely their playground. Gmoser (the founder of helicopter skiing) would soon move on to high snow-and-ice routes on Mount Logan and Mount McKinley. But Greenwood et al. were eyeing new routes, direct routes up the big unclimbed faces of the Rockies. It was only a matter of time before somebody got stuck on one of those walls, unable to move up, or down. Traditional rescues using climbing rope would become very difficult on big faces. Perren had watched Greenwood's progress on the north face of Mount Temple earlier that summer and wondered just how difficult a cable operation would be in such terrain. Well, tomorrow he would find out.

As he drove back to Banff that evening, he considered doing the descent himself, but as the most knowledgeable person, logic dictated he must stay on top and supervise the operation. He thought of the most experienced local wardens he could draw upon for the job. Billy Vroom, Johnny Wackerle, and Bernie Schiesser came to mind. Wackerle and Vroom had the most cable-rescue skills. Before he immigrated to Canada, John Wackerle had learned cable-rescue technique as a sixteen-year-old member of the *Bergwacht* in his native Bavaria. Just the man to second Perren on top of the mountain. Billy would have to go down the face, he decided. He knew this thirty-four-year-old rancher's kid from Pincher Creek, Alberta very well. He had turned into a skilful climber under Perren's tutelage. Bill was a medium-sized guy at five foot seven, but he was wiry and strong. Although a little slow to get started, he was cool and methodical once underway.

For the rest of his team, Perren would need more brawn than experience. Assistant wardens Paul Peyto and Keith Brady were untrained, but Brady was strong, and the eagle-eyed Peyto, related to old-time warden Wild Bill Peyto, was built like Charles Atlas. Andy Anderson had some training, and veteran wardens Ed Carelton, Wally McPhee, and Fred Bamber were tested and reliable, although you had to watch Carelton. He had a tantalum plate in his head, thanks to a German sniper's bullet at the battle of Caen, and though the fit and courageous Ed had done a number of rescues, he sometimes got confused when tying knots. "If I try to leave Ed behind, he will never let me forget it," thought Perren. "John and I just have to keep an eye on his knots, that's all."

The details Perren had to think about were endless. For one thing, in those austere times, some wardens had not been issued with climbing boots. Also, they had no climbing helmets, only the hardhats used by construction workers, and no proper mountaineering clothing or rain gear. They just didn't give him a budget to properly equip temporary wardens. It was frustrating, but Perren refused to let himself get angry about the situation. Banff was a climbing town, and office staff would have to get on the phone and round up boots for his men. Maybe those cheapskates would give him some money to buy gear after this.

Back in Banff, Perren was up late, organizing for the rescue that was set to begin at 5 A.M. Meanwhile, park staff had tracked down pilot Jim Davies and his Bell G3B1 helicopter at a geophysical-survey camp in Jasper park. The helicopter would reach Lake Louise at 9 P.M. Fuel must be obtained; men notified in far-flung districts; and equipment hauled to Moraine Lake by truck during the night.

Warden Andy Anderson was in the most remote location. He was on backcountry patrol at Cyclone Cabin on the Red Deer River when he received a radio message to report to Moraine Lake for the rescue. He had kicked his horses out to graze, and they were out of sight, but Jeanie, the colt of the bunch, was a bit of a pet and stayed close to the cabin. He eyed the colt doubtfully. She was not fully trained. Well, he decided, she had to learn about being under saddle at night sometime, and the time had come. Barbara Anderson made her husband a quick supper, after which he saddled the colt, kissed Barbara goodbye, and left for the trailhead near Temple Ski Lodge, around twelve kilometres away. Barbara would man the station and wrangle the horses while he was gone.

The colt went along well, but she was jittery without the other horses and grew more so as night came on. By the time they neared the summit of a ridge on the way to Baker Pass, the colt was dancing around and fighting the bit in the dark. Anderson knew the trail and thought he must be about even with a scree slope on his left, studded with big boulders and ending in a creek bottom. He was worried that Jeanie might slip off the trail and roll over on him. That's when he heard the "huff" of a grizzly bear clearing its nose to get the man smell out of it. In the dark of night, it sounded like it was about three feet from his ear. Horses can see better in the dark than we can, and what Jeanie saw made her snort with alarm and jump sideways clear off the trail. "She went down over the scree, partly sliding on her back hocks," said Anderson. "All I could do was hang on and hope she didn't hit one of those big boulders." Sparks flew out from under the colt's steel shoes as she finally slid to a halt. Down in the bottom, he listened carefully above the sound of running creek water but didn't hear the bear coming down after them. He dismounted and, talking softly to quiet the trembling colt, ran his hands over her body looking for damage; he was relieved to find no serious injury. "We came out of it alright," Anderson told me, "but the thing is, it was a dead end down there – we had to go right back up the same way we came down." Jeanie nervously picked her way back up the steep slope. Fortunately, the bear was probably just as startled as they were. It had left the trail. They finished their night ride without further incident. He thought that Lady Luck had been riding with them, but it was not the case. The brave little filly had pulled some ligaments. She became permanently lame as a result of that slide down the mountain and had to be put down.

As other wardens prepared themselves for the morning's effort, Perren and his protégé, Bill Vroom, met at the rescue cache in Banff. They had a serious concern. Although Perren had trained his people at lowering operations with the cable, they did not have enough cable to lower a climber 1,000 metres, the effective length for Mount Babel. Besides, the hazards of rockfall at that length would have made the attempt extremely dangerous. Also, they had yet to lift one man, let alone two men at a time, using the cable. They had not obtained the double-action Swiss winch designed for that operation. Perren knew the improvised system had worked on the Eiger on the famous 305-metre lift of two men. Perren would have to improvise a pulley system, and they were short one idler pulley, tripod-mounted, which was needed to prevent the cable from biting into the rock at the top of the mountain. Stan Peyto, part of a family that had deep roots in the warden service, was the garage foreman and a skilled metal-worker. Perren showed him a picture of the specialized apparatus and explained its purpose. Peyto put on his welding helmet and set to work. By 4 A.M. he presented Perren with the finished idler pulley, an accurate match for the original photograph.

Before 5 A.M., the dark of the Moraine Lake road was starred with headlights as the team drove up to the rendezvous site. At Lake Louise, in the chill air after dawn, Jim Davies finished the pre-flight check on his B-1 helicopter and fired up the turbo-charged engine. (The turbo charger is basically an air pump that gives the engine the same air mix it would get at sea level, hence preventing a loss of power at higher altitudes.) Bill Vroom and Walter Perren rode with him as he followed the road below, up along the side of Mount Temple. The Tower of Babel came into sight as they passed Moraine Lake to the right. They ascended towards the summit of the mountain. The rising sun clothed that great bronze lance in ruddy light, and suddenly there were the two men a stone's throw away, huddled together, waving a greeting, the only living things in a vertical world of rock and space. They seemed to be in good spirits but looked totally incongruous, marooned on their rocky porch in the sky with the world falling away from their dangling boots.

The rescuers waved back, then gestured up towards the peak to indicate again that help was coming. They could see the saddle where the gear would have to go; it looked as if the "fall line" was direct from there to the climbers, but in such rugged terrain it was hard to be certain. Bill Vroom stared at the rock, trying to memorize its features. They hovered over the saddle for a few moments. There was no level ground for a landing spot; the site was but a small rocky ramp, angled down the west face towards Moraine Lake, an equally unwelcoming site for a rescue attempt. Conversation was difficult in the noisy helicopter, which had no intercom. "I'll have to set down on top of the peak," shouted Davies over the engine noise. A moment later, Vroom and Perren stepped out of the machine on the summit of Mount Babel. Davies lifted the ship up and angled down in a long dive for Moraine Lake. He would ferry the ten-man crew two at a time, with loads of equipment, up to the top.

Some newcomers were unnerved to be landed with the front skids protruding over a 1,000 metre drop-off: not so John Wackerle. He was used to climbing mountains with heavy cable gear on his back. "For me personally," he remembers, "Babel was an easy one. Riding up and down in the helicopter was like travelling by Cadillac."

Moving at a crouch to avoid the deadly rotors, the men unloaded their equipment. Backpacking heavy spools of steel cable and other gear in their top-heavy Bergens rucksacks (its internal steel frame bit into your shoulder blades at every step), they would rope up and downclimb the ridge of broken rock interrupted by cliff bands, to reach the notch. Perren put his experienced men at the front and tail of each rope to protect the greenhorns. The ridge was narrow, honed to a wedge in one place, dropping off sharply on both sides. Rocks rattled away from under untrained feet, rolling down towards Moraine Lake, filling the air with the smell of sulphur. For Wackerle and Schiesser, it was a walk. But the newer men moved uncertainly, staring wide-eyed down the preci- pice on either side.

Once they were assembled at the saddle in the ridge, Perren supervised setting up the double-cable rescue set. This is an exacting task. The various blocks, pulleys, and clamps must be anchored to the rock with pitons or bolts and an array of climbing rope or slings. Piton hammers soon made the mountain ring. Much care was given to find the most solid anchor points available. One point that had to be used was a large boulder on the edge of the west face; this had to be watched for signs of movement throughout the rescue. To make matters worse, the rescue team had to stay roped up while they worked, which hampered their efforts. Perren belayed Wackerle while he anchored the tripod pulley above the east face. Not surpris- ingly, it was not until 9 A.M. that the team was ready to lower Bill Vroom. His first trip was a reconnaissance, to make sure they were positioned correctly above the climbers. Wearing a sturdy helper- seat harness and equipped with a heavy P-300 Motorola radio, Vroom stepped over the precipice and began walking backwards down the east face as the cable played out over the anchored idler pulley, watched carefully by Perren. Stan Peyto's fabricated pulley worked perfectly. Vroom was clipped into both cables as an added precaution. His teammates, wearing leather gloves, controlled the descent by allowing the cables to run around two hardwood-and-steel blocks. By pulling back on the cable, they could stop the lowering action instantly. In front of the blocks, for extra security, two brakemen allowed each cable to run through one-way clamps called "frogs" due to their appearance. Pushing the frog forward immediately stops all downward movement. This is vital either in an emergency, or while more cable is being coupled in on the uphill side of the lowering block. Walter Perren stood on the edge of the precipice, his jaunty peaked cap on his head, his hands in his pockets as was his wont. There, he could watch Bill's descent and supervise the crew simultaneously. Andy Anderson recalled watching his friend and colleague disappear over the cliff and go out of sight. "I don't remember any of us, including myself, rushing forward to volunteer on that job. It took a lot of nerve to step forward, but we all knew Billy was the right guy at the right time."

The atmosphere on the site was charged and intense. There was no casual conversation, no smoking, no breaks in those early hours. Warden Brady, who had had no mountain rescue training until then, remembered: "It seemed like it took forever to get him [Vroom] down into position. You were in a cramped position, manning the frogs or blocks, or unwinding cable – unable to move much because of the danger of a fall. Walter had to watch and make sure there were no glitches. He didn't have to say very much – one word was enough; all of us knew that Bill's life hung in the balance."

At first, all went well. Vroom walked slowly down the face, his feet wide apart for balance, slightly angled so he could watch for loose rock behind him. He could feel his heart pounding. He glanced up and saw Perren's figure growing smaller, but heard his shouts of encouragement. He had to fight off the urge to grab at the thin cables for balance.

As Vroom descended, the crew could hear his voice on the summit radio. "I'm at a big overhang now . . . Doin' okay."

"I'm stepping over the overhang . . . hanging free now," he reported a moment later. Now there occurred a problem, however, and a serious one. A lot of torque develops in the strands of the cable under load. Because there is no swivel on the cable until you join on the next hundred-metre length, you have to descend quite quickly on shorter lowers; Vroom was being lowered too slowly. When he stepped over the first overhanging roof, forty-five metres down, he was hanging in space, in a sitting position in his harness, and without warning he began to spin with surprising speed, tangling the two cables together.

The rescue crew were alarmed to hear the anxious note in his voice on Perren's radio – "Perren from Vroom – I'm spinning . . . spinning . . . can't stop it!" Perren leaned over the edge. The two cables played out in a perfect parallel line as far as he could see, then went out of sight. But if they were ravelling together, and Vroom continued to spin, the strands might start to splay apart. Eventually some of them could break, seriously weakening the cable. "Stop lowering!" he ordered. Below the overhanging roof, Vroom jolted to a halt as the frog clamps were engaged.

A spin on the cable seems to go on forever when you can't make it stop. The cable scraped across the edge of the roof, dragging him with it, then steadied, as he swayed and spun. Consolation Lakes, some 850 metres below him, whirled in a blue halo. It felt like he was going to flip upside down and bore right down into them. He was on the point of blacking out. A shower of small stones, pried loose by the cable above, clattered down the face and fluttered past like small propellers.

Profanity on the park radio network was a serious breach of conduct. Bill Vroom's wife, Joan, monitoring the radio at their home in Banff, knew something was badly amiss when she heard Vroom shouting as well as swearing on Channel Two. "Goddamn – Walter, do you read me? – I'm spinning – sonofabitch!"

"Bill – take it easy. I know the problem," came Walter's reassuring voice. "Ve make it stop." Walter had his men take off a wrap of cable from each block, decreasing the friction, but it seemed to Bill to take a long time. Finally the frogs were released and he began to move downward again.

Perren's voice crackled on the radio set: "Ve lower you more quickly now. When your feet touch da rock again, it will stop da spin. Let us know when you touch, copy?"

"Copy," came Vroom's muffled reply. "Lower away. Over."

As he sped downward, Vroom fought to control the spin so as to meet the rock feet first and avoid injury. In a few moments Perren's radio crackled again: "Perren from Vroom. Just about there. Ten feet, five feet – stop!" Vroom's boot soles hit the face and he did a brief cakewalk back and forth until he hung motionless, not spinning, but feeling dizzy. He fought off the urge to vomit. Hearing voices shouting a greeting, he looked around in a daze and was dismayed to see the two climbers peering down from above his position. He was about twelve metres below them and nine metres to the north. Vroom had climbed some fairly steep mountains and done some real rock climbs, but when he stared down at the face below, he found it hard to believe the two climbers had come so far up that desolate wall. This was not a place meant for human beings.

The watchful Greenwood, seeing what must be done, had a rope readied to throw to him. When he heard what was happening, Perren had the cables taken off the lowering blocks, then reeved haul ropes, attached to the frog clamps, through two sets of pulleys. The crew on top would haul Vroom up while Greenwood pulled him towards the ledge, drag-line style.

This worked well, and soon he was resting on the tiny ledge and reporting on the party's condition. "They told me Charlie had a broken wrist, and they hadn't had a drink of water in twenty-four hours," Vroom recalled. The news that nobody was critically injured was a great relief. Perren felt a better line could be found, but first, Vroom wanted to try to untangle the cable. "The thing that kept me awake nights afterwards," he once told me, "was the fact that, for some reason, I unhooked from both cables – rather than just one at a time. I was whipping them around trying to separate them – what if I had lost one or both of them?"

Vroom got the cables untangled, and soon felt tension being applied from the top. It was time to return, or as Greenwood laconically explained it, "We had to send him back up for ciga-rettes." Greenwood had him on the rope still, and when his feet left the ground, Greenwood let him out under the overhang on belay, preventing a wild swing against the face that might have resulted in injury.

On the ridge top, two teams hauled alternately on the cables with climbing ropes attached to the frog clamps. Vroom moved up about two metres at a pull, then hung in mid-air for a moment or two between pulls while the frog clamps were reset. He soon found himself spinning beneath the overhang again. It was a lonely, desperate feeling. He remembers trying to count the spins so when he touched the overhang he could spin himself the opposite way to take the kinks out of the cable! Soon he found purchase with his feet and jackknifed his body slowly over the edge of the roof. Perren watched the small human figure come into sight and urged the crew to pick up the pace a bit. At last Vroom came to the ridge crest and the crew was cheered to finally see the top of his helmet, then the rest of him appear at the end of the tether as they heaved at the climbing ropes. He looked a little green around the gills, but was otherwise alright.

Vroom and Perren huddled together and decided no better line could be obtained, due to rock formations on the face that might hinder the cable. Greenwood's assistance would make the first approach workable again. After a brief rest and a drink of water, Vroom felt up to a second trip down the face. This time he packed the Gramminger "rescue diaper" on his back, as well as a pack containing refreshments, including some tobacco to keep Greenwood amused while Locke was carried up. Once again he was lowered down the face, more quickly this time, and Greenwood helped to drag him over to the ledge. Gingerly, he sat down in front of Locke. Greenwood helped strap the injured man into the rescue seat carried on Vroom's back. Then Greenwood helped Vroom get carefully to his feet under Locke's weight on the tiny perch above the abyss as the cable came tight. As he had done before with Vroom, Greenwood controlled their swing out into space with the rope. Vroom took the rope end with him this time. He would anchor it above the overhang to use in returning on the last lower.

This second effort, with Locke's weight added to his own, was far more gruelling. Locke could do nothing to assist Vroom in keeping his balance. The constant spinning under the overhang, first one way, then the other, confused and nauseated the injured man. The thin cables hummed and vibrated under the strain like a bass-guitar string. A wisp of vapour lifted from the edge of the overhanging roof as the cables sawed their way into the soft limestone. Once Vroom's boots touched rock above the overhanging roof, he felt 800 metres of relentless gravity pulling at his waist and shoulders. Slowly, doubled at the waist under Locke's weight, he crept painfully over the roof edge once again and began walking up the steep rock face, hauled by the summit team. As he slowly crept up the wall, flylike, he had to try and follow the line of the cable, but that line was never quite the same as the fall line down the face, because rock projections changed the cable's course. Sometimes the cable lifted up and suddenly sawed across the face to a new equilibrium. Vroom followed like a drunken tap dancer, balancing for two. Due to the elasticity in the various haul ropes and anchor ropes, there was a terrifying back step as the frog clamps engaged at the end of every two metre lift, causing Vroom to suddenly stagger backwards, to the mutual chagrin of both him and his passenger. "It felt awful," Locke remembered. "Every time it happened I thought – I'm going!"

At a point about forty-five metres above the ledge, Vroom found a good piton crack. He eased himself carefully to his knees, grunting with the strain. Sweat ran out from under his helmet edge and splashed the rock. But Locke's feet touched the rock now as he straddled Vroom's back; that helped to keep them in balance. Vroom banged a piton, borrowed from Locke, into the crack. It looked solid, and he clipped Greenwood's rope to it and left it there.

Perren called out encouragement from above. They picked up the pace as the crew hauled away. The edge of the cliff crept slowly closer until Vroom staggered over the lip, where Perren and Wackerle helped Locke out of the harness. There were relieved cheers from the crew.

Perren took a look at Vroom's face as he crumpled down on the rocks to catch his breath, and ordered a twenty minute rest. "Do you think you can make another trip, Billy?" asked Perren, quietly.

"I think I know the way now," cracked Vroom, gamely. "No point in starting all over with a new guy."

"You are doing a good chob here Billy. A very good chob," said Perren.

The whole crew was in need of a break. Sandwiches and coffee were quickly produced as the men relaxed on the rocky ground. Locke, nursing his damaged arm and worried about Greenwood's situation, suggested they hurry it up. Brady recalls Perren taking the young climber aside. After that, the cocky Charlie Locke of other days looked somewhat subdued. Andy Anderson commented later: "You know, we didn't think climbers were very bright in those days, so we didn't expect too much from them by way of conversation."

Greenwood recalls that he wasn't particularly anxious. "The whole operation was very efficient," he said. Locke and Greenwood were part of a mountaineering culture in which people came to each other's assistance when there was trouble. If the warden service had asked Greenwood to help with a rescue, he would have done so. He had interrupted climbs before to go to help others. From his point of view, he and Locke had had some bad luck, so it didn't seem unreasonable that someone might come to their assistance.

After a quiet smoke or two on his solitary ledge, Greenwood felt movement on the fixed rope and looked up. In a few minutes, Vroom backed over the overhang for the last time. The former cowboy and the Brit mountaineer were unlikely accomplices, but they were getting to know each other rather quickly. Carefully, they strapped Greenwood into the rescue seat. The two climbers carefully checked all straps and buckles. On top, Walter eyed the sky, waiting until he heard Vroom's voice again. "Okay Walter, take us up." Once more, Vroom struggled slowly to his feet, helped by tension on the cable. There were some hikers far below, he noticed, watching the action. They looked like ants.

Vroom's final walk over the overhang and up the wall was a tiresome grunt, but he was well-rehearsed now for the struggle. As he moonwalked his way up the cliff, Locke shouted down for them to retrieve his piton. It had cost him $1.37 – an hour's wages in those days. Locke likely meant it as a joke – he had a singular sense of humour. But for some reason, Vroom didn't seem to think the piton was all that important. In a few more minutes he made the ridge crest for the last time, and the crew hauled away with a will until both men were safe on top.

Once Greenwood was unloaded, Vroom collapsed into a sitting position, trembling like a leaf. It was 2 P.M., and the hard part was over. "I think I owe you a beer," said Greenwood. Vroom started walking away in a daze, as if he wanted nothing more but to be alone. Walter Perren hurried after him and put an arm around him to comfort him.

Anderson recalls Greenwood saying that of all the climbs he had done, he was never so frightened as he was coming up the mountain on Bill Vroom's back. Greenwood does not recall that exchange, but it would certainly not be surprising for any climber to feel that way about such a ride.

Keith Brady remembered how the crew felt. "When the first guy came up we were pretty excited. When the second guy is up there and standing there and he's alive, there was a feeling of euphoria. There they were, living and breathing. We had done it. Walter went around and shook hands with each man in turn and thanked him personally for his effort."

The bubble of tension had burst. The crew, tired and thirsty, wanted only to get off the mountain and repair to the Cascade Tavern in Banff, where an informal debriefing would be conducted over a tableload of cold draft beer. Fred Bamber recalls the historic event seemed like a typical Canadian operation; once it was over, the attitude was "Well, now we've done that. Wonder what will happen next."

Brian Greenwood would return to Mount Babel with climber John Moss in 1969, to complete the east face route. They used a bolt-and-pendulum technique to surmount the crux pitch above the ledge. Charlie Locke recovered from his injury; he and Chick Scott were with Greenwood on the first winter ascent of Mount Hungabee that December.

Greenwood continued climbing and racking up first ascents until 1975. "It was just something I enjoyed doing," he told me, summing up in a few words a passion for which he'd quit his career in the Alberta oil patch that summer of 1966. Ironically, it was not a fall from a mountain, but from a ladder, during a roofing job, that injured his knee and finished his climbing career at age forty-one. He has a new passion now – gardening.

At his home in Duncan, B.C. in February, 1999, Greenwood, a grey-haired but hale-looking sixty-five years old, told his side of the rescue story over dinner as his wife Nancy and I listened. It had been a matter-of-fact account, with little display of emotion. "I went over to Walter, after we got sorted out, and said, 'That was a very well done operation, Walter.'"

Greenwood paused; I glanced at him and was startled to see his eyes were filled with tears as he recalled Walter's quiet words to a fellow guide. They contained no rebuke. As a mountaineer, Perren understood that Greenwood's accomplishments and reputation were not tarnished just because he and Locke had had bad luck. "He said 'Brian, the helicopter is waiting. Take care of your client.'"

Walter Perren's eldest son, Peter, followed his father's example and joined the Banff Park warden service, where I worked with him for awhile in the 1970s. He recalls that in 1967, his father began to experience debilitating tinnitus in his ears. Other symptoms soon followed. "The doctors suggested it was ulcers," recalled Peter, "that he was too tense. But my father was the most relaxed of men. It was aplastic anemia. He had no platelets left in his blood. They only diagnosed it correctly two days before he died.

"It must have been hard on him that his body let him down like that."

The first thing Walter Perren had climbed when he arrived in the Canadian Rockies were some rock formations called the Needles, on Mount White above Lake Louise. Although his children – Peter, Martin, and Mark – were often after him to take them climbing, he always demurred, saying they were too young, although he would gladly take them fishing and skiing. He told his wife, Pam, that they should wait until their lungs and heart muscles were more developed. So Peter, age thirteen, was surprised when his father finally asked him to come climbing at Lake Louise one summer day in 1967. Peter didn't know what was wrong with his father. "In those days, they didn't tell the kids too much about fatal illness," recalled Peter. "Dad had never been ill in his life until then, but he wasn't feeling very well. At Lake Louise, he rented a horse from the Brewster outfit. I had to hike behind while he rode the horse up to the Lake Agnes teahouse. I asked if I could ride for awhile, and I was surprised when he said 'No, Peter – you can ride on the way down.'" Once they reached the Lake Agnes teahouse, they made their way slowly up the goat paths to Mount White and climbed the Needles.

Although he didn't explain it at the time to his young son, Walter Perren knew that one day it would all be clear to him. It was the first climb Walter had done in Canada and it would be his last, but now it would be Peter's first mountain also and they would climb it, this first and last mountain, together. The circle was complete. Walter died, on December 29, 1967, aged fifty-one.

You won't find him mentioned in the current *Canadian Encyclopedia,* but Mount Perren, straddling the Great Divide, commemorates his name.

CHAPTER SEVEN

Cruising for a Bruising on Mount Huber

A s a middle-aged former mountaineer, I long ago settled into the mode of the scrambler and ridge rat who knows how to use a climbing rope and ice axe when necessary. I'm out there for the scenery and the exercise, and something indefinable that has to do with nurturing the soul. The mountains are where the prophets went to commune with God. I think that's where He goes to roll his dice, and I think He loves to see His little gamblers at play among the building blocks of chaos. You can lean on His rocky windowsill and speak to Him informally there. Sometimes He will put his finger on your throat, ever so gently, so that a lump forms suddenly and threatens to choke you with mountain love and with grief. Grief, because looking at the world below, you will see how beautiful the world is He has made, and know how much of it we have destroyed.

When I was eighteen, I loved to don the implements of the mountaineer as if dressing for a war. My arms were the piton hammer and the ice axe, and I learned how to yodel and make the mountains ring. I liked to go bounding down a scree slope in giant strides, my pitons clanging together like an array of short swords and daggers. It's a good thing Canada had no wars for me to fight; I probably would not have lived this long.

By the time I reached thirty, grim experience in mountain search-and-rescue, along with the responsibilities of being a parent and husband, would knock the edges off the old bravado, and I began to wonder if I could continue at wardening and still reach forty. But looking back, I see that though I was brash, I was by no means a totally fearless climber to begin with. I was a slow starter at climbing because I was slow to make friends and shy about asking more experienced climbers to take me along. That changed when I started climbing with Bernie Schiesser.

There was no need to worry about Bernie's ability; I soon learned that it far surpassed mine. I came to dread hearing five familiar words from my partner: "Why don't we wander up . . ." followed by the name of some horrible feature I had not thought of climbing before. Another word that gave me pause was the word "interesting" when he used it to describe a route.

I was the perfect partner for a guy who wanted to practise for his guide's licence. As lead hand, he could use me as a pretend client on any mad whim that came into his head. Early in the season, he had said, "There's still too much snow around here. Why don't we wander up the left-hand side of Takakkaw Falls? I've often looked at that and thought it would be interesting."

Takakkaw, I thought. Sounds like a word invented by a crow with a bad cough. The falls, which empty part of the meltwater from the Waputik Icefield into the Yoho River, are some 380 metres high, and the cliff there had not been climbed previously. The cliff proved extremely "interesting" to climb – for me, that is. It was probably an advanced rock climb overall, by our standards then, and was steeper than anything I had climbed before. The waterfall thundered in our ears, and I could feel the rock vibrating under my fingertips. Spray from the falls wet the rock here and there, so the holds were not exactly user-friendly. A lot of debris washes down glacier-fed streams. I worried about boulders tumbling down the falls and ricocheting in my direction. After a while, I stopped worrying and just wished for a set of ear plugs.

What stands out now, looking back, is belaying Bernie while standing on a narrow ledge a few feet from the edge of that incredible tumult of water. In *Men for the Mountains*, I wrote that we crossed the stream above the falls. What got chopped from that account was the way we crossed. Bernie waded the stream at the top, on belay from me, and we set up a sort of mini Tyrolean traverse, an aerial crossing using a climbing rope between two short cliff faces – "just for the exercise." Perhaps setting up such a traverse was on Bernie's forthcoming guide exam. I crossed hand over hand, belayed by Bernie while suspended from a carabiner with my feet wrapped around the rope. Perlon rope has a lot of stretch in it. I bounced up and down, my hind end dipping in the rapids, much to Bernie's amusement, with my testicles shrinking at the kiss of glacial water. I couldn't help staring at the lip of the falls downstream, where the river formed a flat table edge and fell into the sky. My eyes were as big as saucers by the time we rappelled, spiderlike, back down into the forest above the district warden cabin. I looked at the cabin, which sits close by the falls, and thought, Man, I wouldn't want to work in earshot of all that racket – little knowing that I would be doing just that only two years later.

I had often looked at the bare profile of Grassi Ridge above the O'Hara cabin when I worked at the lodge, marvelling that anybody could find a route up such a precipitous bluff. Occasionally, I would look up on the ledges there and see a goat looking back. "You can have it, friend," I would mutter. One morning, Bernie was gazing up pensively at the ridge, like a young swain admiring a desirable woman. "Are you thinking what I'm thinking?" he asked.

"Christ, I hope not!"

Bernie chuckled. "It's a beautiful day. Why don't we wander up the Grassi route? Don Vockeroth says it's quite interesting."

"Don said that, did he?" I shivered involuntarily, imagining the kind of vertical horrors Don might find "interesting." "I dunno, Bernie," I protested. "Interesting is probably not a strong enough adjective for that route. Frightening comes to mind first, although I think absolutely fucking terrifying would probably sum it up best for me."

Bernie shook his head and laughed. "You can do that route."

"No way."

"Bullshit!" he scoffed. "I know I can lead it, because I've done harder climbs than that on Yamnuska. And I know you can second it. Hell, you could probably lead it yourself."

I stared at him doubtfully.

"It's probably easier than Takakkaw," he added.

I didn't know how to react to his estimation of my ability. Male role models who paid me compliments were a new phenomenon to me. I was more used to the arse-kicking naval version of my sea-cadet days – as in "stand clear of the gun mount, fuzz-bum."

"You know Sid," he added, "It's not the mountain you have to overcome. It's only yourself you have to master."

Wisely (for a change), I resisted the urge to make some cynical rejoinder. Bernie obviously believed in the truth of his statement.

And so I found myself following that master of the golden cliché up Grassi Ridge. The ridge was so interesting, I nearly wet my pants when Bernie suggested I try to lead on the crux, a shitty little gully of soft, crumbling shale shaped like a half-section of crumbling clay sewer pipe, too rotten to get a decent piton in for protection. It's the kind of place where you have to fight off the urge to chop steps with the sharp end of your piton hammer – a practice greatly frowned upon by real climbers. In fact, some purists might try to pillory you with turgid prose in club journals for this offence. The "Conquistadores of the Useless" are not amused by those who would deface a beloved route like Grassi Ridge. I flailed my way up the bugger somehow, and fought off the urge to give the grinning Bernie a piece of my mind when he zipped by me to take the lead again.

But a funny thing happened. When I came to the most exposed portion of the climb, a big red cliff, steep but full of excellent holds,

I suddenly lost all patience with the idea of fear itself. My own timidity sickened me; I wanted to vomit it out, or tear it off me like an old dead skin. I came alive in a way I'd never done on Takakkaw Falls. Okay, I thought. I'm angry with myself. Let's work with that; let's harness the fury. I relaxed, stopped hugging the rock like a dog in heat and let my feet take the weight, bouncing up and down a bit in the secure holds like a boxer or a dancer, and let my hands keep me balanced, just like Bernie had told me. When you feel confident on a wall, you can lean back and get a view up to what lies ahead. Clouds scudded by above the cliff where the rope went out of sight. I could feel Bernie's reassuring presence through that red perlon umbilical cord that joined us together. When you relax, you think clearly; you can read the rock and find the pattern, like a choreographed score, that will lead you from one move to the next.

I yelled for slack on the rope and gave it a tug as a signal, wanting to choose my own path. A strange little voice came into my head; it said *You could lead this route.* I laughed aloud at the notion. But in fact I went on to lead it on several occasions after that.

Before Bernie got through with me, he would have me leading a three-man rope up the Tarrant Route on Mount Odaray, which was not climbed frequently in those days. This is the striking northeast buttress of the mountain as seen from the Elizabeth Parker Hut, an awesome Roman nose that rises some 900 metres above the scree slopes that drop into Linda Lakes. Nowadays it's rated (in Sean Dougherty's *Selected Alpine Climbs in the Canadian Rockies*) as "mostly easy fifth class." (He rates the hardest move, which is very near the top, at 5.7).

All this encouragement of my climbing abilities seemed to go to my head after a while, as is often the way with young men. I went from being nervous on exposed pitches to being cocky, without any intervening period of common sense. Dressed in my uniform shirt and a pair of German climbing pants made of grey leather, I strode the trails of Lake O'Hara as if I owned them. I thought of Locke's misadventure on Mount Babel. "Pride goeth before a fall," indeed. Did an element of *schadenfreude* creep in as I considered how the mighty had fallen? Did I harbour lunatic notions of dancing on the cutting edge myself someday? Perhaps – but only for a self-deluded moment. I think it was more the reflected glory of being one of Perren's chosen few that went to my head. The khaki uniform identified me as one of the rescuers; the "rescuees" were the other folks, the civilians. I was not a civilian, ergo, I would not make any embarrassing mistakes. As my old man used to say, "Son, you're cruisin' for a bruisin'."

Abbot Pass Hut was a place I took a special interest in. Maintaining the place was our responsibility. (It has since been handed over to the Alpine Club.) There were a few younger alpinists who delighted in leaving the place untidy, knowing we would have to clean it up. It was usually the wandering teenage backpacker who committed the worst offences, such as leaving crap on the outhouse seat, and, for an encore, leaving every piece of crockery, cookery, and cutlery piled on the counters, unwashed and swarming with flies. I had an obsessive desire to catch these types in the act, like Vitus Germann before me. I left some comments in the hut log about people's bad habits, which make me wince when I read them now.

Many backpackers thought there was a trail up to Abbot's Hut. In fact, the way up the scree slope is scrambling terrain; it's a mountaineering route, and too often people tried it without proper footwear or overnight gear. One spot where they sometimes came to grief was on a steep slope of hardscrabble at the corner of Mount Victoria where the goat path washed out quite frequently. Grassi had cached some hand tools, with which to maintain the path, under a shelf of rock, but our orders were to leave the path au naturel, since maintaining it just lured inexperienced people to attempt the Abbot Pass scree slope.

Occasionally, there were complaints from hikers about this dangerous spot on the route, to which I responded that mountaineering routes have many hazardous spots – that's what made them different from hiking trails. If you can't handle the hazard, back off – or words to that effect. Once upon a time, wardens who didn't think you were competent enough to travel in the backcountry would order you back to town, sometimes siccing their cougar hounds on those who tried to outflank them. I used to have a sneaking admiration for my predecessors' frontier attitude; eventually I grew up and realized that it was contrary to the whole spirit and purpose of national parks. People have a God-given right to go out and risk their necks if they want to, as long as they don't start whining and assigning blame and suing the authorities should they come a cropper because of their own stupidity.

But it's hard not to adopt a proprietary attitude, as a "guardian of the wild." The warden is the proprietor in the park, but only on behalf of the citizen. Sometimes you forget that you are first and foremost a public servant; sometimes it takes a confrontation to force some self-evaluation.

One morning I was building a new culvert above Mary Lake, below the switchbacks that lead up to the Opabin Plateau, when I heard the sound of a bear-bell tinkling. I looked up and beheld a bizarre sight. A man, dressed in saffron-coloured robes, walking staff in hand, was working his way down the switchbacks. I thought at first I was hallucinating, the result of drinking a wineskin full of Zing the night before. (This was a cheap bingo sold in Alberta liquor stores; it should have been sold in hardware stores instead.)

As he drew nearer, I saw this was no imaginary figure, but a real person, whose legs were bare and dirty from the trail. I seem to recall a battered straw hat, which, when flourished about, revealed a shaved poll beneath. At first I thought he was barefoot, but he was wearing "Jesus boots," a kind of leather sandal imported from India, held on by a strap around the big toe, the kind you still find for sale in city head shops. His feet looked bruised and battered, and were zig-zagged with scratches.

The spectre, smiling beatifically, bowed its head. "Greetings," he said. He was a youngish man, perhaps a few years older than I was, tall and lean of build, his face tanned from the mountain sun. I had the impression that he was an American. What few possessions he had were in a haversack slung over one shoulder.

I gaped at him, at a loss for words. "You're wearing sandals," I blurted at last.

"That's true," he agreed, seeming to marvel himself at the notion, and following my gaze down to his battered feet. "I was lucky to find these. They have rubber grips on the bottom. Good on ice." He cocked one foot up so I could see the rubber grips. The soles were made from old car tires.

"Ice?" Here I gaped openly at him.

"Indeed."

"You came over the Opabin Glacier, wearing sandals?"

"I sure did. From a place, Moraine Lake, I think it's called."

"Who else is in your party?"

He smiled. "No one corporeal. But I never feel alone in the mountains."

"Neither do I," I said lamely, after a pause, as if waiting for the punchline; "at least not around these parts."

"I think I'll wash my feet," he suggested. "They look a little discoloured."

I looked down at them again. There was an inflamed tinge to the edge of his feet, darkening ominously on the little toes. "Cripes. It almost looks like you have a bit of frostbite there, friend."

"Oh, just a little bruising, I think. The flesh is such a weak container, isn't it?"

"It is so. That's why God made Italians."

"How's that?" he asked, taking the bait.

"Because He knew they would invent hiking boots."

The guru humoured me with another smile. "There are so many gods. I got these from the god of sandals."

I shook my head, not quite believing this encounter. Of course I had to lapse into park-warden mode eventually. I started talking about the dangers of crevasses on the glacier, how easy it would be to disappear without a trace, travelling alone and unroped.

"I have to tell you, Mister," I concluded sternly, warming to my theme: "What you did was very foolish. You're lucky to be alive."

You would have thought I'd never slunk across a glacier solo in my life to hear me talk.

He looked at me quite steadily. "I could say, that in talking to me this way, as if I was a child, you yourself are being foolish. You don't know anything about me. So why do you assume that I'm not aware of taking risks? Could it be that I choose to take risks?"

That made me colour a bit. There was a good trail beaten down across the glacier, and the holes there were fairly obvious. It was still dangerous, of course, I was not exaggerating the risk, though I was enough of a philosopher to appreciate his point. "It's my job," I said, feeling defensive, "to advise people when they are clearly doing something silly and dangerous, foolish as that may seem to you." Of course that did not answer his questions. I wasn't willing to debate the issue.

The guru dipped his feet in the brook, and smiled sadly up at me, acknowledging my omission. "It seems we are both fools then. There is a saying I've always liked: 'The fool pursues his folly until he becomes wise.'"

"Only if he lives long enough," I said darkly. Old Edward Feuz would have applauded my words, no doubt.

For some reason, he thought that was pretty funny. "Then I hope we both become wise first," he said, gaily, "before we become dead. Again."

"Again?"

"Yes. It's all part of our journey, isn't it?"

"It is?"

"Indeed it is. And speaking of which, can you direct me to the right trail for the Abbot's Pass?"

I frowned. "Abbot Pass is another mountaineering route."

"Really? But I understand there is a hermitage up there, no?"

I stared at this quixotic traveller, wondering what tack to take next. "Why don't you meet me down at the warden cabin, and I'll give you some more information, maps and whatnot."

"If you wish."

I told him how to find the place. With a nod of his head and a sunny smile, he resumed the descent while I packed up my tools.

I have long ago lost the notebook that contained the name of this singular pilgrim. Eventually I learned to memorize people's names and not rely on paper to remember them for me. He would not be the last lone mystic I would encounter wandering the hills in the sixties and early seventies, but he was by far the most intriguing.

I believe the guru had not registered out at Lake Louise, but I let him off with a warning instead of an appearance notice. Afterwards, he became for me the equivalent of Wordsworth's leech gatherer on the lonely moor; Wordsworth didn't learn much from his guru, either. Mine was kind enough to promise me one thing: that he would not attempt to cross Abbot Pass in sandals, "since it seems so important to you."

I met up with him once more at the warden's cabin later that afternoon, where he allowed me to doctor his battered feet, "if you feel its necessary." I urged him to seek a medical opinion on those toes, but was called away to the lodge on some errand, and when I returned, my guru was gone. Perhaps he thought I was not ready for further enlightenment. I never saw him again, except in memory, coming down the trail to Shangri-La only to be up-braided as a fool by one of its gatekeepers before he had a chance to tell his story.

It was not long after this encounter and the rescue on Mount Babel that Bernie and I set out for Mount Huber one weekend to look for a party of overdue climbers. This peak, first ascended in 1903, is one of the popular "eleven-thousanders" of the area. With us was my friend George Schwieger, who was assistant manager of the Hudson's Bay Company stores in Banff. Myrna and her pal Donna Hayes were also visiting. The weather was hot, and the women had taken a rowboat out to explore the lake.

We climbed up the goat path that switchbacks up above the lake to the Wiwaxy Gap at 2,532 metres. Far below, I could see the little boat leaving a long ripple on the still surface of the lake. I stared down through my field glasses and waved my arm. Staring back through her own glasses, Myrna waved back.

"I'm going to marry that girl some day," I told George.

"I know," said George patiently. "You have told me this many times. You have also told her this many times. Pass the water bottle."

The radio crackled and a message was broadcast: "Lake O'Hara wardens, Lake Louise warden office," but they did not hear our responses until we reached the gap, where we could trip a nearby radio repeater and get through. Our overdue quarry had checked in at last. They had elected to climb Mount Victoria and descend via Lake Louise rather than Lake O'Hara.

"Now that's ambition," commented Bernie. He had some business in town that afternoon, but George and I planned to climb the peak since I had not been up it before. Bernie described the route. I asked him to take the heavy PT-300 radio (it was powered by eleven flashlight batteries) back with him. It was around 2 P.M., a bit late in the day for that peak, as we started up through broken terrain to gain the west arête, and the West Huber Glacier. The usual route led across this body, then you ascended by the upper glacier and the northeast ridge to the summit.

Huber looms over you in a domineering sort of way, but the lower slopes above Wiwaxy Gap are just a scramble on big ledges and up scree couloirs that you climb unroped. George followed along, trusting my route-finding skills. His trust was misplaced; I had been seduced into trying to shortcut the climb by following some cairns an earlier party had left behind.

I reached the arête and rounded it, then stopped, alarmed at the view. Right in front of us, the top edge of the glacier, engrailed by sun and wind, swept across the face of its headwall. I looked down towards the gentler lower slope of the main body of snow-covered ice I had been aiming to reach. It covered most of the lower face; no doubt it has retreated quite some distance over the years. We were at least a hundred metres too high for the usual traverse. I did not have an altimeter – couldn't afford to buy one – but a glance at the map (it was still in imperial measure then) indicated we were at around 9,800 feet (close to 3,000 metres).

"Shit," I muttered. "I've gone and taken us up the wrong route." I explained to George that the cairns had probably been left by someone following W. E. Stone's guided ascent on the west face, done in 1913. (Stone was one of the old originals. He had died in a fall from the summit of Mount Eon in 1921.)

"Why don't we just do the Stone route, then?" said George, ever the game one.

I glanced at my watch. It was already two-thirty. "We'd have to be stoned to try the Stone route today," I said, staring up the arête to the ledges above. "It's a longish rock-climb. Supposed to be a lot of loose junk on it."

I could not see the bergschrund below us, the main crevasse that cuts laterally across a glacier close to where it joins its headwall. It is wise to always know how this hazard lies. I concluded, wrongly, that it was probably covered by a snow bridge. The 'schrund is a sort of moat protecting a peak from intruders, which it swallows without pity if they are not careful. I remember being concerned about the time, and a change in weather predicted by mare's tails drifting across the Goodsir Towers to the west. You hate to lose altitude on a mountain – every metre of climbing costs you energy – but a more experienced leader would have downclimbed the ridge to where the route follows the gentler slope of the lower glacier, then followed the normal route up the northeast ridge.

I thought about it briefly. We didn't have a lot of time to get up this peak, and I wanted to get up it. It was not a hard peak, but it was a notable peak, a favourite of the old Swiss guides and one of only fifty-one summits in the Rockies exceeding eleven thousand feet. I had yet to climb an eleven-thousander, let alone lead on one. Myrna the ever-desirable was waiting down below; a night of wine, women, and song awaited us. When they casually asked, Did you make it? We both wanted to modestly say, "Of course – could there be any doubt?"

There was a band of broken rock leading across the cirque above the ice margins. Given a few thousand years, it might one day become a ledge. It looked like thirty minutes of effort, sidestepping on our toes and boot edges mainly. It would lead to more broken ground with lots of holds, and we should come out on the usual route on the northeast ridge. Cleverly, I would turn my error into triumph. But we couldn't use the rope. We had brought no pitons to protect a fall – there was no need for them on the standard route – so we had no way of belaying each other on such a tentative spot.

"Can you follow me across that, George?"

"Sure."

That's what I wanted to hear, of course, instead of rationally considering my partner's experience and ability, as a good leader should. "We'll have to rely on our feet there and just balance against the rock with the hands."

"It doesn't look so bad," he said stoutly.

I glanced down at the hard névé snow, streaked with ice below us. It was fairly steep, but manageable, I thought, in case of a fall. "We have to climb with axes in hand. If you come off, you'll slide down onto the ice; first thing you do is a self-arrest with the axe. You remember how to do that?"

"Put the pick end in on ice – not the adze."

"That's right."

"Then what happens?" asked George.

"Then I reverse myself, downclimb the arête and throw you a rope end – if you need it."

"And what if you fall? You've got the rope."

"Uh . . . then it gets more 'interesting.'"

"But we're not going to fall on that anyway," he said confidently.

"Right on!"

I led off and we were soon in the shadow of the mountain, our sweaty bodies rapidly chilled by the mass of ice below our feet and the cold rock under our hands. The rock was fractured and crumbly on the band; I had to kick loose pieces off at times to get any purchase on the holds, which were mainly slanted downward. Rock pieces flew down the ice in long bounds. George followed along behind me: the holds were giving him a bit more trouble than I thought they would; his knees were trembling a bit. Maybe this was not such a good idea.

Glancing down the ice slope below, I was dismayed to see how steep it looked from directly above, how it seemed to grow steeper the farther we traversed towards the centre of the cirque. The wall of the cirque, scooped deep in shadow, angled up overhead, slightly overhanging at the top, as I recall. At least any falling rocks, loosened by meltwater from the summit glacier, should be deflected safely outward. And now I could see a dark line in the glacier below, and realized the bergschrund was not covered at all, but open – a real danger if we could not self-arrest on the ice. I stopped moving then: this was far too steep for a self-arrest. We had to get the hell out of there . . . but easy now, go carefully. Then I heard the axe clatter on the rocks a few metres behind me. George cried out, but when I turned to look he was gone from his holds and doing a somersault down the rock. He hit the ice right-side up a metre or so down the ice slope, and there was a loud crack.

"Self-arrest, self-arrest!" I yelled. "Use the pick!" But the axe, in two pieces, flew away on either side of him. In fact, he had landed on the axe, broken it in two, and cut his knee wide open on the metal of the axe head. I have this image of him scrabbling at the ice with an imaginary axe, but it couldn't have been more than an instant, and he was gone, head over heels down the slope.

I had often imagined how a man in free fall would be gone like a bullet; but as I stared down, frozen on my holds, I couldn't believe the speed of his tumble, end over end down the ice. He was a rag doll, coming apart at the seams. First his hat flew off, next the glasses, then the gloves, one then the other. His watch (as I discovered later) flew off and finally his pack tore loose and tumbled down behind him. An orange shot out of the pack and wandered off on its own tangent, then swerved back and chased him all the way to the bottom.

To George, the fall seemed to take a long time in its beginning, but that is only the brain trying to save itself; that is only the ego's disbelief. George remembers yelling or thinking "Shit! Shit!" over and over again. He was amazed at how mundane our thoughts can be in moments of extreme peril. He said it was a very scenic fall. "I saw blue sky, mountains, snow . . . blue sky, mountains, snow . . ."

As I watched, transfixed with fear, the tumble turned into a high speed slide right toward the 'schrund. Should he fall into its depths, he would either be killed in the plunge or wedged in where the crack narrowed further down and quite possibly die of asphyxiation before I could get him out. The névé snow, streaked with blue where bare ice showed through, was a slick chute in the cold shade of the mountain, ending in the gaping bergschrund. But the ice edge was higher on the uphill side of the 'schrund. His speed shot him right over the opening, which was some two metres wide. If he kept going now, he would hurtle over the ice cliff at the terminus of the glacier and smash onto the rocks below. But where the mountain's shadow ended, the snow was softened by the August sun. Gradually, he slid to a stop.

I yelled his name over and over as he lay there. I saw how a trail of blood streaked down the ice where he'd fallen. Oh Christ, I thought; this looks bad. Then there came a wonderful sound – the pained wail of his voice, crying out on the ice, echoing from the wall of Mount Victoria to the east. Better still was to see him moving, thrashing about like a bug, but with all four of his limbs in motion – no back injury!

"Hang on, George!" I yelled. "I'm coming."

He was sitting up now, his back towards me, tiny and forlorn-looking in his pain. Cursing myself and my own stupidity in trying the traverse, I worked my way back across the shale band to the arête and descended the rough terrain in minutes, then worked my way out over the glacier, probing for crevasses with the axe shaft.

George, lying in the blood-streaked snow, was pale and nauseated by the trauma of his fall and loss of blood. His back and neck were bruised but otherwise uninjured. There was a hole in his knee, the size of a fifty-cent piece, where white bone showed through, his hip was paining him badly, and his hands were cut and covered with blood from the knee wound. I eased my rucksack under him to get him off the ice. He was able to help as we taped a war-surplus wound bandage on his knee, then splinted the leg with wire splints from my first-aid kid. Groaning with pain, he struggled hard to get past it and focus on treating his cuts. Thank God it's not worse, I thought. Now what the hell do we do next?

I stared around at the silent peaks and valleys, feeling terribly alone and powerless. I left George for a few moments, worked around the 'schrund, then chopped my way up the slope to retrieve his scattered effects. He was amazed that I found his watch, both straps blown off but otherwise intact. I was struggling to get my shit together, to think clearly about the next move.

George was shivering uncontrollably from shock. I helped him into his warm down jacket, which he had carried in his pack. "How far do you think I went?" he asked weakly.

"About four hundred feet."

"Wow! They won't believe that one back at the office." He seemed oddly pleased with the number.

It was time to get moving, if we could move. We were somewhere below 2,900 metres; the weather was fair but subject to violent change without notice. It is always best to get down off a mountain under your own power if you can, and besides, I knew the park rescue team was already engaged elsewhere.

"Do you think you can walk, George?"

"I don't know. I'll try. What about . . . a helicopter?" he wondered.

"Chances are we won't find one close enough today, even if it was approved. You might wait until morning, then they might decide to take you down on a mountain stretcher anyway."

"Oh man," he groaned. "Let me try to walk then."

"Are you sure?"

"I'm not staying here. Help me up."

"George, this is all my fault. I'm so sorry about it."

"Oh bullshit," he said. "I'll be okay."

"Four hundred feet!" he grinned wildly. "I can't believe it." I helped him up, and he stood, legs trembling like jackhammers, swaying like a drunk until his head cleared a little. "Where's my pack?"

"I'll carry that, no fear."

"And you found my watch! I can't believe you found my watch."

His watch. I stared at it: the straps were gone, the crystal was broken, and the hands were torn away. I could have wept, I was so mortified. It seemed miraculous that my friend was still alive.

We had to descend several hundred metres in altitude spread over a distance of a kilometre to reach Wiwaxy Gap. I tied George into the climbing rope before we moved off the glacier onto the arête. We would climb together down the scree slopes and couloirs to the col, sometimes with George leaning on my shoulder, other times with him limping down using my axe for a cane while I belayed from above. He sent loose rocks crashing down the mountainside in front of us, filling the air with the smell of sulphur.

By the time we reached the windswept saddle between Huber and Wiwaxy, the sun was resting on the ridge of Mount Odaray to the west. The adrenalin rush was long gone and George was in real agony. "I can't do this," he said. "I'm going to have to stay here."

I stared down towards the lake. The little boat was long gone. Down at the cabin, Myrna would be pulling some cold bottles of beer out of the lake about now. Bernie would be telling them about the rescue on Mount Babel. My tongue felt like a puffball stuck in my throat, but George was far thirstier than I. There were streams on the slopes of Wiwaxy below us, where we could get all the water we needed. There were only two kilometres between us and the cabin, but it was little more than a goat path, dropping five hundred metres in altitude. Could I carry him down on my back? One slip on that trail, once we were hooked together, would mean a horrendous tumble.

Well, don't slip, I told myself. Lake O'Hara wardens don't leave their friends behind.

I took the climbing rope off my shoulder and started coiling it in a big loop to make an improvised rescue seat, a trick Don Vockeroth had shown me. With the rope draped over the back of my neck and under my arms from front to back, the bottom half of the coil was a seat for George to ride in, padded with my emptied rucksack. I strapped a lightened pack on George's back and stashed excess items to pick up later.

"You can't carry me down that goat path," George protested as he cradled his injured knee.

"Sure I can. Hell, I've been training for this all summer. I'll just pretend you're a frigging highway sign." I hesitated. An unpleasant thought had come into my head – that Perren might think I was a total screw-up if the crew was called out for this. I shook my head involuntarily, furious with myself, saddened by thinking of my own interests at a time like that. I stepped to one side and stared down at the water below to talk it over with my conscience. Are you trying to save your job, or are you trying to make the right decision, you dumb shit: which is it? I went over the options in my head. His spine is alright; he has no internal injury; his leg is stabilized; the bleeding has stopped. I'm not going to increase his injury by packing him down. I'll get him down lower, less exposed to lightning in case a storm blows in later tonight. At the very least, I'll get him down to where there is water, which he really needs badly.

Go for it, then!

"I don't think this will work," he protested, as he worked his legs through the loops of coiled rope. "Oh Christ, man, it hurts!"

"George, the sound of your complaints is music to my ears. It means your tiny brain is not injured."

"Fuck you, buddy."

Gingerly I leaned forward, got my feet under me and stood up with my arms crooked under his legs. "This is not bad," I said. "I can do this, if you just stop grabbing me by the windpipe."

I put my beret back on my sweaty head.

"I will do this, George, or my name is not Alpine Technician."

"Ow – my leg!"

"Sorry."

"You don't . . . look like a German . . . Volkswagen mechanic," rasped George. "You look like a French queer."

I had to laugh, the sound of it working against my own worries, restoring confidence.

We started down the upper switchbacks, George hanging on gamely, trying to maintain his balance for my benefit; trying not to scream right in my ear when I jarred his injured leg. Far below were the sparkling waters of Lake O'Hara. It felt like we were climbing down the sides of a monstrous well shaft and for a while I doubted my own resolve in making the attempt. For George, helpless on my back and staring down the mountainside, it was far worse. Once, I tripped on a rock and had to take several running steps to recover, causing him to convulse with fear and grab at my neck.

"Sid, if you do that again, I'm going to piss all over us."

"George," I gasped, "That would piss us both off."

"Ha – ah! Don't make me laugh. It hurts even more."

It took every ounce of concentration to keep my feet under me. The climbing rope sawed into my shoulders and the deerflies and mosquitoes, drawn by the smell of blood, clustered on our necks and arms like skeins of black lace, then crawled under our shirt collars and down our chests, biting us to distraction. In my mind's eye I pictured the cover illustration of Jerzy Kosinski's book *The Painted Bird.* It's a painting by Breughel: a demon, carrying a sinner to hell in a basket: I was the demon, inflicting pain on both of us.

At last we heard the underground muttering of a brook and found a rivulet washing down into a shallow pool. I eased us down against the slope; we drank greedily out of the glacial melt like horses, and rested until the biting flies goaded us to move on. Painfully, we got under way again. I inched my way down the steepest switchbacks of the trip, which were imbedded in a slope of hardscrabble clay and shale. We encouraged each other through tight spots like that with insults. It's a guy thing: "You are a heavy, fat little swine – did you know that?"

"Oww! And you're the clumsiest goddamn mule I ever rode. Please don't . . . fall down here and kill us . . . especially me . . . oh God!"

Night came on slowly; the sun slipped down below the rim of Mount Odaray; lights came on at the toy lodge far below: a lantern blazed forth suddenly from mid-lake like a comet. It was a boat. I had a small flashlight which I used sparingly, saving the batteries. I blinked it three times, then three more, and yodelled to get their attention. A man's voice, a questioning tone, called back to us from the dark water. It turned out to be Bill Bird, a friend of George's.

"Tell the warden we need help," I shouted. Then, swallowing what was left of my pride: "We need HELP!"

I could not make out the words he called back, only the tone, which promised assistance. At the cabin, Myrna and Donna were worried about us. To reassure them, Bernie had jogged around the lake, and had found us with his spotting scope in the twilight. The light was bad, but he'd seen enough to know we were in trouble. He stopped at the lodge and collected some of the staff to form a stretcher party. As I crept slowly down into the timbered slope where the route switchbacks down through an avalanche path, I was cheered and energized to see the lights of the warden cabin. Bernie and party were on their way up. Suddenly I saw a headlamp coming up through the trees. Bernie's voice answered my shout of greeting with a cheerful yodel.

"Thank God," said George, fervently, as I carefully set him down to rest.

In a few minutes the group surrounded us while I explained what had happened. We bundled George carefully onto the stretcher and lashed him on the deer-toter, a ladder-like conveyance equipped with a bicycle wheel, but there were no hand-brakes on that early model, as I recall. We still had an unpleasant hour of work trying to roll that thing down through the shintangle while Bernie belayed it from above with a climbing rope. The rough going made George yell quite a bit. (What we didn't realize at the time was that he had an impact fracture in his hip.) I thought that I might have bothered people needlessly; it was actually easier for George on my back.

We got him down to the Mineral Springs Hospital in Banff sometime after midnight, where they kept him overnight without detecting the crack in his hip, or the bone splinters in his knee. I returned to O'Hara in time to drink a subdued nightcap with my friends.

Bernie was supposed to file a rescue report on such incidents with Fred Dixon. Fred's only comment, over a cup of coffee one evening was, "That rescue practice on Mount Huber – went okay, did it?"

"The rescue . . .? Oh – yes. That went very well."

"Yeah. You can learn a lot that way from a spon . . . a spont . . ."

"Spontaneous?"

He nodded. "From that kind of a practice."

"You sure as hell can," I said, ruefully.

A few days after the Mount Huber mishap I headed up to Abbot Pass on a routine patrol. As I crossed the rock slide above Lake Oesa, there were some people working their way cautiously across the hardscrabble. It was a family group, and there was a teenager stuck in the middle of the path, terrified by the steep, gritty slope that terminates in rocks. Her father quickly retraced his steps and grabbed her hand. In a minute, the tension was over, and they continued on.

I skipped over the narrow path without incident. Grassi's tools were still cached under a ledge above the trail. I carried them down and went to work widening the tread, as Grassi had done many times before, though I knew it would only be carried away again by the next heavy rain. I believe Bernie did likewise on other occasions.

My friend George returned the next summer and seconded me on a climb of the Tarrant Buttress. He was the best man when Myrna and I married the following year; he and his wife Celia named their

youngest son after me. Eventually he moved away from the mountains. George's knee has bothered him all his life, and he has had
several operations to remove bone chips, as well as a hip replacement
operation. He gave up climbing early on.

George and Celia parted company some years ago; she changed
her son's name. I don't blame her; Sidney is favoured now more for
girls than boys, it seems to me. That's what I tell myself, anyway.
The last time we were together, and the story of his fall came up, I
had forgotten that he descended to Wiwaxy Gap partly under his
own power. George reminded me of those details: I'm glad he did.

When I think back on it now, knowing what I do about human
nature, I no longer see the rescue as a one-man effort, though I can't
help feeling a little bit proud of the physical strength of that young
man I was. The carry was something we did together; George let me
carry him down that hill, and fought to stay balanced all the way
down, though it added to his pain. He let me try to undo the
damage I had done in the name of self-aggrandizement, in the name
of folly, though I don't suggest he thought it through that way at the
time. He trusted me, despite my mistake; paid me the supreme
compliment of climbing with me again. And have I become wise,
like the guru on the Opabin switchbacks? A little wiser, perhaps,
step by painful step, sometimes up, sometimes down, on the switchbacks of the years.

Someday George and I will meet again around a table of beer and
talk about Mount Huber. Maybe we'll argue about what mistakes
were made; what was learned; who rescued who; or whether it's even
possible, ultimately, to save anyone or anything, and to keep laughing
at the follies of youth, even when there is nothing left to remind us of
youth but scars, like a winter count, on our aging bodies.

CHAPTER EIGHT

Black Bears, Poem Bears

ernie qualified with the Association of Canadian Mountain Guides in 1967 and started a climbing camp for youngsters, called High Horizons and based at Lake O'Hara. I spent that O'Hara summer working alone, living in a canvas frame-tent while skilled timberman Len Tober and his crew built a brand new log cabin at Sargent's Point. There was no work available in the warden service that winter, so I went to work as a by-law cop for the City of Calgary. All winter, I looked forward to taking up summer residence in that deluxe facility at O'Hara. It sported its own office, and, more importantly, a private bedroom which I was dearly hoping to tempt Myrna the Muse into sharing, should she be inclined. She had decided to marry me that autumn.

But the summer idyll was not to be. A teenaged assistant warden, newly married, was hired and it was decided the new cabin would be his honeymoon suite for the summer. Neil Woledge, the new chief warden, apparently had a romantic heart under his thick cowboy hide. So Tristram and Isolde moved in, and immediately painted the entire interior of that handcrafted log cabin baby-scat yellow – or was it pink? At any rate, I found myself transferred to Takakkaw Falls, home of the Thunder God. It was there that I became an equestrian, albeit reluctantly at first – being educated in horsemanship by an ornery government gelding name of Shawn. I would beg advice on handling horses from any veteran warden passing through the area, but Shawn was my professor of equitation, and I later critiqued his pedagogy, bruise by bruise, in my book *Men for the Mountains.*

Aside from the equine component, there was another important difference in the Yoho River Valley where I now worked, and that was the constant presence of American black bears and grizzly bears, especially black bears. Neither species had been frequent visitors at Lake O'Hara in my time there.

The point was sharply brought home to me one morning when I went outside and found the sign of a black bear sow and two cubs on the freshly scrubbed decking of the front porch. Does a bear shit in the woods? You bet, and if your porch is in the woods it may shit there, too. Bears would become a constant interest and concern every summer I spent in the warden service. I learned to track them just by dint of daily practice. Eventually I was trained to trap and tranquilize them when Myrna and I moved on to Jasper Park in 1970. Part of every week of my summers was spent making observations on their habits, degree of aggressiveness, on the food they ate and the scat they left along my path. Oft-times I might be encountered along some remote trail, dismounted from my steed, which was staring over my shoulder, ears pricked up in wonder as I muttered to myself while pondering a gloved handful of bear shit under a magnifying glass. I was looking for telltale signs such as deer hair, soapberry seeds – and sandwich wrappers – which would tell me something about the habits of the bear in question. This interest in bears continued when we were transferred to Banff National Park in 1972.

If I were to select a family totem, I think it would be a carving of a black bear. It has been a fundamental irony that although as a warden I constantly warned people to view bears only from a safe distance, it is my own close encounters with bears that inspired a number of poems published in my first book, *Headwaters* (1973). My memories of black bears are generally happy ones, which wasn't always the case with grizzlies.

The American black bear is the species of bear that most people are familiar with, since it still inhabits sizable parts of its old range throughout North America. Run-ins with black bears are legion throughout its range, and mostly people come away from these without injury. I remember some of the exceptions, such as the guy who stepped sleepily out of his tent in the middle of a moonless night to have a pee, inadvertently hosing down a black bear that was apparently standing there watching him. It didn't occur to the bear, which looked like an ink blot in a coal mine to the camper, that it was invisible.

"Well, piss on you too, Pal," thought the bear (or would have if bears could think as we do). Its armoured paw came out of nowhere and swatted him hard on his naked buttock, making him squeal with pain and fear and leap back into his tent, pronto. The bear left the area, growling under its breath about the lack of manners in the woods these days.

More fearsome exceptions are the black bears made desperate by sickness and old age combined with famine (as when the usual berry crop fails), who have been known to stalk and kill human beings on rare occasions. Renowned bear expert and author Dr. Steve Herrero has described a number of such attacks in vivid detail in his book *Bear Attacks, Their Causes and Avoidance* (1985) – required reading for anyone who ventures into bear country – and there have been other fatalities from black bear attacks since his book was first published. Bert Freeman, an Alberta fish-and-wildlife officer (now retired), once told me of a fisherman who was killed by a scrawny black bear up in Alberta's Coal Branch country. When the bear was tracked down, it was found to be a mature bear. The head was of normal size, but the body was so emaciated that the bear weighed only eighty pounds. It was so weak that an officer held it at bay with a stick, but it had still been strong enough to kill its victim, having attacked the man from behind.

By now most outdoors people are familiar with the concept of playing dead to escape being seriously mauled by an attacking bear – especially in the case where you have come between a female and her cubs. Herrero believes that it does no good to lie down and play dead if you encounter the desperate type of black bear and it seems intent on stalking you. Although a black bear sow may occasionally charge you as a bluffing tactic, the desperate bear typically charges once and presses home the attack with tooth and claw. It is better to stand and fight with whatever weapon you can find, including your bare fists and feet if you have nothing else, than to let this bear tear at your flesh. Of course, the trick is to know enough in the first place to figure out what kind of bear you are dealing with.

The healthy black bear sow with cubs seems less inclined to attack people who get in her way – but "seems" is the operative word. A black bear sow in Banff Park that accepted my presence when I encountered her on horseback chased my patrol truck on another occasion when I met up with her. Bear expert Charlie Russell, who has worked at closer range with more wild black and grizzly bears than anyone I know – without trapping or tranquilizing them, that is to say – got in between a black bear sow and cubs while hiking with his son on the Waterton Park boundary one day. A chunk of elk antler that Anthony Russell was carrying made all the difference in beating this bear off. Both father and son had to duke it out like tag-team wrestlers with this smallish bear and they didn't escape without several painful bites and scratches.

It takes a lot of field study to read the body language of a bear. His face is a mask, as writer Edward Hoagland has pointed out, that tells you little about his inner emotions, though if he (or she) bristles up, flattens the ears, and runs at you – watch out. Unlike the cat family, Blackie has no twitching tail or whiskers. His small eyes are not the windows to his soul as with the cat family, and he doesn't have the mobile grin and pout of the canine species, though a display of his teeth in your direction is a clear message. I have heard bears tell me I've infringed upon their space with a variety of noises including huffing or woofing, snorting, moaning and making a disconcerting popping or chopping noise with the jaws. Swatting at the ground, at trees and of course at you are also really good indications that it's time to think about your options. Watch for these and other signs the experts write about; be aware that the experts have different opinions on how to deal with bear encounters. But remember, when you pitch upon a bear, you have to reach deep inside yourself and listen there for the message your eyes and ears are conveying, because not even the bear itself is completely sure about what's going to happen next. What you do or fail to do in the first few moments of that encounter has a lot to do with the outcome, and the more you know about bears and bear country – and about yourself – the better the end result will be. And to keep it all in perspective, it helps to realize that you are far more likely to be in a car accident, or be bitten by a domestic dog, than you are to be attacked by a bear.

One of the reasons that black bears have fared so much better than grizzly bears in surviving the onrush of our modern syphilization is their amazing tolerance to human beings, including those who are stupid enough to offer food (a practice which is illegal as well as dangerous). A few tourists will run away screaming at the first close-up sight of a begging black bear – not usually a good idea, since it may encourage the bear to chase after you. But for many others, black bears, especially roly-poly smallish bears, seem to bring on a sentimental fit of what I would describe as Teddy Bear Syndrome. Teddy always was a real bear in the child's fantasy world, and now here he is again, by the park highway or campground picnic table, magically animated like a Disney cartoon, reminding the adult of a happier, more innocent world. The fact that he may be grazing on vegetation like an old milk cow and standing there with a bunch of flowers in his omnivorous mouth only adds to the tranquility of the scene. Hard to believe you are looking at a critter that can beaver his way through a small fir tree with his teeth or kill a steer with a cuff of his paw.

Teddy Bear was a black bear cub. He came into being as a popular symbol of conservation as a result of a famous incident in 1902 when Teddy Roosevelt was out hunting in Mississippi. According to author Charles Panati (*Extraordinary Origins of Everyday Things*, 1987), Roosevelt was offered the chance to shoot a black bear cub, which had been captured expressly for him by his hosts – and flatly refused. The incident inspired a cartoon in the *Washington Star*. That inspired the creation of "Teddy's Bear" by Brooklyn toy salesman Morris Michtom. Teddy's Bear became the most sought-after toy of the era, according to Panati, and Teddy Bear has been with us ever since.

Winnie the Pooh was my favourite teddy bear as a child. Christopher Robin's Pooh Bear represents a connection with idealized nature – a utopia where children and wild animals roam in peace, and speak the same language. We have forgotten that language now, or perhaps we just can't hear what the bear has to tell us through the white noise of everyday living. No doubt there are many instances in the human experience with bears that are the roots from which the myth flowers. And the instances keep recurring, as if the bears were trying to tell us something we need to hear.

Edward Feuz recalled a child who wanted to speak to a bear though it had not yet learned its own mother tongue. It was in 1903, in the days of Mount Stephen House, a CPR hotel at Field, B.C., where the railroaders kept a black bear on a chain for the amusement of the tourists.

A black bear thrives on loneliness. He wanders through the shades of loneliness all his life, the solitary essence of the mountains given animate expression, but is not saddened so long as he is free to roam. Never does he appear so lonely, however, as he does when surrounded by humanity. This bear, first captured in a pit trap, then tethered by man's whim, grew fat on many offerings of food but retired to the den that he'd dug in the ground to brood at times. A brakeman there used to give his chain a tug and tease him out to wrestle. Preceded by a furious burst of disturbed flies, the bear would emerge, frowning like a dark-suited banker dragged forth from his beloved vault, lazy and suspicious, responding to a familiar voice that promised yet more increase. His handler would shake the chain and wrestle the bear up onto his hind legs so the wealthy tourists could photograph him with their Kodaks.

One day Edward was hanging around the station house waiting for the train to come in so he could find some clients to take out climbing or hiking. He was a young guide and a foreigner, his legs tethered to a contract, probably as bored as the tethered bear.

From the corner of his eye he noticed movement in the bear's pen up the road. A child, a mere toddler that had somehow escaped its mother's eye, had come down the hill from the town of Field. She squeezed between the slats of the fence around the bear pit. "By God," recalled Edward, "that little kid walked up to that black bear." As Edward jumped to his feet in alarm, the black bear, which usually seemed so docile and slow, seized the child in its jaws by one arm and dragged her into its den. Bear and child disappeared from the world and descended into the realm of myth.

Black bears have been known as opportunistic predators of small children from time to time. Edward feared the worst.

"Oh Jesus, my heart broke now, that little kid," he said, remembering the event. He'd rushed into the office and in his broken English called for help. One of the workers, used to caring for the bear, tore over to the bear pit. He didn't hesitate but crawled into the den at once.

He was relieved to hear the child's voice, prattling away as if to its mother, though he could not name the words. It took a moment for his eyes to adjust to the light. At last he could make out the little girl, her hands gripped in the bear's fur while it lolled on its back, its eyes gleaming. It was probably while being dragged back into the human world by a stranger that the child began to cry in protest.

"The bear was playing with the kid!" cried Edward. "That's the biggest surprise I ever had in my life."

Amerindian legends abound with similar stories, though centred on a far-distant time when men and wild animals interacted and spoke to each other.

The bear, which stands upright on two feet at times, looks eerily humanoid, especially when it is robbed of its hide. In Indian legends, the grizzly bear, which typically addresses humans as "brother," comes to the assistance of those who call out for help. In the Blackfoot story of Mik-a'-pi, Brother Grizzly carries a wounded warrior back to camp after dressing his wounds with mud. Sometimes, however, an evil spirit takes the form of a bear that returns to camp to harass and frighten former enemies.

Christopher Robin has grown up, become a stockbroker, has never seen a bear outside of a zoo, and suspects they no longer live in the wilds. Doesn't know shite from shinola about the hazards of approaching wild animals anyway. But suddenly, on a sunny holiday in July, a docile-looking black bear wanders out of the woods to the side of the road, where it waits patiently among the wildflowers looking for a handout. It's Winnie the Pooh redux. He's a grown-up bear now, but he seems like that same, non-threatening Pooh Bear of childhood, simply looking for the next pot of honey. Something in this crazy, sick world has remained innocent and kindly – or so thinks our jaded Christopher Robin as he snaps a picture. Don't tell him about danger: don't tell him this Pooh Bear could rip and tear him or his loved ones. He comes from the world of drive-by shootings and youth gangs armed with guns and meat cleavers. Muggers don't wear fur coats. Blackie looks so cute and cuddly. Go stand beside him, dear, while I take a picture; here, give him some potato chips.

Fred Nelson, an assistant warden many moons ago, once did something that some game wardens have been sorely tempted to do: he kicked a beggar bear and punched a bear-feeding tourist all in the same go-round. At least that's the story that went around the parks for years after Nelson left the service to become a helicopter pilot. The truth is a little bit different, according to Fred Nelson.

Driving up the Big Hill near Field, B.C. one summer day, Nelson came upon a bear jam at the Spiral Tunnel Viewpoint, and was alarmed when a black bear suddenly charged at a group of tourists that had approached it on foot. Blackie was trying to feed on vegetation like an honest black bear should, but the tourists were harassing him, coming too close and offering snacks to try and get him to pose for a picture. As Nelson made a U-turn, Blackie made another bluff charge, driving more tourists back to their cars. Nelson had no peace-officer status to prosecute people for feeding bears, but he pulled over to stop people from approaching the animal. He got out and began warning people, including a motorist whose daughter, a girl of eight or nine years, was just about to get out of the car with her camera in hand. "I know the bear looks tame, but it's not," he warned her father. "It could strike out at any time."

The father pointedly ignored Nelson's well-intended advice. After Nelson's back was turned, he told his daughter to go and get a picture of the bear. According to one account, the little girl jumped out of the passenger side door, ran around the back of the car, and darted towards the bear. Thinking the child was attacking, the startled bear reared to his hind feet in alarm. The child ran into its belly and bounced back, falling flat on her back as Blackie scythed one paw at the air where her head would have been a split-second earlier.

Nelson was still close by when he heard the girl scream in fright. He rushed at Blackie and kicked at him to get his attention, which gave the little girl time to scramble over the guard rail and get back to safety. Confronted by a determined adult, Blackie retreated. Nelson, furious now, went back to chastise the father, who had remained in his seat throughout the entire incident.

"Hey! I just told you two minutes ago that bear was dangerous. You just about got your little girl killed!"

The motorist glared at him. "Look you, mind your own business. Don't try to tell me how to raise my kid!" he snapped.

The frustrated parks employee lost it: he tried to punch the man through his open window, but fortunately, or unfortunately, depending on how you look at it, he instead smacked his fist into the protruding edge of the open no-draft window typical of those days, just about breaking his wrist. Shocked by the pain, Nelson stood there wondering how much trouble he was now in with his employers. The driver shifted into gear and drove off. He hadn't learned a thing, but fortunately, he elected not to complain about Nelson trying to punch him.

Nelson drove down to Field and confessed his sins to Chief Warden Andy Anderson, who chewed him out thoroughly. He later admitted to Nelson that it was something he had wanted to do himself for about twenty-five years.

The little girl was very lucky, but if black bears attacked every person who ever confronted them or offered them food, the emergency wards in bear country would be crowded with victims all summer long.

By now, we are all used to cute news stories about how some bear wandered into town, was tranquilized by the local game warden and whisked off into the wilderness, end of story. This is folklore. There was limited hope for bears who became habituated to human food in the 1960s, and there is even less hope now. The idea that these bears can be trapped and relocated successfully should be treated with skepticism. There are still some happy endings, but in the populated latitudes of southern Canada and the northern U.S.A., there is just not enough wild land left to relocate bears with any guarantee of success. Like humans, bears are creatures of habit with a strong sense of home. They often migrate back to their home ranges, and they have been known to travel over a hundred miles to get there. Repeat offenders wind up being destroyed because they are a hazard to the public, and there is also the matter of legal liability in our "sue the bastards" age. Despite these uncertainties, the trapping and relocating of "problem" bears continues, mainly because the only other option is to destroy them.

In the Canadian Rockies, the American black bear is a creature of the shadows, looking over his shoulder all the time to watch out for Brother Grizzly, who is ever ready to eat Blackie's lunch. When there is a shadow where there is no tree or rock to cast it, that shadow may be a black bear. My old rucksack carries the marks left by the first one I saw up close. That was on the Ottertail River in Yoho Park where I was employed clearing trail, in the days when I knew little about bears myself. He stepped out of the darkness under a spruce tree into a clearing and, pausing there among the Indian paintbrush flowers, took utter possession of my attention in an instant.

Muskwa came up the trail behind us
from the Ottertail.
He wanted to rob our lunch

Jerry tried to bluff him with the chainsaw
he put his hackles up . . .
It was a stand-off until the chainsaw
choked up; water in the gas

Muskwa is a Cree word for black bear. I'd felt like an alien on an unknown planet in the insouciant command of his roly-poly, pigeon-toed approach. We backed away, Jerry still yanking away on the saw's starter cord to no avail.

That bear was a totally corrupt little beggar, a highway bear, and he followed his nose straight to my rucksack. He pounced a forefoot upon it, catlike – before it could get up and run away – and tore the flap open with his teeth. Then he slipped his dainty meat hooks inside and fished out our lunch bag, ignoring my protests:

and scoffed the whole works
wax paper and all

before our famished eyes
as Jerry got the saw going
and chased the little bugger
down the trail,
and him grinning all the way.

Grinning inside at least, and leaving me the pack with a hole in it for a souvenir, trading me a poem for the bullcook's mundane Wonder bread sandwich – not a bad deal in the end.

That was the first of many close meetings I would have with black bears. On too many occasions, the bear was on the wrong end of a tranquilizer gun. I helped to drag their inert bodies into cages, peeled back a top lip from the gums to tattoo it for ID purposes, examined their teeth, measured their girths, and generally treated them as if they were rats in a science project, all in the name of wildlife conservation. But those are not the black bears I remember.

When Myrna and I first went to Jasper National Park we were posted at Pocahontas, a station near the east boundary where my supervisor was Warden Abe Loewen. We lived in a tin trailer close to Abe's house on a low-lying stretch of forest and swamp near the Athabasca River. The place was lifting with several varieties of mice. At night I kept an array of boots and running shoes by the side of the bed, and managed to kill mice in pitch darkness just by throwing shoes at the sound of scurrying feet. Oddly enough, Myrna was not all that impressed with the results of my marksmanship.

Black bears ruled at "Poco." One of them took a liking to our trailer, whose screens were covered with big luna moths every night and with mice (the ones that had gone outside) hunting the moths. The bear seemed to enjoy licking both mice and moths off the door screen, late of a summer evening. We never opened that door at night without turning a light on first. I appreciated his work on the mice, since we had no cat, but did not enjoy his proprietary attitude to the trailer.

Bears create "scent posts" to mark their territories. They will rub their backs against a favourite tree, leaving guard hairs stuck to the bark, and "blaze" the tree (strip bark away) with their teeth as high as they can reach. I think this leaves a kind of scent profile for the next bear along, something that says "This is how big and mean I can be – now buzz off." I suspect Blackie saw our trailer as a kind of tin tree, because he took to scratching the outside of our bedroom wall with his claws. This made an unnerving sound, like somebody scratching a blackboard with a set of crampons a few inches from our ears.

One day Myrna was away visiting her parents in Calgary. I came home after a hot July day which I'd spent along the CNR right-of-way, helping to put out spot fires caused by faulty boxcar brakes. Blackie, meanwhile, had been snooping around the local motel as well as scratching paint off the Loewen's kitchen door and generally being a furry pain in the neck. Abe had decided the bear needed a change of venue away from the highway. I had been daydreaming of a cool shower and an ice-cold beer, but first I had to set the culvert trap up in the station yard.

I caught a glimpse of Blackie in the woods when I drove into the station. His presence there was so familiar that I no longer took much notice. He was snooping around a big squirrel cache under a spruce tree in a desultory fashion. I secured the guillotine-style door on the trap, making sure that Abe was not around first. Some wardens have a sick sense of humour when it comes to bear traps. A favourite trick we had in those days was to sneak up, camera in hand, when a colleague was cleaning a trap, and trip the steel gate behind him. The gate would slam shut with an unnerving crash. Then the victim would be photographed with his hands gripping the steel bars of the gate, getting angrier and angrier. Some pranksters liked to wait until a bit of saliva was drooling out of the victim's mouth before snapping the picture. The usual penalty for being caught was a bottle of whiskey and a promise not to beat hell out of whoever trapped you. I did not invent this tradition, by the way – I was merely a slave to it.

Anyway, I don't recall Abe drinking whiskey. So I crawled inside to clean out the bear crap and urine left by the last occupant, and the maggots growing from the old bait. That was always an unpleasant task. I punched holes in a can of sardines we kept handy for fresh bait and tied it to the trip lever to work its aromatic magic, then headed for the trailer, thinking to get some old wieners out of the fridge as further enticement. Nothing like a little mystery meat to intrigue Blackie. More importantly, I would grab a cold beer while I was at it.

But it seems that Blackie was on the same wavelength as me; maybe he was longing for a cool brewski himself.

When I stepped into the kitchen, the fridge door was open. Glancing down the hall, I noticed the rear door was ajar. That door opened on our bedroom. There were a lot of people hitchhiking on the highway at the time; I stopped in my tracks, thinking the place had been burglarized, thinking, Some hobo sonofabitch has stolen my Pilsner! That's when a matched set of black claws appeared over the edge of the white fridge door and Blackie stood up to peer at me in the dim light.

> "Woof" you said
> startled while trying the fridge
> I forget what I said
> Your black fur made quite a contrast
> against that white porcelain

Looking back, I'm not sure the poem did the moment justice. It is amazing, really, how wild and scary a mere black bear looks, standing on your kitchen floor while outlined against a home appliance.

> Being both timid
> we turned simultaneously
> and attempted to exit
> in embarrassed haste

You see, the way I looked at it, it was a government trailer and Blackie was a government bear. If he wanted that tin mouse-condo, he could have it. Trouble was, Myrna had waxed the floor the day before: my cowboy boots spun out and down I went, expecting the bear to run over top of me. But Blackie was spooked by my intrusion. He tried to run the opposite direction and went into a treadmilling skid, his claws rattling on the shiny lino. Then he got back on all fours and ran the length of the trailer to the bedroom in about one half of a second. The aluminum door hardly gave him pause. In fact, he took the entire door, wrapped around his neck, partway into the swamp with him. I found the various parts of it later, bent around a tree like tin foil. That poem concluded with me loading the shotgun in a temporary fit of pique, thinking:

Boring days will never come again
To this sleepy warden station.

I never did catch that bear.

My black-bear memory switchbacks forward in time to 1972, when I was on boundary patrol during the provincial sheep-hunting season. The idea was to make sure that hunters stayed out of the national park, where all hunting is illegal. I spent part of my time at Miette Cabin on the south side of the Athabasca River, a lonely outpost well-known to bears and wardens. We worked twenty-four-day shifts, and I patrolled the valleys and ridges along the park boundary mostly alone during my time there. I missed my wife and infant son and was sometimes in a cantankerous mood as a result. It got so bad that my horses refused to speak to me, even when I walked out to jingle them at dawn, shaking oats in a tin pail. At night, I found myself in an argument with a sub-adult (two-year-old) black bear who was apparently feeling as cantankerous as I, probably from having been recently kicked out by its dam to fend for itself. What seemed to offend his (or her) sense of propriety was an enamel washbasin that I left on the front porch after washing up for supper. Blackie followed a trail down the escarpment above the cabin every night. Whoever built the cabin had placed its front porch across this ancient pathway. Rather then deviate from his route, Blackie simply walked across the porch. The basin was directly in his way. He refused to step over it or around it. With an indignant snort, he would backhand it out into the meadow with a loud clatter and wake me up.

This seemed to happen every time I stayed at Miette, but like a bushed-out old trapper, I was too pigheaded and ornery to put the basin away at night. Instead I would rush out – stark naked, as a rule – yelling threats at Blackie, who retired to the meadow to watch my performance. A bear is like a wild man of the woods, his expression frozen from facing into solitude. You can't tell when he's laughing at you, but I wonder now if I wasn't providing him with comic relief – or just a bit of company. I'm sure he enjoyed the way I spooked my own horses with my wild-eyed appearance in the middle of the night, sending my hobbled ponies off with kangaroo leaps of fear across the meadow, the lead mare's bell ringing like a fire alarm. Maybe to Blackie, I was just a strange, naked bear whose den this was:

Who now sits on his porch
pink skinned, having given up on sleep
to stare at the world revealed by a silver moon.

I learned to live with bears like a close neighbour, cultivating a respect for them which I feel they returned. It wasn't prudent to encourage them to come too close, especially when I was travelling alone in the bush. But often I have travelled on horseback with black bears ambling through the bush alongside of me, sometimes ahead, sometimes behind when we happened to be travelling in the same direction. Bears find our human trails quite convenient to use at times. And I would sing to them, songs that I made up for the occasion, warrior songs, bragging songs which I thought they would find amusing.

The fascination that humans feel towards bears was explored in fiction by the late Marian Engel in her notorious novel *Bear* (1976). Engel's heroine is Lou, a lonely, sex-starved archivist who comes to catalogue the library and contents of a historic house on an Ontario island. The property is inhabited by a tame black bear, which she must feed and care for as part of the contract. Over the course of the summer, Lou falls in love with "Bear." Not content with merely wrestling and swimming with the docile creature – and allowing it other, more intimate, contact – Lou eventually becomes obsessed with the idea of mating with the bear in accord with an old Finnish legend: "The offspring of a bear and woman is a hero, with the strength of a bear and the cleverness of a man."

Just as in many other contacts between humans and wild bears, it is the bear that draws the line and shows a kind of common sense that humans often lack, and that brings Engel's heroine back to reality, albeit painfully.

On the subject of bears and human sexuality, there was a theory being kicked around in 1976 that bears were somehow offended by human beings making love in the woods. The theory came about, in part, after an incident in Jasper Park in which a naked couple were discovered by a bear while in flagrante delicto and chased out of the woods and back to their car – stark naked of course, and without their car keys. They had to clamber up on the roof for a while to avoid the bear, creating a startling sight for passing motorists until Warden Daro Stinson came to their rescue. Maybe the bear was just jealous. After Stinson had set his dog on the bear and treed it, he'd found the woman's clothes had been ripped to pieces though the man's were intact. Stinson recovered the car keys, but the woman had to wrap herself in a picnic blanket for covering.

Our higher-ups worried, briefly, that the public should be

educated against the hazards of doing what comes naturally in bear country. Chief wardens amused themselves by trying to design a universal sign-symbol that would describe the activity and the hazard – without being pornographic. After a while, the notion was forgotten.

Engel's prodigious writing talent made her description of Lou swapping spit with her furry playmate seem plausible, at least to anyone who has not smelled a bear's breath close up. But it's strange how life can sometimes imitate art. Once, after a poetry reading, when I was still working on the poems for my book *Nobody Danced with Miss Rodeo*, I was told an incredible story about an encounter between a woman the informant claimed to know and a black bear. This woman had a terrible sunburn. She was lying naked in her tent, covered with cold cream, when a black bear walked through the tent door. The lady froze, played dead, and without much preamble, the black bear began to lick off the cold cream – all of it. Then he wandered off in search of dessert, leaving his victim uninjured, though emotionally debilitated – to say the least.

But how fortunate for the victim of this encounter that a certain ambitious and rather humourless warden I knew at the time had not come upon this fraught scene. For there is no doubt in my mind that he would have immediately charged her with "unlawfully touching wildlife and enticing it to approach by setting out food-stuffs or bait, contrary to section 4.1.(f) of the National Parks Wildlife Regulations."

As long as there are black bears and human beings to keep them bemused, anything is possible, and what you only dreamed of today may happen tomorrow. But there is a moral to this story: don't set out food for bears, especially on your body; keep your beer tied up in a sack suspended at least fifteen feet off the ground on a rope between two trees; and don't camp across a bear's trail. But do learn to sing to bears, especially when you can't see them, and not just to scare them away, because deep in the woods when they are all alone, they remember the melody you taught them and they dance for you.

It is their way of praying for us to leave them alone. Though it's not the dance of a circus bear, though it might be hard to describe it even as a dance, though you might think they are only scratching their back on a tree and moaning, they are dancing.

I suspect they remember many things, including music, including the sound of our voices, which stays inside their heads, and therefore in the wilderness, long after we are gone.

CHAPTER NINE

Sling Jobs

"You whack 'em, we pack 'em."
> — Unofficial motto of the Banff National
> Park mountain rescue team in days of yore

The sky lowers over the Livingstone Range like a dirty black canvas. Deerflies – "face flies," I call them, due to their modus operandi – careen around my head in ever diminishing circles, drawn by the smell of blood on my scratched-up hands, seeking only to implode their tiny jaws into my flesh. I crank the handle of the wire stretcher tight, glance up at the sky with steel fence staples protruding from my mouth like vampire's fangs. The still August air is heavy with the threat of an impending storm. Twelve miles east atop the Porcupine Fire Tower, fire lookout Laurie McAllum is waiting to count the lightning bolts, and plot their fiery strikes on a map to be investigated later by the Alberta Forest Service heli-attack team.

Lightning plays over the ranges farther north as I drive in the staples with the fencing pliers. The hair on my arms is standing at

178

attention. Better give up on this chore in case lightning hits this fence and grounds me out like a cinder. Last year, not far from where I live, thirty head of cattle drifted into a barbed-wire fence corner like this one during a storm. Lightning walked down the fence and jumped to the herd, killing $30,000 worth of beef on the spot. The same day, it hit a rider on the top of his head, burnt a hole right through his body and through his saddle, killing him and his horse stone dead.

Now there comes a distant sound as if the canvas of the sky was being shaken out by two mighty hands – *whup, whup*, growing louder – WHUP WHUP WHUPWHUPWHUP – and a forestry helicopter comes into sight high over the Livingstone Range, heading north from the Crowsnest Pass, a small object dangling underneath it on a long cable. It's probably a monsoon bucket, used to douse spot fires. But I never see a helicopter slinging a load beneath its belly without remembering what it's like to hang underneath that machine in a rescue seat on the end of a sling rope (a doubled climbing rope). I remember how it felt, sitting in the sky, facing backwards mostly, staring up at the white ventral surface of the craft overhead with the wind rushing past my helmeted ears. In a yellow anorak and bright climbing harness under the rescue-seat harness, hung with shining metal climbing hardware, I was a lure trolled through the clouds for that big sky-pike name of Death.

The first rescues I participated in required the use of my own back muscles for transport of the injured. In 1968, I graduated to horses, and employed them to evacuate several people who were sick or injured on park trails over the years. Helicopters, which came into their own as airborne ambulances in the Korean conflict, long ago transformed mountain rescue operations in the western national and provincial parks. But the old-fangled attitude of national park officials towards those machines is remembered well by retired pilot Jim Davies of Banff, the most distinguished mountain rescue pilot of his generation. Davies, a dark-haired, bearlike man, is also a talented wildlife artist. He is the son of the late Bert Davies, longtime Banff

Park warden, so Jim came by his interest in mountain rescue and wildlife conservation naturally.

In the Canadian Rockies, helicopters were employed on a few occasions prior to the Mount Babel rescue, most notably on Mount Blane the Kananaskis in 1962. On that occasion, the helicopter's operating ceiling was very limited. A warden rescue team had to carry and lower an injured man hundreds of metres to where the helicopter could land – and that was only after park workers built a hasty log landing-pad of felled trees. Still, the presence of the machine shortened the total evacuation time of the casualty by a considerable margin. In 1965, a climber was injured in a crevasse accident near Mount Daly, seventy crow-fly kilometres from Banff. Davies, flying for Bullock Helicopters, was based in Calgary, and as a commercial pilot, was not allowed to keep his helicopter in the park. He offered the use of the machine to the park superintendent, Harry Dempster, whose gruff reply was "No bloody way." Chief Warden Bob Hand informed him: "We have thirty-five wardens and forty-five horses. That's the way we will do the rescue."

Horses on a glacier. It has been done before, of course, though not without great risk. At his home on Tunnel Mountain in 1999, overlooking the Banff warden office and the old helicopter hangar that he personally built in the seventies, Davies frowned at that memory. "It took them three days and the entire warden service to get that guy down. They injured a warden doing it. It would have taken about twenty minutes by helicopter. That caused them to really start rethinking their attitude." It was probably one reason why Walter Perren got permission to use Davies's helicopter on Mount Babel the following year.

After Perren's death, one of his protégés, mountain guide Peter Fuhrmann, took over the alpine specialist function for the southern mountain parks while guide Willi Pfisterer performed a similar function in Jasper National Park. The two guides were well aware that helicopters were becoming more powerful and efficient. Davies had demonstrated that when he set an altitude record by landing his

G3B1, with two passengers aboard, at 17,147 feet (5,228 metres) on Mount Lacania in the Saint Elias range. Helicopters allowed rescuers to get people to hospital in hours or even minutes where traditional stretcher-carries took many days. "Helicopters saved them [rescue teams] a helluva lot of work," said Davies. "But most importantly, the helicopter reduces the risk to the rescuer, because it reduces the amount of time you are exposed. It's just seconds in some cases."

Despite the technological advances, there are countless places in the mountains where even the most advanced helicopters will never be able to land. Cable winches were an innovation that allowed flight rescuers to reach stranded and injured climbers. "But when you went to meetings with rescue experts in Europe," said Davies, "they all talked about winch accidents." Peter Fuhrmann thought there was a better way. In *Men for the Mountains*, I described how he introduced the idea of using climbing ropes tied to the frame of the helicopter to sling rescuers in and out of places where the helicopter could not land. According to Davies's flight log, he and Peter did the first training flights with the sling on June 3, 1971. A chance to try it out on a live rescue wasn't long in coming. On August 6, 1971, Jim slung Fuhrmann and a critically injured climber off a ledge on Mount Edith and landed them at the door of the Banff Springs Hospital minutes later, astounding the naysayers in the park administration building, which was known to us mere grunts in those days as "the Kremlin." After that, training in the new method became part of the advanced rescue courses in the mountain parks.

In 1972, in the days when the technique was still considered experimental, I took my first ride under the helicopter. It was not an auspicious beginning. I had not been issued with uniform-type climbing pants so I was wearing my old grey leather knickers. I was unnerved at first by the noise of the machine and the hazardous nature of the exercise. In short, I was scared. The rope, some eighteen metres (sixty feet) long, formed a sharp angle between me and the machine. Instead of walking quickly underneath the helicopter as it rose, a technique which maintains a vertical line and a smooth lift-off straight up, I sat down in the harness too soon. As a result, I took a trapeze-like swing on the gravelled strip – and found myself being dragged backwards along the gravel on the seat of my leather pants, leaving a plume of dust behind me until I finally bum-skied up into the sky. You could say that my first sling job was a real pain in the arse. It didn't help to look way down below and see my colleagues rolling around on the ground speechless with laughter. I was too humiliated to be frightened as Davies whirled me around the perimeter of the airstrip several metres above the ground. I managed to land correctly – feet first, that is – and unclip from the O-ring, my face burning. "Now we know why you wear those leather pants," wheezed Warden Jay Morton, still wiping tears of laughter from his eyes. "You're gonna have to stop it, Marty," he protested. "These stunts of yours are killing me."

I was always glad to provide my trusty cohort with comic relief, although it was workmate Tim Auger, with his propensity for clowning, who handed Jim Davies's wife, Sue, the most laughter after his own first training flight.

"Why so glum, Tim?" she had asked as he gathered up his gear after his first flight one spring day.

"I thought I would fly like Peter Pan," confessed the aging flower child, sadly, from under his seventies mop of jet-black hair. Smiling wistfully, Tim had gotten up to demonstrate what he meant, his arms flung wide, dancing *sur les pointes* – of his climbing boots – with balletic grace. He fluttered spastically to a halt. "But I couldn't fly like my hero Peter Pan, Sue," he said, glumly. "I just hung there . . ."

In 1998, I was talking over my first flight with retired warden Monte Rose. Rose, who started out life as a dirt farmer's son, has retired now to a little shack out on the prairie like a modern-day homesteader. I had gone to talk to him about a dramatic rescue he pulled off at Moraine Lake with Bill Vroom in 1972. The first time I'd met this lean, sandy-haired warden with the sardonic sense of humour, he was tied in on a ledge below an overhang on the east face of Tunnel Mountain, high above the Banff Springs golf course, and I was being lowered down to "rescue" him on the end of a steel cable.

"Ha ha!" chuckled Monte, savouring my helicopter mishap. "Funny thing though," he mused, in his satirical rasping way. "Sounds like old Morton forgot to mention what happened on his first flight."

I pricked up my ears. "Tell me about it."

"Well, it was another sling exercise back in 1972 also. Maybe before you transferred to Banff. Anyway, Jim was flying the Alouette II back then. I clipped in and he yanked me off the ground like a cork out of a champagne bottle and whipped me up towards that second big hump on Mount Rundle above Banff. So naturally he didn't take me right up there and just set me down on the rock. No, no. In his own sick mind he thought it would be fun to fly right out where it drops away to nothing. He knew I was in his power. So he flies a loop out there first to give me a thrill. Finally he tires of the sport and sets me down. He goes back for another victim and it's Morton. So here comes Morton, just a little speck hanging under the helicopter at first, but getting closer and closer. Finally I can see the sun glance off Davies's grin up there in the cockpit and just then Morton gives a half turn and I can make out his face as he comes whipping towards me on the sling rope, then passes by overhead. He looks as white as Casper the ghost. You see, when he went to snap in, he missed the O-ring on the end of the sling and hooked the carabiner around that doubled sling rope instead. He gets the gate jammed in the open position. Now all his weight is on it, so he can't close it. The 'biner is just kinda casually resting there now, like the hand of fate, waiting to be jarred loose."

Monte puffed on his pipe, relishing the memory. "So Morton is staring at the carabiner, kinda hypnotized by it all," he went on, "as Davies whips him out over that drop-off. I thought he was going to throw up there when he finally got his feet back on the ground."

There were many faux pas as we tried out the new method. The training flights were sometimes more difficult to endure than the missions themselves. Mine were few in number and quite straight-forward compared with the many complex operations done by my friend and former colleague, Tim Auger, and other public-safety wardens and rangers in the Rockies. But when I asked Tim which sling job stands out in the history of the service, he didn't mention one of his own. The one that we both thought of first was the 3–3 ½ Couloir escapade that Monte Rose, Bill Vroom and Jim Davies pulled off.

There were fifty to sixty search-and-rescue operations annually in Banff Park in that era and the regional alpine specialist could not be available for all of them. On this particular fraught occasion, Vroom and Rose had to put all of Perren and Fuhrmann's training into practice on their own. They could not have done it without the skill and experience of Jim Davies.

The notorious 3–3 ½ Couloir, which rises above the inlet of Moraine Lake in the Valley of the Ten Peaks, lies between Mount Bowlen (Peak 3) and a peak known as 3 ½, part of the Wenkchemna Range. Mount Babel is part of this group, as is Mount Perren, iron-ically enough.

At one time, climbers mainly used this particular high-angle (fifty degrees) snow-and-ice route to get to the Graham Cooper Hut for climbing in the Ten Peaks area above the lake. The hut was named for a mountaineer who was – ominously – killed by rockfall while descending to Moraine Lake after helping to assemble the hut in 1964. A number of people have been killed and injured in this couloir over the years, mostly by falling rock I believe, including three people who died in one party in 1980 and a man killed there the day the hut was finally disassembled in 1983. The tiny Cooper memorial hut was replaced by the modern Neil Colgan Hut, named for a young warden who died while on duty in 1979. The couloir is a natural funnel for everything falling or dripping down the moun-tain walls that feed into it. Rockfall is the main hazard. It is so constant that Peter Fuhrmann once told Jim Davies, "The next time we have to sling in there, we're going inside a forty-five-gallon drum." The 3–3 ½ Couloir route remains extremely dangerous to this day, especially in summer when the heat of the day or sudden rainfall melts rocks from their moorings on the mountain walls above it. Yet it is a tempting, adventurous feature for edge-loving types who enjoy ice climbing. Most parties these days use a nearby rock-climbing route to get to the Colgan Hut.

On August 9, 1973, two young climbers – David R. Smith, twenty-one, and Marshall Ralph, twenty-six, both members of the Wastach Mountain Club of Utah – were ascending the ice gully on the road to summer adventure. Due to the injury he suffered, Smith's memory of that day ends with the crossing of the inlet stream of Moraine Lake. Smith, whom I tracked down by telephone in 1999, recalls that they were headed for Mount Fay. He says that when he looked up at the couloir the day before he had thought, "What a beautiful way to get up to the hut!" He laughed ruefully at that memory.

The two climbers were well equipped, properly roped up and climbing in good form. "I guess our mistake was that we didn't begin the climb early enough in the day," Smith confided. At 10 A.M., the party was about 230 metres from the top of the couloir, near a feature in the ice known as the Hourglass, but the sun was already softening up the mountain. A chunk of rock fell into the chute and exploded like a bomb, sending fragments flying. Smith, the more experienced of the two, was tied into an ice screw, facing downhill and belaying Ralph with the rope around his waist. He believes he was hit twice by rock: first on the helmet, which was pushed forward, cutting him above the eyebrow and exposing the back of his head; then on the back of the head, which rendered him semi-conscious. He wound up hanging from the ice screw, no longer able to belay his partner. Ralph, only three metres below him, made a fast sidestep on his crampons to dodge the missiles, came off the ice, and instinctively grabbed at the slack portion of the climbing rope, which was tied off through the ice-screw anchor to Smith's

harness. The quick move stopped his fall and probably saved both
their lives, since a full-length fall would no doubt have pulled Smith
off the mountain. Other climbers have wound up mangled on the
rocks at the bottom of the chute in cases like this.

Ralph told Smith afterwards that he (Smith) was able to respond
to Ralph and move his feet as long as Ralph kept shouting at him.
Ralph either helped or belayed the dazed Smith on a fifteen-metre
traverse to his left where a rocky bulge in the mountainside afforded
some slight protection from further rockfall.* Ralph set two tubular
ice screws for anchors and tied off his friend's climbing harness so he
would be secure beneath the rock bulge in a gap where the ice meets
the mountain wall. He managed to stop the bleeding and bandage
his partner's wound, then wrapped him in a sleeping bag to try and
keep him warm. Then he set off, downclimbing and rappelling
down the ice to get help, no doubt expecting a rock to strike him at
any moment, but forced to move very slowly and cautiously in
descending seven hundred metres to Moraine Lake. According to
the rescue report, it was 6:00 P.M. before he finally reached Moraine
Lake Lodge and the nearest telephone. Monte Rose, acting area
manager at Lake Louise, got the call, and immediately notified
Banff, where the dispatcher rounded up Bill Vroom, Jim Davies,
and other wardens on duty to begin the operation. (The dispatcher
rang my number as well, but I was out of the park on days off.)

At 8:20 P.M., Jim Davies, guided by Marshall Ralph, eased his Jet
Ranger helicopter in between the rocky ridges hemming the couloir
near the Hourglass so that Bill Vroom could plan the evacuation of
the injured climber. "There was no room to turn," Davies remembers. "It's like a narrow canyon. I had to hover straight in and hover
back out again." The ice sheet and its forbidding borders of rock
loomed over the helicopter, filling the field of vision.

From his position beside Davies, Bill Vroom could see the
bright-coloured square of Smith's sleeping bag and a patch of

---

* I was unable to track down Marshall Ralph for his account.

blood in the snow where the accident had occurred. The ice was pockmarked with rock fragments. Smith's crumpled form was dwarfed by the immense rock wall, streaked black with dripping water, that towered overhead. He slumped, sacklike, in his harness. He stirred slightly, reacting to the engine noise, but appeared to be basically unconscious.

"I can't sling you in beside him," came Davies's voice in Bill's headphones. "Not enough room for the rotors."

Bill noticed a protruding rock to the right and below Smith near the centre of the couloir. He pressed his microphone button and pointed out the spot. "If you land us there, I figure once we get him in the rescue basket, we can slide it down a rope from where he is, and then hook him on the sling rope."

"That should work," replied Davies. He eased the ship carefully out of the col, and circled up to land on top of Peak 4 (3,054 metres), which rises from fields of ice broken by rock peaks. Vroom got out to ready the sling-rope and climbing gear, not bothering to admire the view of Moraine Lake to the north. Davies flew back to unload Ralph at the lodge and pick up Monte Rose. Rose always enjoyed helicopter rides, but the steepness of this ice chute did not please him. "I remember seeing what I thought was some brown birds flying erratically around, at great speed," he told me, "including one very large one. Then my tiny brain suddenly realized – hey, those aren't birds; those are falling rocks! Somehow the chopper ride wasn't fun any more."

Soon both wardens were ready to sling off the top of the peak and down to the ice ramp 460 metres below. Vroom was quiet, absorbed in the task ahead. The usually ebullient Rose was taciturn too. He was brooding over the hazards of the impending rescue, but also over a domestic upset earlier that day, caused by the death of a family pet. As they readied their gear, they could see outriders of a coming storm cresting the western peaks.

In the old rescue reports, there was a section for weather conditions. Weather in the mountains can change by the hour. Under weather for August 9 and 10, Vroom and Rose had circled the words "Calm, Warm, Cool, Cold, Sunny, Cloudy, Drizzle, Heavy Rain, and Lightning." Monte recalled that it was also Windy for a while that night, but he considered it a blessing that it was not also Freezing and Snowing.

Bill Vroom reached under the machine and clipped the sling ropes onto the load brackets. Monte Rose double-checked the connections. Jim Davies brought the engine up carefully to flight-idle speed while Vroom backed away and clipped into the O-ring. Rose would bring the steel rescue basket (stretcher) in on his flight. In a moment, Davies opened the throttle and lifted the machine up from the mountaintop and Vroom could hear Davies's voice in the headphones built into his helmet as he reported his take-off to the Banff Park dispatcher. Then the straps came tight on Vroom's thighs and shoulders and he was flying off the edge of Peak 4. Monte Rose vanished from sight above and behind him and Vroom was looking down between the toes of his boots into the waters of Moraine Lake some 1,000 metres below. There was the lodge at the end of the lake where other wardens were handling radio communications and standing by with their rescue gear if needed.

Davies circled around to the couloir and side-slipped his way between the gap in the ridges near the Hourglass. The ramp of ice grew steadily closer as Vroom talked by radio to his pilot, who had taken his window off in order to see the rescuer dangling below him.

How easily we surrender to the birdlike freedom of flight, even tethered flight like this. It takes no time for your legs and feet to fall happily asleep. Vroom banged his boots together to make sure he could feel his feet, then turned in his harness, bracing for his return to earth – or rather, ice. The ice came up, closer, hostile, streaked with rock chips. Rotor blast and engine noise shook his whole being, rattling his concentration. A blur of red swept by, and for a heart-stopping moment, Bill Vroom thought Smith had come off and fallen down the chute – but it was the sleeping bag, blown away by the rotor blast. He reached out with his axe and sank the pick with vicious, wounding intent into the surface as if harpooning a white whale, then kicked the front points of his crampons in to take his weight. He felt awkward and unbalanced now on the cold, hard surface. His winged heels turned into heavy clay once again. His heart was pounding, his knees already trembling, and his mouth was dry; he felt far from secure on the steep slope. Glancing down, he could see the rocks far below waiting to receive him if he fell. While the helicopter hovered above him, he chopped down to blue ice, then turned a couple of ice screws in and attached slings to them, which he grabbed onto with one grateful hand. Vroom told me that the helicopter couldn't have moved more than a few inches in the time he stood there placing the ice screws, a kind of precision that was typical of Davies's work. Davies said that was the hardest thing to do, maintain the hover that went on for four or five minutes, eyeing the arc of the rotors, gauging the distance from the ice, cocking an eye upslope for falling monsters, while both hands and both feet worked the controls.

Now Bill Vroom hesitated: it was another one of his existential moments. He wanted to hook into the anchors (ice screws) before he unclipped from the sling. But small rocks were whizzing by like bees, making him very nervous. If he was knocked unconscious by a rock, the helicopter would be tied to the mountain, where it would hover until it ran out of fuel and crashed – so Vroom told me afterwards.

I asked Davies about that in 1999. "No," he said. "I had enough power to pull the anchors out – but I doubt I could have done it without injuring him, pulling him between the machine and the ice screws like that. It's the kind of thing he would worry about, though, being Bill."

Instead, Vroom unclipped from the machine and waved Davies away. "Needless to say," he reported later, "I did a very fast and very cautious job of snapping myself into the two sling ropes." Now he worked at placing ice screws for Monte Rose to use. He stared up at the still form of Smith huddled fifteen metres to his left. He shouted a greeting, but there was no reply. The figure, suspended in the harness, looked corpse-like up there. Were they risking their necks for a dead man?

Except for the clatter of falling stones, it was quiet. In the fading light of evening, the couloir funnelled upward to a vanishing point of sky. Bill thought he heard the injured man groan at one point, but could not be sure. Then he heard the machine taking off from the summit above, the noise echoing from the walls of Pinnacle Mountain across the lake. In a few moments the helicopter was circling down in a wide arc, drawing nearer, then hovering slowly in between the canyon walls again with Monte Rose dangling underneath. "Moraine Lake looked like a blue teacup down between my feet," Rose recalled. Soon Vroom made out Rose's crooked grin, as he swung in to the ice with the rescue basket suspended at waist height in front of him. Rose dug in the front points of his crampons and, helped by Vroom, who grabbed one end of the basket, he hooked himself and the basket into the ice screws Vroom had ready for him. It seemed to Rose that it took ten minutes to secure themselves and the stretcher properly before they could finally wave the chopper away. This is going to be one big problem, thought Monte Rose.

Rocks were still coming down the chute at intervals. "I have never seen so many falling rocks in my life," Rose told me. They would have to leave the heavy rescue basket in place for now and get to cover fast. Hurriedly, the two roped up. They lacked the modern ice tools used today. Vroom, helped by the pick of his axe and the front points of his crampons, climbed carefully up to Smith, belayed by Rose, then brought his partner across. There was only a twenty-five-centimetre-wide shelf of ice and imbedded stones to stand or sit on next to Smith. The rescuers drove in some pitons and tied themselves in to prevent falls.

Smith was weak from loss of blood and was unresponsive. They might have given him a little water but nothing else. The climbing harness was interfering with his circulation. Occasionally he would talk incoherently or cry out in pain. They bundled him into an extra down jacket and taped fresh compress bandages on his wounds.

It was twilight now and they had not yet been able to retrieve the basket. The pilot's voice crackled over Rose's belt radio: "Rescue Team, Helicopter V-H-I."

"Go ahead, Jim."

"Monte, there's a storm front coming in. We should get you guys out of there, copy?"

The first drops of rain were already pattering down. The rescuers exchanged looks. They might be able to sling out themselves, but it was impossible to retrieve the basket and lower Smith to the pick-up point in the moments of daylight they had left. Leaving Smith behind was out of the question. Hypothermia was a real possibility given his condition. At least they could keep him warm and dry for the night, and try to let him know he was not alone in this miserable, exposed aerie in the dark.

Vroom radioed back their decision. Davies acknowledged. There was barely time to make one last flight from the lodge to bring in rucksacks containing food and water, wool blankets and a mickey of whiskey that one of the wardens there threw in at the last moment. Monte Rose claims they never found that whiskey. It's probably just as well.

While Vroom belayed, Rose traversed on his front points across the chute to the pick-up point. The sun had gone down over the edge of the western mountains and the light was growing dim in the couloir. Rose watched the helicopter approaching for the last time that night, the red and green lights blinking and its landing light on to illuminate the approach into the dark couloir. It represented the future at a moment when present dangers were overwhelming; a doorway in the sky leading to a safer tomorrow, a door tantalizingly close but impossible to enter now. The sling rope swayed towards him, and he grabbed the packs on the end of it. The rain was steadily increasing now, rattling down on his helmet. The coloured lights made eerie splashes like Christmas-tree lights on the ice sheet. A fog bank was creeping up the valley with the rain.

From the shelter of the rock bulge, Vroom watched, horrified, as two large rocks hurtled down out of the dark shadows above, into the bright cone cast by the Jet Ranger's landing light, and passed by either side of his partner. Busy with the packs and deafened by the roar of the turbine, Monte never noticed. Vroom felt himself trembling with the shock of that sight. Both rocks could have either killed or critically injured his partner.

On belay, Monte made his way back to the rock bulge with the packs. "About this time," wrote Bill Vroom in his report, "the rain started falling heavily. As Monte reached the protected area at the base of the cliff, the storm hit in full force, heavy rain, very dark, and a lot of lightning."

The most useful items inside the packs were the blankets and some plastic sheets. Smith at least was clad in quality protective clothing – not so his rescuers. I have a picture taken by Vroom of Monte Rose standing on the narrow ledge later that night. Although Gore-Tex was unheard of then, Monte does not even have a nylon cagoule to ward off the weather. Nor does he have either warm climbing pants or a down jacket. He is wearing brown corduroy pants to save wear and tear on his uniform pants, a summer-weight uniform jacket – "sackcloth," he called it – and a down vest. He likely had his parka along in his pack, but our parkas took on water like a sponge. We were not issued with sleeping bags back then. Wool blankets were actually more useful; wool stays warm even when wet.

Rocks kept clattering down the chute. They could hear them whanging off the side of the steel basket. From time to time a rock glanced off the opposite cliff faces and ricocheted over their heads like a bullet.

The lightning lurked and flared on the black summits around them. The two rescuers must have been half glad that the steel rescue basket was not right next to them. Smith sat crumpled unawares between them. Vroom, his face streaked with rain, took a bite from a soggy sandwich, tried to chew it, and remarked: "Well, Monte. I guess this is about as close to hell as it can get."

"You think this is bad?" scoffed Rose, his mind idling back to the tears and arguments at home that morning, "I got a dead guppy to deal with when we get through with this."

Bill started to laugh wildly and had to spit the sandwich out to avoid choking on it.

"It was black as the inside of a raven's throat up there," Monte recalled. "Funny the stuff that goes through your head when you get in a situation. I was thinking of some girl from the Moraine Lake Lodge who used to really crank my tractor. Your mind is in a kind of mental vacuum lock at times. Then a rock would go zinging by your nose and snap you back to reality."

After a while the rain stopped. The two wardens strapped head-lamps on their helmets, then Bill traversed out to the stretcher on belay from Monte and they managed to drag it back to their position, though the effort drained Vroom of energy. They anchored the stretcher to the rock, eased Smith into the foam-lined interior and wrapped him in more warm blankets, then lifted it up to hang at a comfortable angle. With the pressure of his harness finally removed from his legs and chest, Smith groaned with relief. His circulation was improved now, but head-injury cases can become manic. Twice that night the injured man began to struggle violently in the darkness, unnerving the rescuers clinging to the narrow ledge. "He fought hard to get out of the stretcher," Monte remembered. "Lots of crying, moaning, terrible cursing, and inhuman strength." Smith managed to slip halfway out of the stretcher before the two rescuers could control him. After that they lashed him in cocoon-style and had no further trouble.

Daybreak couldn't come early enough for the two wardens trapped below the Hourglass. They wanted to make their escape before the sun and the mountain started up their rockfall duet. "Twirly," as we called Davies back then, was already idling his rotors down at the lodge, discussing the plan by radio with the rescuers.

A light rain began to fall again as Vroom, belayed by Monte, eased the stretcher down the fixed rope hung by a sling and carabiner at its far end, and by a sling and prusik knot arrangement at the other so Vroom could brake the descent with the one-way prusik knot when needed. By the time he reached the take-off zone, Davies was hovering overhead, directing the weighted heli-sling rope to within reach of Vroom's outstretched hand.

The strain of the situation was becoming harder to bear as the minutes wore on. The first pebbles were already rattling down the ice. Vroom took out his knife, opened it, and clamped it in his teeth. His plan was to slash the light slings that held the stretcher to his climbing rope, once it was clipped in to the helicopter sling rope.

He grabbed for the ring, missed, and felt his body jerk off-balance. Eighteen metres above him, Davies peered down, one hand on the control stick, feet on the rudder pedals working his magic with a 400-horsepower motor. Easy now, Vroom warned himself. Don't mess this up at the last moment. Here came the ring, straight to his hand as if Davies had sent it on invisible wires. One hand closed eagerly on the cold steel like a handshake – hello to the end of this nightmare. He clipped the stretcher's steel cables and Smith's climbing harness into the O-ring separately – just in case.

Now he called Davies on his belt radio through the microphone attached to his helmet. "Okay, Jim. Take him up a foot or so."

"Roger."

The weight of the stretcher now came off Bill's climbing rope, but it was still tied to the mountain. "It was the only time I ever flew a mission where the machine was hooked both to the rescue party and to the mountain at the same time," recalled Jim Davies. From the look on his face, I could tell it had not been a pleasant feeling.

It was now or never and Vroom did not hesitate. He warned Davies of his intentions, had him lift the basket up tight against the traveller slings, then cut both free with the knife. The stretcher swayed out from the ice. "You've got him, Jim!" warned Vroom, and he waved his free arm.

"Roger that," came Davies's reply. The stretcher slipped away into space, described a lazy couple of turns below the helicopter, then straightened out on its long tether.

Vroom traversed back to the bulge where he and Monte packed up their gear. It was nearly over now, but caution was more important than ever in these last, exhausting minutes. Monte Rose kicked his way across the ice to the pick-up point. In his mind, the couloir was a kind of vertical arena in a frozen hell in which he and Vroom were duelling with the home team, the Mountain Demons. Standing out at "centre ice" as he called it, waiting for Davies, Vroom endured several dangerous slapshots. The worst attack was a free-falling rock "about the size of a wheelbarrow" that threatened to cross-check him into oblivion. Falling rocks can flutter like a propeller, whistle like a kettle, buzz like a bee, and warble like a bird from *The Twilight Zone*. "This one went by screaming like those artillery shell sounds you heard in old World War One movies," he told me.

"You ever believe you can actually smell death coming?" Rose had asked me pensively. The prairie wind blew eerily through the wooden fence outside his cabin. "I can," he said grimly, not waiting for an answer. "I could smell the stench of his molten sulphurlike breath. Seemed to me like I heard an eerie rasp of a voice squeal out 'Shit! Missed 'im.' Then another rock, smaller this time, went by my right leg. I was hopping back and forth like a young chicken trying to roost."

The helicopter approached, the sling rope swung in, and Rose clipped gratefully into the ring and quickly released himself from his ice-screw anchor. He swung out into space, free of the ice. "Suddenly I felt quite brave," he recalled. "In fact I was angry – getting the hell out of there." He glared at the evil spot by the Hourglass, and swore at the opposing team of invisible trolls and minions of Satan, his fists clenched, as the helicopter carried him to safety.

Shortly after that, Davies would return and sling Vroom back down to the lodge. Smith would be on his way to an intensive care unit in Calgary to recover from his head injury. There was nothing left behind to mark their passage but a few ice screws, a swatch of red climbing rope, and a red bloodstain in the snow as a warning to the next party up that route.

"Well, and probably a few piss stains, too," I can hear Monte Rose adding. "When ya gotta go, ya gotta go."

As my years in the government employ went by, the casualties were mainly strangers met for the first time, sometimes in peril, sometimes beyond help. What I remember of those other rescues are mainly pictures zooming into close-up, as from a remote camera hanging underneath a helicopter.

Gendarmes of rock rush into view; we look down between our feet and see them slide by as the machine lifts us over a pass where nothing goes but eagles and the spore of a lichen and the updraft on the lee side cuffs the machine violently, rattles the straps on our plastic helmets. It bats the tail boom sideways above us as we clear the rock and fall into another well between the peaks. Where there was no turbulence there always seemed to be more assurance of surviving the training flights, or the actual rescue of whoever needed our services. In the calm air, there was the comforting feeling that Death was hunting elsewhere, that this was little more than an elaborate amusement ride in an overgrown theme-park – the Sling-O-Rama Ride.

In the early seventies, our dead people mostly arrived with faces intact: a middle-aged drowning victim who shocked me mostly because he somewhat resembled my father; a young rancher's daughter, doll-like and surprised to have stepped backwards over a waterfall. She was stopped later by an exposed tree root in the bottom of the river, tucked under her leather cowboy belt. An avalanche victim, frozen stiff but miraculously intact after a half-kilometre ride in a falling cornice. These were the friendly dead: mere sleepers still fresh to the touch, ready to be cradled away in a mother's arms one last time. These were the dead worth waiting for, who had one last comment for the living etched on their faces. We searched for them with avalanche probes and rescue dogs, with ropes and grapnels by the river's edge late at night. Our head-lamps flickered greetings across the starlit waters. We were fishers of men in the foam, hunters in the snow.

Some of my worst memories of rescues are of ones I played no part in, like the 3–3 ½ Couloir story that gave me nightmares. Or like the time Willi Pfisterer's Jasper Park team lowered Warden John Turnbull from a cable through a freezing cold waterfall in Ogre Canyon to pick up the dead bodies of two teenage boys; the poor kids had fallen into that trap like mice into a bucket and drowned.

With two children and a wife to think about, I found myself less and less interested in climbing as time went by, except on training exercises and searches when I was being paid to do it. I still enjoyed the climbs, but only within the elite circle of the mountain outfit. Being involved with bear-trapping operations in front country, conducting long backcountry patrols on horseback, then working on avalanche control during the winter offered all the adventure I needed. At the time, I felt that as a family man I had to cut down my exposure to risk and not go out looking for more. But after hearing about the 3–3 ½ Couloir caper, I developed an unreasonable dread of the helicopter sling; I went through a brief period of active dislike for mountain climbers as a group.

Thinking back now, I date the beginning of this sad-sack period, when I eyed all alpine technology with Luddite wariness, to a night spent not on a mountain, but on a stretch of mountain highway that I would rather not name here. I was returning home at 1 A.M., dead tired from night shift, when I saw an eerie fluorescent glow in the night sky. Rain washed over the windshield, and rounding a corner, I found myself driving down a funnel of brilliant flares ending in a blinding array of flashing red and blue lights. I flicked on my own flashers in acknowledgement. Vague creatures moved in and out of the revolving auras, involved in some alien ritual; then a radio voice suddenly broke the silence inside the truck cab, as I geared down to pull over.

"Your timing is superb."

The Mountie – I think his last name was Creaser: I certainly hope so – hung his microphone up and closed the door of the cruiser as I braked to a stop. I saw the car then, pulled over in the ditch, the windshield webbed into splinters. The top of the hood was strangely damaged, massed with some dark shadow. The other officer, wearing his traffic vest and yellow slicker, was bent over on the road; his flashlight beam made a scarlet circle on the asphalt.

"You ever believe you can smell death coming?"

I stepped out of the truck and smelled its passage, like something redolent of a killing floor spiced with the scent of spilled beer. "We can use some help," said the constable. "This guy's all over the road. Gotta pick it all up."

I stared at him in confusion, then noted the bloody plastic bag in his hand, and was unable to think of a reason to deny him. Anyway, it wasn't a request. Wardens are also peace officers, and often help out the RCMP when needed. Behind him I saw what was left of the motorcycle. The rider had come over the centre line and hit the car head on, dying instantly. An elderly couple had been in the car; the driver had tried her best to get out of his way. The couple was safe at a motel back in town right then, trying to drink an entire bottle of rum, though they were both teetotallers.

I had known but not seen up until then just how fragile a human body is. Every day brought collisions between vehicles and animals on those roads; a plethora of bashed-up bears, inch-thick coyotes, and dismembered moose; proper tributes to King Automobile, who rules supreme. But those were not human beings. I had not dreamed how someone's father or husband might turn into fallen Humpty Dumpty in a nightmare. I had not seen how Death might sow our precious blood and bone – that a mother had lovingly nurtured for so many years – like seeds into the jaded roadside grasses. I saw Everyman: I saw my own body lying there. Anyone who dislikes the police should spend some time helping them clean up after a vehicle accident. I've done it a number of times. You'll come away with a whole different understanding. The shrouded corpse was amazingly small, lying in the back of the truck under the moonlight, as I drove back to town. I felt old and lonely, and colder than the man in the moon.

Back home I stumbled into the shower. When I came out, I saw the stain on my boots and threw them out into the night. Towards dawn I crept into bed, trembling with a dread foreboding, and wrapped myself around my sleeping wife like a drowning victim, drinking in her warmth with every nerve-end until the very intensity of my emotion frightened her into wakefulness. She held my hand over her womb, made me feel the new baby kick, kept my hand there pulling me back from the images in my head, back into the new life she believed we could plan for, until I fell into a fitful sleep.

Later on, I thought of the motorcyclist when I imagined my own death, bouncing downward like the Mexicans on Mount Victoria from ledge to ledge: turning into a streamer. At age thirty, I developed an ulcer from constant worrying and other frustrations of the job. Then one day, patrolling alone on the Dormer Pass, I was kicked in the back by an ornery government pack horse. Unable to breathe for a long, desperate moment, I lay in a pile of rocks clutching my saddle horse's reins, wondering, who will rescue the rescuer so far away? And it occurred to me, as I finally got my breath and pulled myself together, that only a fool imagines he knows how his life will end.

Two months later found me driving up to the Sunshine Ski Hill turn-off, slated to spend the morning making hand charges and blowing up cornices under Warden Keith Everts's skilled direction. An impatient driver pulled his muscle car out of a long line of perhaps twenty left-turning vehicles and blew down the solid line to pass. I don't know what caused me to hit the brakes – it was nothing I remember seeing – but the muscle car blew by in that instant with a few centimetres to spare. I managed to complete the turn, then pulled over and sat shaking, having missed the chance to even get his plate number, grateful only to still be alive. I would have given almost anything I owned to spend just five minutes with that stupid sonofabitch in a locked room.

"You ever believe you can actually smell death coming?"

Oh yes; I've caught that odour reeking from my own affrighted sweat. But as you get older, and friends start keeling over, and you start to see that we are all ducks in a shooting gallery anyway, death loses some of its power, though none of its dominion. There was no guarantee that Death rode herd on the helicopter sling-rescue technique; in fact, Death favoured me dying behind the wheel of the patrol truck above all else; that's where I spent a good portion of each winter day and entire shifts in the summer. That's where two wardens had died a few years earlier in a fiery crash with a semi-trailer truck, yet I had never worried about driving before that day at the turn-off. The constant sense of dread subsided and the ulcer eventually disappeared. Fear became something you put on, like a chest harness, and took off again when the shift ended. Fatalism brought its own measure of relief.

As it turned out, some aspects of rescue work became more and more demanding as the routes climbers attempted became more technically advanced, and as ice-climbing, usually on frozen waterfalls, came into vogue. Several wardens (Tim Auger was the first) qualified as professional mountain guides. Now these wardens led on the difficult rescues; the rest of us backed them up as needed.

It was just as well. You have to maintain some serious interest in climbing to do this kind of work. Once, when I was slinging in to land on a ledge with Lance Cooper, my legs fell asleep and as I stumbled to get a grip on the rocks where a backpacker was comforting his injured partner, I struck the man in the jaw with one heavy mountain boot and had to grab him quickly to keep him from falling. The memory saddens me even now. We worked hard, rehearsing frequently for our "role," wanting to be skilful, and under our cool veneer of professionalism we hated our mistakes to distraction. Cooper, a quick and competent flier now, was a light and quick young man. I don't remember him ever making an error, but then few people I know are as willing to admit to their errors as I am. I think I've made a kind of vice out of it: it's a part of my half-British background, to believe that I can't improve as a human being without acknowledging my mistakes. In those early, shakedown days of the sling job, some mistakes were unavoidable.

One of the things that gave me pause was the attitude, approaching resentment, displayed by a few of the climbers rescued by warden service crews. They were the ones who could not forgive themselves for screwing up, for not getting a chance to correct their own mistakes. That was my impression. What Tim Auger didn't like, still doesn't like, is being taken for granted. As he puts it: "I've had young people we've rescued say to me afterwards, 'So how do you get a job like this? It looks like it would be fun to do.'

"I just have to walk away from that."

The tourists – lost in the woods, stuck somewhere without an extra ski tip, or stranded on an island in the Bow River with a punctured raft after blundering stupidly over Bow Falls – were different; they expected to make mistakes; they could forgive themselves their own follies and were glad to see us coming.

What does a rescue man want? Back in those pioneering days, we didn't ask for much, although if you do it for a living, you want to be paid properly for the risk you endure, not with the pathetic wages that were doled out to us in the early-to-mid seventies ($12,000 per year, maximum). When it got right down to it though, you were not doing it for the money. You wanted good equipment, good training, competent leadership, and the same kind of people backing you up that you would want going into a dark alley to face a guy with a switchblade. A handshake and a word of thanks was about all you wanted from the survivors. Marshal Ralph knew that when he wrote the park superintendent to praise the "extraordinary courage" of Vroom, Rose, and Davies. "Anything Dave or I could say," he wrote, "seems pretty feeble. It was a fine, superb thing to do." Ralph was a class act; he took down the names of the ground support party at Moraine Lake Lodge and included them in his thanks: "Larry Gilmar, Darryl Grams, Cliff Milroy, Lorie Collingwood, Dale Loewen and Cpl Neil Stanley, RCMP. . . ."

But blessed too are the fools. I remember them along with the alpine heroes, seeing in them something of my younger self. One of my favourite temporary fools was young "Banlon Bill," as we dubbed him. He was named for the style of hosiery he wore. We performed perhaps the fastest rescue in park history on the unfortunate Banlon.

Banlon Bill set out for a snowshoe trip just after Christmas one winter, racquetting down the road from the Banff School of Fine Arts and headed, apparently, for the fleshly delights of the Banff Springs Hotel. He was wearing a kind of Oxford walking shoe and a pair of thin Banlon dress socks for foot protection. When we plucked him out of peril not long afterwards he had no hat on and no gloves. In other words, he was a typical Canadian teenager much like the two that Myrna and I raised.

There is a curve in the snow-covered road, footed by a cliff above Bow Falls, where tour buses have no trouble turning. Either Banlon was going so fast that he blew the turn, or else he thought he would take a shortcut to the hotel that was on the other side of the Bow River. Anyway, he took a fall down a steep gulley with his snowshoes on. It is not a high cliff, but it's high enough to kill you. He landed in a big snowdrift on a shelf of ice, right above the open water of Bow Falls. He was not badly hurt, but he was soon desperately cold. The kid worked his way upstream for some reason, then tried to climb back up the snowy cliff, about eighteen metres, but got stuck near a tree and started yelling for help. A passerby heard him and called the cops, who called our dispatcher.

Timberline Jim Deegan, the warden dispatcher, alerted Monte Rose, who was on duty that night. Deegan was a perspicacious old-timer with a thirsty memory, and soon tracked the rest of us down at the King Edward Hotel tavern where we had repaired at day's end. Annoyed at being rousted from our boozy soliloquies, we were in a mood to expedite Banlon Bill's rescue *tout de suite*. Monte Rose was already on the scene with a climbing rope. He had tied off on a tree, rapped down the cliff, and secured the young fellow, who was trembling uncontrollably from exposure (hypothermia had not been invented yet).

Earle Skjonsberg, being a sober and upright relic of World War Two, drove us back to the office, siren wailing, where we grabbed some ropes and lights and headed for the falls. Arriving at the scene, I tottered out first and stuck my head in the nearest snow-bank to try and get a grip, causing an attending RCMP officer to frown. Peering over the edge with a radar light in hand, we could see Monte straddling a tree trunk down there like a squirrel and cradling the kid in his arms.

"Sure fun, eh guy?" called out Monte, sardonically. It was a favourite expression of his.

Cooper and I set up a pulley on the edge of the cliff. Cooper lowered a Gramminger rescue seat down to Monte and he strapped the kid into it to carry him up on his back. Normally we would have used a cable, but on a short pull like this the climbing rope would be enough. But how to haul him and the kid up?

"We'll have to set up an improvised pulley system," said a sober voice.

"Bullshit!" cried another, vehemently. "The bar will be closed by the time we cobble that shit together."

"Use the Cornbinder!" came the gleeful suggestion from one of us – I can't remember who.

Everybody hated the Cornbinder, which was what we called our International Travel-All. It rattled in every joint, but on this occa-sion the old tank was a perfect mule for the task. Its bumper was bombproof. Lance wrapped a heavy web sling around it and we clipped the end of the climbing rope in. Somebody jumped in and eased the brake off. We were on a hill and I don't recall if he even bothered to start the engine. He just let it roll slowly down the slope. Up the cliff walked Monte Rose with the victim on his back, working hard under the kid's weight. "I remember I was puffing, blowing, and whimpering," Rose recalled. We quickly wrapped the victim into a sleeping bag, slipped a stretcher under him, and whipped him into the back of the Cornbinder before the poor kid had time to squawk a protest. Somebody jumped in beside him like a good EMT (Emergency Medical Technician) should and off he went to the warmth and comfort of the Mineral Springs Hospital, red lights flashing and siren blaring. He had suffered some frostbite during his brief ordeal. The rest of us piled in with Monte Rose to return to the pub. I checked my watch. From start to finish the whole thing had taken less than thirty minutes – another rescue first. And how fitting a rescue for the Bow Valley of Banff National Car Park – mountain rescue by automobile, in the montane life zone where the automobile rules supreme.

His shift over, Rose turned his jacket inside out to hide the badges and came in to join us. "And can't you see him lying there," said Warden Rose, puffing contentedly on his pipe back in the tumult of the old King Eddy later that evening, "perched there beside that gigantic icicle. He sees the Christmas-tree lights of the Banff Springs Hotel floating in the sky above him; he can see people in the windows over there, laughing with merriment as they quaff hot toddies by the blazing yule log. He can almost smell the roast turkey. While his little beady eyes slowly frost over."

Banlon Bill recovered and shuffled out of my ken, like so many others. I hope he is happy and healthy somewhere out in the big world, and agrees with me that if you do something silly in the mountains and die, it's a tragedy. But if you survive – and fortunately most do survive – it's just another chapter in the human comedy that only made you stronger. And you have a story to tell to your grandchildren.

CHAPTER TEN

The Bear's Mouth

Picture a man with his head in a bear's mouth, his skull clamped in its jaws, his face turned into the bear's maw. The man I speak of was a trapper and travelling alone when he pitched upon a bear without warning. Now death made animate has him in its grip. As remorseless and unyielding as the jaws of his own steel traps is the grip of those jaws on his head. It would seem his fate is decided – yet he is determined to survive, determined to reach for the last weapon he has and make the one move that might save his life.

I received a letter one day in 1998, printed by a trembling hand, from one Gordon K. Burrows, an old-timer from Jasper demanding to know why I had never written about Jim Christie's fight with a grizzly bear. In his letter he told me the tale as he remembered it. I looked into the story, and thanks to the generosity of several informants, uncovered a few remembrances of the man himself.

James Murdock Christie was born in Perthshire, Scotland, in 1874. Just when he came to Canada is not known. He was a small, dapper Scot standing 5.5 inches tall and given to wearing a sandy-coloured moustache. He was fair-haired and hazel-eyed. He listed his profession as "guide" when he went overseas with the Canadian Expeditionary Force in the Great War. Later he would sign on as a warden in Jasper and Banff national parks, from 1921 to 1931.

I soon discovered that, as with most bear stories, there were several different versions of Christie's ordeal. Burrows claims Jim Christie was a warden when he tangled with the bear. The fight happened back in the twenties during a backcountry patrol. He said that Christie carried the scars of the bear's teeth on his skull all his life. Indeed, the scars were noted by an army doctor – but in 1914, not in the twenties.

Burrows had Christie being jumped by a grizzly while going to his root cellar for provisions at a backcountry cabin. His young assistant warden found him lying with his head gripped in the bear's jaws. The bear was dead and Christie was unconscious when his helper freed him from that grip.

I had never encountered any records of Christie's ordeal during my researches in national park history. But then I remembered Henry Ness, an old-time warden from Banff Park who at age ninety-one has outlived most of his contemporaries. I called him up while visiting the park one day in 1999. "Sure I knew Christie," he said, to my delight. "But the story will cost you a cup of coffee."

I met Ness in the basement of a bizarre multi-level shopping complex on Banff Avenue that would be right at home in Los Angeles or Tokyo. What this monstrosity is doing in a national park could be the subject of another book. If the place seemed alien to me, whose memories of Banff start in the late fifties, I can't imagine how strange the place must seem to Ness, who was a warden here when the sidewalks were still paved with cinders left from the old Bankhead mine boilers. Ness is a sharp-featured old-timer, greyhound lean and blessed with good walking legs still, whose face has taken on the hue of a weathered pine trunk stripped of its bark. He is as chipper and bright as a red squirrel. The luck of his genes, combined with an outdoor life in the mountains, seems to have blessed him with good health.

Ness filled me in on the version of the story he knew. He'd known Christie as a warden, but in his version, Christie tangled with the bear while he was employed as lineman for a telegraph company near Telegraph Creek, B.C. He caught a grizzly breaking into his meat cache and he shot and wounded it. The bear came after him, as wounded grizzlies are wont to do to people who injure them. Going down a bank on his snowshoes, Christie tripped and fell, and that's when the bear caught him and fastened its jaws onto his head. Christie was alone at the time. Ness did not recall how Christie escaped this dilemma.

I should not have pointed out the discrepancy between his story and Burrows's to Ness. A cloud of self-doubt came over his features. "Well, when you are as old as I am," he said ruefully, "it could be that the whole damn thing was just a dream. And it became so real for me that it seems true."

But Ness was not dreaming. Some readers will by now suspect that Christie is the Jim Christie featured in a famous bear story they read in Laura Beatrice Berton's book *I Married the Klondike* (1954), in which he encounters the bear while trapping on the Rouge River, Yukon Territory, in October 1908. I believe she has the most accurate version of events; she lived close to the scene and the protagonist. Yet if I had the time, I wager I could collect a dozen other versions that people would claim to be the real ones.

Bear stories have a life of their own, like morning glory vines branching through rich garden soil; they are too rife with wild surmise to be tied to the written word. That's why it is important not to jump to conclusions when we hear a blood-curdling tale about bear maulings. What is often missing from these graphic accounts is the explanation for what caused the bear to attack in the first place, which is precisely the detail that is most important to know to avoid attacks in the future.

Berton's account covers the whole epic scale of Christie's ordeal. Here is a brief summary: Christie was trailing a grizzly after it raided his meat cache. The bear, aware that he was trailing it, attacked suddenly from cover, and although Christie shot it twice at close range, it kept coming. It knocked him down, mangled his head, broke his jaw and one wrist, bit him on the thigh, and eventually died while he was in its grip. Christie dragged himself clear. His torn scalp was hanging over his eyes and he had to tie his gaping jaw shut with the sleeves of his jacket. Worse, he had to stagger six rugged miles to his cabin, where his partner found him in this horrifying condition. His partner and two Indian hunters dragged him out by toboggan on a four-day trek to the nearest trading post. The Indians, being practical souls, endeared themselves by asking at intervals "Are you dead yet, Jim?"

At the post, Christie recovered enough strength to start by dog team for Dawson, breaking trail with snowshoes, and finally reaching the hospital there in January. Eventually, Christie was shipped off to a Seattle hospital for some serious repairs.

From other sources, I learned that Christie had a silver plate fitted in his skull to close off the head wound. They had to rebreak and reset his jaw, but he recovered with only a few scars on his scalp for a souvenir. In 1914, two months short of his fortieth birthday, he enlisted in the Princess Patricia's Canadian Light Infantry, where he served with great distinction overseas. According to Berton, he was mentioned in dispatches and awarded the Distinguished Conduct Medal and the Military Cross. Others claim he was a sniper and the record shows he was promoted to lieutenant. After his years in the warden service, where we know little at present of his doings, he retired to Saltspring Island sometime after 1932, a "white, agile little man, living quietly with his wife," when Berton paid a visit decades after the mauling. According to another family friend, the Christies lived pretty much on clam chowder, the west coast equivalent of oatmeal porridge, and Christie made a living of sorts hunting seals – with a rifle.

A brave man; a tough little nut in a tight corner and a canny wee Scot. But there is something omitted from Berton's account that Christie revealed to the Burrows family – or was it something that he embroidered into the tale? It is something that seems to be in accord with his nature.

The man in the bear's mouth can hardly breathe for the dragon-breath stink of the bear. What he sees through skeins of his own blood is the dark maw of the bear's throat. But he can hear, and he can feel those ivory teeth scraping on his skull under the torn scalp, scraping there like nutcrackers, and he can feel his own bones breaking. He can hear the ferocious growling of the grizzly in answer to his strangled, broken-jawed cries.

He pries at the bear's jaws to no avail. Its teeth have punctured his skull but his brain is working, still functioning as the bear's canines tickle its dura mater, still able to control his panic by the force of his will to survive. He reaches quickly, with his good hand, for the one weapon that can save him, the big war-knife a trapper carries on his belt. He slips it up alongside his head to aim it – and drives it up through the bear's palate with all his strength in an attempt to penetrate to its brain. That's probably when the bear let go of his head – if the story is true. Then naked bear and real bear rolled, steaming, through the snow, laved in each other's blood until the bear lay still.

I have a reason for being absorbed by this tale: it reminded me of another good man's fight with a bear – this time in Banff National Park, in 1973. He, too, was a kind of trapper who looked into the bear's mouth. But this man was no hunter; he carried no gun or knife. Distracted by a camera lens, he forgot to use the one weapon we all carry with us.

The history of the European settlement of North America is also a record of the displacement of wild species from the more productive lower-altitude habitats coveted by man. Bison, black-tailed ferrets, prairie owls, and swift foxes are but a few of the animals who cannot make a living after the white man turns the grass wrong side up. In the year 1690, Henry Kelsey, the first European to wander west from the Hudson's Bay posts to explore the interior of Canada, had found the grizzly bear at home far out on the plains of Manitoba. Of it he wrote "He is man's food, and he makes food of men."

Before the advent of Europeans armed with firearms, the Black-foot people of what is now Alberta and Montana greatly feared the White Bear, as they called the mature silvertip grizzly with its whitened guard hairs. Their lances and arrows were a poor match for a charging bear; only the bravest and strongest hunters collected a grizzly bear's claws and lived to tell the tale. With the advent of firearms, the bear was extirpated throughout much of its former range, which once stretched from Alaska far into Mexico. The remnants of the southernmost American population survive today in Yellowstone and Glacier national parks.

Of grizzly bears in Canada's more populated latitudes, some survive in the Swan Hills of Alberta. The rest are confined to the mountains and foothills of Alberta and British Columbia, centred on the national parks. There are supposed to be 800 grizzly bear in Alberta (including national park bears), although some biologists believe the number is much lower, and about 16,000 in all of British Columbia. In 1999, the best estimate for the Banff National Park population is from 60 to 80 grizzly bears, down from Warden Bill Vroom's 90-to-110-bear estimate of the mid-1970s.

Grizzly bears are intelligent animals and after the advent of firearms they gradually learned that man was dangerous and should be avoided. On the prairies, it was hard to hide from men, so the knowledge didn't do them much good. Some critics of national park bear-management policy believe that grizzly bears have lost their "natural fear of man" within our national parks, where hunting has long been prohibited. Grizzly bears are dominant over all other predators in this part of the world, including man when he is unarmed. It is misleading to think that grizzly bears are "naturally" afraid of us, simply because they learned to avoid us. When we leave

food out for them, including garbage, we encourage this opportunistic omnivore to change his avoidance behaviour and approach
omnivorous man more closely. This is a recipe for tragedy.

It is often said that the grizzly bear is a kind of canary in a coal
mine, an indicator of ecological integrity. The bear, like other large
mammals, thrives best in the same lower-altitude habitat where
man stakes his claim. Making room for bears to live and to breed
successfully makes room for the other plants and animals that
cohabit with it, from hummingbird to bull moose. This kind of
sharing is a formidable challenge for us naked bears. A mature male
grizzly in our relatively dry climatic zone may need 1,500 square
kilometres or more to make a living; a sow with cubs, up to 500
square kilometres, some of which intersects with a male bear's
range. This remnant population is increasingly under threat due to
the fragmentation of habitat, both within and outside the mountain national parks, because of human incursions such as roads,
townsites, ski resorts and other urban-type developments. There is
simply not enough room in the islands of wilderness called national
parks to support viable populations, unless the bears have access to
adjacent lands at times.

We know that if bears are to survive, we must be prepared to give
them room to live and breed. That means we assume some degree
of risk when we venture into bear country. If we ever decided, as a
nation, that we did not want grizzly bears to inhabit Banff Park, we
would no doubt wipe them out within a few years. Grizzly bears
survive because most Canadians want them to survive. In Alberta,
where people see the Rockies as the boundary of a wild frontier, the
grizzly bear epitomizes the Spirit of the West.

As someone who was once part of the bear industry, by which I
mean the informal coalition of hunters, trappers, wildlife biologists,
and game wardens, including park wardens and rangers, I preached
the party line: Bears are dangerous and unpredictable beasts. From
this general agreement flow two other assumptions. One is that of
the hunters: Bears can only be approached by brave marksmen

armed with heavy-calibre rifles. The other is that of the biologists who maintain that only bear experts, well-trained in bear behaviour, and armed with leg snares, culvert traps, and tranquilizer guns, have the expertise to approach bears.

Yet until Myrna and I transferred to Banff National Park in 1972, I had lived at peace with grizzly bears. I had seen the playful side of bear nature, watched them sliding down the snow of an old ava-lanche slope just for the sheer hell of it; met with Mustahyah and found him willing to share the country with me without aggression. I was privileged for a time, lulled, some critics might say, into think-ing it was possible to live in harmony with the great bear. Part of that has to do with the fact that I spent a lot of time in backcountry work and met with grizzlies that had not been corrupted by expo-sure to human food and garbage. Significantly, these encounters of mine were all on horseback, which I believe is still the safest way to travel in grizzly country even today.

In Jasper Park (1972), I spent much of my time patrolling alone in the Moosehorn area on twenty-four-day shifts. For company, I had two pack horses and a saddle horse. We shared the valley with a lone male grizzly bear. I had seen his tracks on my back trail several times without actually seeing the bear; I knew full well that the bear had seen me. One of his bedding sites was on a bluff right above a trail I used almost daily. He was a mature bear with paws some eleven inches long. One night I heard the horses snorting and blowing out in the dark meadow, and in the morning, there were his big pad marks circling my cabin, the points of his claws form-ing an exclamation mark on each toe-print. I could see his sign where he had been grazing on horsetails – the plant, that is – quite close to the horses.

I had gone to sleep thinking about grizzly bears, of a story Jasper outfitter Tom Vinson had told me. How an old-time ranger at Rock Lake had woken up one time to discover a dark head looming through his window, and believing it was one of his horses, he gave it an irritated slap on the chops. The indignant growl this horse emitted had sent a chill through his spine. It was a grizzly bear. Fortunately, the bear had retreated after this rude reception.

Rock Lake was only nineteen kilometres east of my cabin. You would think that I would have closed my own window, in light of that story. Instead, I left it open wider than ever. I'd been told how George Busby, who had built some of the trails in the area in the teens of the century, had never closed the door of the shack in summer, let alone the window. I admired that, though his attitude to bears sums up a much wilder era. Busby patrolled on foot, leading his pack horses, and once shot two grizzlies that decided to chase him, dutifully recording it in his official diary, as required. J. B. Harkin, director of national parks in Ottawa at the time, was what we today would call a "micro-manager"; he read each warden diary as it was sent in. Although the policy then was to have wardens shoot predators such as wolves, coyotes, and cougars on sight, bears were normally protected due to their value as a tourist attraction. (Tourists were seldom seen where Busby patrolled). Anyway, Harkin wrote the chief warden demanding to know why Busby was shooting bears. Busby apparently told his chief, "Well, I cut that trail out and I cut it out for me. When I'm not on it, the bears can have it. When I'm on it, damn them, they've got to get off, or else."

Apparently the chief warden told him, "Well, you know, if you've got to kill them, don't put it in your diary."

Out on that north boundary of loneliness, I used to dream occasionally about meeting up with that bear. It was well before dawn one restless night, when something cold and wet nuzzled at my face. I shivered in fear and woke up in one of those paralyzed moments where you don't move a hair, where you have to will your eyes to open. I found myself staring into a massive oblong shape looming through the open window a few inches from my face. I heard the thing drawing breath; something wet dribbled on my chest – saliva. Something luminous and eye-like regarded me from within this dark mass and I just about wet the bed. Then the thing gave a very loud, enquiring snort, blowing some snot into my face and sounding like a trumpet in that tiny shack. It floated back out the window.

I lay there, weakly cussing Rivets, my imperious old pack horse, who had stuck his head through the window to tell me it was time to get up and hand out my cheapskate rations of oats. I decided to close the window at least partway after that.

I knew that I would meet up with this old boar eventually, but I was so used to seeing his tracks and cowlike droppings, full of soapberry seeds, that I began to suspect he had accepted my presence in his territory. One autumn day I headed up Kephala Creek on China, a wall-eyed pinto gelding, through a stand of trembling aspen whose yellow leaves rustled underfoot. The route I followed was little more than a game trail. It would take me up to a ridge overlooking provincial land where I could keep an eye on some bighorn-sheep hunters based at Moosehorn Lakes. I came to a spot where the old boar had been digging up rotten logs and rolling around rocks the size of a kitchen range, looking for ants and larvae. I stopped the horse, wondering if I should continue up the trail. I could still smell the tang of that musky old outlaw among those displacements. I felt the flat muscles in my stomach tense; felt the draft of cool mountain air blowing up my shirt-sleeves and smelled moss perfuming a stream bed a hundred feet away. Being on horseback, I had a better chance to avoid the bear. The horse would hear him or smell him sooner than I would, I reasoned, and I would spot him more quickly from horseback than I would have done on foot. I've never heard of a grizzly successfully attacking a person who was on horseback; if it has happened, it has been a very rare occurrence.

I was supposed to carry a rifle while on patrol, for a number of reasons. To dispatch crippled big-game animals for one, and for another, the hunters carried guns. But a rifle is an awkward thing to carry on horseback in rough country. Its stock tends to hang up in deadfall snags and it rubs against the inside of your knee in an irritating fashion. So I left the rifle behind that day.

What surprised me most was the fact that China took me so close to the old boar grizzly when he knew full well it was nearby. His ears were up, but he rounded a corner in the trail with a will and there was the boar coming quickly towards us, swinging his head from side to side. I felt my hat rising above my ears on my thrilled hair-ends. China stopped in his tracks and would have grinned sheepishly if he knew how to. The bear stopped some twenty paces away. His humped back shone with silver guard hairs; his whole stance was focussed and alert.

At the time, I had been reading heavily in the realms of Plains Indian mythology. The words of a Bear Society song drifted through my head:

Hey-yah. My teeth are my weapons
Hey-yah. My claws are my weapons

A cold fever washed through every nerve in my body. I felt the horse's belly tighten and swell against my legs.

Speak to this bear
for he may know you
said a voice
in my frozen senses.

I began to talk softly, endearingly, you might say. China swivelled one ear back at me and kept the other one trained on the bear like a radar cone, to hear his reply, I suppose.

I think it was good luck that I met him without the temptations of a rifle to muddle the encounter. A person's whole manner of being in confronting a bear is different when he is armed: a bear is like a living lie-detector; it can smell what we are hiding in our sweat. Instead of thinking about the rifle, I had to think only about the bear and the horse under my reins. That sentient beast was a translator of emotions between bear and man. He would know before I did if the bear meant trouble, and what I had to do was hang on and go with the flow.

We took a step backwards and the bear reared in a blink on his hind legs, towering over everything around him, over the trees, big as they were, and the mountains themselves, and cleared his nostrils with a loud "huff." He stood there swaying his head, inclining it towards us in a formal acknowledgement of the gravity of this situation, peering at me in that near-sighted way that deludes you into thinking that bears can't see very well. He saw me quite clearly. It might have been a hornet buzzing by his nose that made him hook the air tentatively with one big paw. It might have been an invitation to parley for trail rights. I backed China up, still talking softly to both bear and horse, not making direct eye-contact with this keeper of the trails.

As we backed away, the bear dropped to all fours and stood still, gazing from side to side as if considering his options. The horse stopped of his own volition, watching the bear as if expecting some kind of entertainment. He had divined, through the bear's body language, that the crisis was past. With what sounded like a bemused grunt, the bear shambled, in an unhurried dignified way, up the hill among the pine trees. He waited there, peering down at me over his shoulder in an enquiring manner. I saw nothing threatening in his actions; he had given me the trail; but he was in the dominant position. So I urged China forward again though he was reluctant – but then he was always reluctant, except when returning to the hay-shed – up the trail, watching the bear without staring directly at him. At the first set of switchbacks, I stopped the horse. The grizzly had descended, crossed the trail to go down into the stream bottom, then continued on his way downhill and blinked out among the aspen boles.

Later that season, the old boar made a fatal mistake. Not aware of invisible boundaries drawn on maps, he wandered out onto provincial land, where he was shot by an outfitter who claimed the bear was hanging around his camp. The outfitter was prosecuted for killing the bear out of season. I learned later that the bear weighed out around eight hundred pounds, a good size for a mountain grizzly bear.

The bear's absence from the valley changed the whole set of my nervous system. Even my posture slumped. The valley had become altogether too safe; its wilderness character was an expression of the bear, which was the physical manifestation of what the word meant. Somebody had assassinated the Emperor of the Pristine. At night, by candlelight, I wrote:

Now the lake is tame, sullen
The only thing that moves in the wind
is Kakakew, the greasy raven

A few days later, lulled into carelessness by the sun's heat, I fell asleep momentarily in the saddle. China rounded a corner only to confront another terrifying sight – a spruce grouse, rearing up at least thirty centimetres from the ground. The grouse probably clucked worriedly like the species of chicken it is; China, threatened by this, panicked and shied violently to one side, half unseating me above a pile of rocks and broken snags before I snapped awake. The spruce grouse strutted off.

It occurred to me afterwards that China and the grizzly were old acquaintances from sharing the meadows along the creek. The horse had travelled that country with other masters before me. I believe that this bear, which had been close to me several times without my ever seeing it, knew the sound of my voice, knew the shape of the human form that went with that sound.

What was it he tried to tell me, as he stood up there on the trail? I think he was puzzled that I did not recognize he meant me no harm. I'm aware of the anthropomorphism I'm displaying here. This happens when you live alone in the mountains; you begin talking to the animals as if you were reverting to the time of legends, when men and animals all spoke the same language. There is such a language, a language of scent and sound and body movement for both people and bears, an inarticulate dialect that can be learned, but only through experience and by devoting much time, time which we never seem to have enough of in this frantic, high-speed era.

Once, we were more like bears, in that we lived at the same pace they lived at. Now we speed like arrows from birth to death, encapsulated in our technology, and can only snatch glimpses of that old life through the chinks in our artificial carapace. That's why the precious time we spend wandering in the backcountry is so important for our peace of mind. I think our sanity depends upon the idea that there is still wilderness for us to roam. But not only do we have to make room for bears and other wildlife, we have to make time for them, which in the end might prove the hardest sacrifice.

I brought my live-and-let-live attitude toward bears to the high-visitor-use area of Banff Park when we transferred there in 1972. The attitude was hard to maintain in the face of unpleasant reality, since I had arrived during a kind of peak period for bear-human conflict. Furthermore, we were living at the Bankhead Warden Station hard by the Cascade Fire Access Trail, which led into the heart of grizzly country. Down that road and through our yard trooped the bears, headed for their main food source, which was the Cascade Sanitary Landfill Site (read: garbage dump) just a few kilometres downhill.

Two million people went through Banff Park every year in the seventies. There were 8 million by 1997 and 4.7 million of those were considered park visitors. In high summer, minor conflicts between bears and people were almost an everyday occurrence, but some of the disputes got ugly. Biologist Steve Herrero lists five human injuries in Banff Park, including one death, due to grizzly bears from 1970 to 1973. Four of the injuries, including the death, were caused by grizzlies with a history of garbage and campground foraging. From 1972 to 1973, nine grizzlies were destroyed and one died accidently while being handled. In 1972 alone, thirty-one grizzlies and seventeen black bears were trapped and relocated in Banff Park. I was personally involved in some of those operations.

The most grievous shortcoming leading to this mayhem was a lack of political willpower in dealing with the one factor that caused the most conflict between people and bears, and that was the access bears had to human garbage and foodstuffs in Banff Park. The warden service had a mandate to go after sloppy businesses and residents, but when push came to shove, we didn't have the administrative and political support to force compliance, especially when dealing with big business. The park superintendents preferred we take the "educational" approach with restaurateurs and innkeepers in the park. In other words, they de-fanged us.

There is nothing sexy about garbage, it's true; nothing high tech in the greasy slump of it. It represents the plastic husks, the pulp and bone from which the profits have already been squeezed. Garbage belongs to the people who pick it up. What they did with it was their business, as far as the average restaurateur was concerned. To the park administrator, who must budget for its control, garbage represented a fiscal headache. It was expensive to collect, store, and dispose of. And if you hung on for a while, bears would go into hibernation – problem solved. Especially if your promotion came through for a transfer before next spring rolled around.

But to a grizzly bear, for whom fat is a narcotic, garbage was, and is, golden. I would watch them trooping down from the Cascade Valley and surrounding hills of Two Jack Lake to tunnel their way under or rip their way through the "bear-proof" fence into the sanitary landfill. Wilf Etherington, studying bears for the Canadian Wildlife Service, counted seven fully grown bears one moonlit night in 1973, rolling in unsanitary splendour through humanity's discards like furred Midases, snorting and moaning with pleasure. At a 1972 bear conference, a study group "rejected the idea that any further research was needed on the subject of bears and garbage. The problem is clear and the solutions are obvious." The solutions included bear-proof garbage containers and more frequent pick-up. In other regions, garbage was hauled away for disposal outside the national parks or incinerated, and bear problems declined as a result. One administrator mentioned the cost of such improvements. The reply, which proved to be somewhat prophetic, was that one successful lawsuit against Parks Canada would be a lot more expensive. In fact, the last garbage dump in the park would not be phased out until 1980, and bear-proof bins were slow in coming. A successful lawsuit against Parks Canada would eventually come (in 1988) but it would cause more public embarrassment than financial loss in the end.

The other problem was harder to solve – a problem of space: the politically difficult solution would have been to close off large areas of the park from human beings, which is contrary to the whole purpose of national parks. Something had to give, and that something was the bears themselves.

The war with the bears was a miserable affair that went against the grain of most park wardens, who saw themselves as protectors of wildlife. It was a sad, unequal fight and it preyed upon my conscience until the day in 1978 when I finally kicked over the federal trough and resigned to write full time.

When I look back at it now, the dark absurdities of the affray still stand out. Its surreal icon, as was the case with sling rescues, was the Jet Ranger helicopter, a grizzly bear pendant beneath it in a cargo net, blazoned on a sky shield of *bleu céleste*.

Perhaps you saw it, gentle reader, flying up the valley from the direction of the park townsite you had so eagerly left behind you. Slung beneath it was something large, hairy, and dangerous: the winged *Ursus arctos*, tongue lolling, eyes glazed from the effects of some arcane pharmaceutical. What is he thinking about, on that sky-journey, after the hell of being manhandled? That was the question that kept coming back to haunt you on your wilderness quest. Or perhaps you simply turned around and went to find another valley.

On occasion, the difference between a bear's life and death depended on whether Davies could fly on any given day. Bears could not be held indefinitely; they became too dehydrated and weak in the bear jail to be tranquilized for removal. If no warden was available to go out with him, Davies's choice was to fly the mission by himself or to know that the bear might be destroyed. Davies opted to fly by himself on some occasions. He would set the bear down at the release sight, and would get out and free it from the cargo net as the rotors idled overhead. Then he would move the machine away and watch to make sure the bear recovered from the tranquilizer before returning to base. Such dangerous extras were not part of his contract with Parks Canada. They were done because of his genuine concern for wildlife.

The majority of grizzly problems in the era I speak of centred on Lake Louise. Leading the control actions there was none other than Monte Rose of 3–3 ½ Couloir fame.

Trapping bears was a no-win situation for the warden service. Its mandate was to protect the park from the visitors and the visitors from the park, in accord with the overall goal of preserving the parks unimpaired for future generations. It is good to have impossible goals; it keeps you interested. But in a way, this meant that whatever wardens did with bears was wrong, depending on how you looked at it. If we destroyed a bear that we believed was hazardous to the public, we were destroying part of the gene pool for what was already a declining population. To make matters worse, it was usually the females with cubs that got into trouble with people; females only breed about every three years to begin with. But if we took a chance and let a "problem" bear go, we risked exposing some- one to injury from that animal in the future – not to mention a lawsuit for negligence against ourselves and our employer, the federal government.

It's hard on your head, this being wrong all the time, but Monte Rose, with his penchant for savouring cosmic ironies, tended to see the humorous side of the thankless bear business. From 1964, when he started as a warden, until 1981, when he retired, Monte Rose handled scores of bears, most of which were captured and relocated. With the bears came the stories, each bear being a personality who specialized in a particular kind of mayhem, from breaking into cabins, to mugging picnickers, to chasing cars in the campground, depending on its whim.

Chasing bears back in the seventies was exciting, if nothing else. "It was kind of like a war," Rose once told me. "I got so I looked forward to nightfall, when the action would begin."

In 1973, for instance, the Lake Louise wardens were absorbed with capturing a bear named Spassky. He was a huge boar, weighing in at over 1,000 pounds and named after the famous Russian chess master. Even on all fours this grizzly would tower over the top of a small car, yet he moved through the dark campground like a ghost whenever a warden came into sight.

"Everybody liked him," recalled Monte, during my visit to his prairie cabin in 1998. "He wasn't really aggressive at all – just big."

"What was he doing there?" I asked.

"Oh, nothin' much. Just break-and-enter, stealin'," drawled Monte. "He'd rip a tent up occasionally. Just kinda stick a toenail in the side of one and walk around it like a zipper – to see what was inside."

Spassky had a habit of going through a campground and flipping over the dumpster bins of garbage, picking daintily through the half ton of waste before moving on to the next one, chewing on a delicacy as he ambled along. This would be described by Rose as "Spassky making his move." When reports came in, Monte Rose et al. would rush to the campground with the tranquilizer gun, but Spassky, as if gifted with sixth sense, would have already slipped into the timber and loped off.

Culvert traps were set, but the big boar was far too smart to go in them. One night two young black bears were caught. They peered woefully out through the trap bars and moaned at Monte. "Spassky is just sacrificing a few of his pawns," he told them. "It's gonna be checkmate soon for the big guy. You tell him that, next time he puts you up a tree."

The black bears didn't always appreciate this lack of respect for their species. One of them tried to strangle the bear guy one night to teach him a lesson. Rose was up on top of a trap, peering down at a black bear through the inspection port when the end of his green uniform tie slipped through the hole. Bears are incredibly manipulative with their claws; they can peel a pine cone like a squirrel with tooth and claw. In a flash this one grabbed the tie in its claws and quickly pulled down on it, cutting off Rose's air in a second. His face was being dragged closer and closer to the porthole; he could see the black bear's tiny eyes gleaming up at him and he had time to realize what would happen if his face got close enough to one of those claws. But he got out his belt knife, unfolded the blade, cut the tie in half, then wrenched it off his neck so he could breathe. I think he probably changed to pull-off-type ties after that.

Many were the bait concoctions that wardens offered to the Spassky bear, without success. It took a bait sack full of Lobster Newburg, filched from the garbage cans behind the Chateau Lake Louise and tied lovingly to the trigger of the bear trap, to tempt Spassky finally into making that wrong move. Once captured, Spassky was flown out by Twirly to the Cyclone area, where he soon peeled off his radio collar and vanished from human ken.

Other wardens had told me "get Monte to tell you the story about Coolidge," and one day back in 1977, over a cup of coffee, he obliged.

"I was up at the Lake Louise campground, going after a couple of grizzly runts" (young of last year) "that had got separated from their ma. They were ripping their way through the campground – tent by tent – trying to find her.

"This was during the day, so pretty soon I had a whole gallery of spectators trailing after me." (Monte's seasonal warden kept them back out of harm's way.) "I felt just like Arnold Palmer. They were ooh-ing and ahh-ing and making little bleats and blats of fear whenever they spotted the bears.

"I had one dart loaded and shot the first bear in the bum. He made a few bites at his behind, and then went out like a light. The gallery kinda sucked its breath in as I aimed at the second bear. But the damn dart didn't inject when it hit the bear, as per usual, and I was roundly hissed at. So there I was, having to mix up another dose of Anectine. Knowing I had blown my birdie and was looking at being one over par on that hole.

"Anyway, while I'm loading the dart, the other bear comes over and starts wrestling with his pal. The crowd was suddenly very quiet. I looked up and saw the second bear had taken advantage of the situation. He had mounted the other bear and was humpin' away like a madman. The second dart was ready. It was going to be a case of coitus interruptus. Just as I'm drawing a bead, I heard this woman's voice comin' kinda shrill from the back of the crowd. 'Oh look,' she said, 'He's trying to revive his friend!'

"Well now, to get on to Coolidge. We no sooner got those two bears out of there, but we had to set the trap again for another one. There was this little man rushing around there that wanted to get into the thick of things. I just couldn't get him quieted down at all. 'Can I help, can I help?' he says. 'Is there something I can get? What can I do?'

"Well I didn't want to tell him what he could do. So I said, 'We could use a little honey – to bait the trap.' He rushed away and I was just congratulating myself on getting rid of him when he comes tearing back with a little teaspoon of honey stretched out in front of him.

"'Thanks very much,' I said. I made a great show of pouring this drop of honey over the bait sack. So there we were, trying to get the trap ready with people crawling all over thick as flies and any moment expecting one of them to stick their head in the trap and be decapitated by the gate. You had to watch 'em every moment. While this little man strutted up and down with his chest puffed out like a rooster. He seemed to have the crowd kinda mesmerized.

"Then he says to me: 'My name is COOLIDGE! Do that name ring a bell?'

"'Well, no,' I told him. 'At least it doesn't ring my bell.'

" 'Well,' he says, getting huffy, 'I'll have you know I am the great-grandson of the thirtieth president of the YOO-NITED STATES of AMURICA!' And he puffed out his chest again – just strutting up and down.

"I kinda scratched my head, at a loss for words. Then it came to me. Tell you what, I said: when we catch this bear, we'll name it Coolidge! Now how'll that be?

" 'Well,' he says. 'That would be just right.' "

As winged bears sailed out into the bush – at great expense in helicopter and man-hour time – visitation increased and the garbage problem grew in proportion. The employer felt the need to do something about garbage. It decided to back a film designed to educate tourists on the dangers of feeding bears and allowing them access to campers' garbage.

This initiative, which came from regional office in Calgary, as I recall, was not completely wrong-headed; tourists did need education on this issue, just as private park businesses and park managers in regional offices and in Ottawa needed educating on the garbage management issue. It was the way the filming was handled that raised my hackles. We got off to a bad start when a cameraman showed up one day and got into the thick of a bear-tranquilizing operation I was working on in Banff townsite. Local managers had not bothered to inform us peons about the film project.

We were using Anectine (succinylcholine chloride) in those days. It is an extremely dangerous depressant of the respiratory system and we were constantly concerned about the risk of hitting each other, or an innocent bystander, with one of those darts; there was basically no antidote short of an iron lung. The cameraman was told to get the hell out of the way, and stay out. A black bear cub died during that operation, which was extremely upsetting, but not unlikely given the nature of the drug. Nobody wants to kill a bear to begin with, and a cub is about the most lovable critter in creation.

The film project had a high priority with the employer, and I had my tail chewed on by the area manager for being rude to the cameraman. My partner and I were ordered to haul the sow and the cubs up the Cascade Fire Access Trail and then re-tranquilize them so that the cameraman could record the action. Our orders were to co-operate fully with Bill Schmalz, the filmmaker.

The sow and the two surviving cubs were stressed out, hungry, and dehydrated, and the sixty-kilometre trip up the road to Scotch Camp was not going to help them. I explained (either to Bill Schmalz or his assistant), as diplomatically as possible, that we would not be tranking bears in that condition, orders or no orders. I wasn't going to risk killing another bear unnecessarily. As I recall, he agreed with my decision. I believe he filmed the bears on location while Scott Ward and I released them from the trap.

I remember thinking I was working for an organization whose management was as out of touch with reality as a tranquilized bear.

I was glad to go out on backcountry shifts, to step back into the past through the magic of the backcountry world that had made me want to be a warden in the first place. One man who I occasionally saw on my trips out to the Panther River was Canadian Wildlife Service technician Wilf Etherington, who was engaged in a bear-management study in the mountain parks, directed by biologist Laszlo Retfalvi. We thought of Wilf back then as a seasoned wildlife technician, due to his age (fifty-two). I was surprised to later learn that in fact he had only recently completed a degree in zoology after a career as a pharmacist in Edmonton. With his daughters Beverly and Carol both launched on professional careers, he had talked things over with his wife, Sheila, and decided to go back to school and do what he had always wanted to do – become a zoologist. He was a likable, good-natured man with a deep love of wildlife, doing work that he enjoyed doing. I think he had a soft spot for bears. I remember the tears in his eyes as he stood over a dead grizzly bear sow and her three cubs down at the Canadian Wildlife Service (CWS) lab in Banff one day that summer. I was told that he wouldn't carry a firearm while working around trapped or tranquilized animals. That was also the policy of Laszlo Retfalvi.

I saw Etherington on September 5, 1973. He was cooking a pot of soup over a Primus stove near a stream on the old Cascade road, and we talked briefly about his work before I continued on to Windy Cabin. I remember how cheerful and enthusiastic he was about studying bears in such a beautiful landscape.

On or about September 23, 1973, Lake Louise wardens trapped a large grizzly bear that had broken into a cabin at a bungalow camp. The bear was a three-time loser that had obtained garbage before, though it had not offended anywhere else, or injured a person. Being opportunistic by nature, the bear had broken into a building this time – just exploring – and scored big, finding the groceries that were being stored there over the winter. The bear, a 527-pound male grizzly, was later reported as being "in good physical condition except for worn teeth and a broken canine tooth. One eye pupil was white and the bear may have been blind in that eye." The bear trashed the kitchen and dragged foodstuffs all over the place. Etherington noted that park administrators in Banff ordered Monte Rose to get the bear out of the area and stop the destruction of private property.

There seems to have been some debate at the time about whether to destroy this bear or relocate it. Ultimately, it was held for two days in a trap, pending relocation, a decision that was criticized later by Retfalvi, since it put undue stress on the animal.

Bill Schmalz heard about the capture of this bear and saw it as an opportunity to film a grizzly in a release operation, perhaps for the last time that season.

Etherington was on hand September 25 to tranquilize the bear, since he kept tabs on events at Lake Louise. He and Monte Rose used to make friendly bets with each other on the weights of all bears captured. Etherington was a very careful man, according to his daughter Beverly Kemsley, a physician who apprenticed in pharmacology with her father for twelve months. His character shows in the clear, meticulous handwriting in his 1973 field notebook, which contains observations on radio-collared bears and lists of plant species in his study plots. The last entry in his notebook reads: "Sept 25/73 L. Louise Grizzly 1241" (the time) "Administer 200 Mgm Sernylan 125 Mgm Sparine."

Sernylan (phencyclidine hydrochloride) was an immobilizing agent, a type of disassociative anaesthetic. Sparine was a tranquilizer, useful in preventing convulsions. These were new drugs to the warden service; only CWS personnel were licensed to use Sernylan. Etherington wished to observe the effects of the chemicals on a bear as it recovered use of its limbs in a remote release setting.

Now the story gets complicated.

Bill Schmalz told me (1999) that he had arranged with the pilot to fly him in with the bear, but Wilf Etherington wanted to go along with him.

Laszlo Retfalvi, on the other hand (1999) believed that it was Wilf who had arranged to go in, to observe the bear recovering from the drug, and that he allowed Schmalz to come along "out of the goodness of his heart," and contrary to Retfalvi's instructions regarding dealings with the filmmaker. Retfalvi was opposed to helping Schmalz obtain close-up shots of grizzly bears. He thought this sent the wrong message to the public. However, Beverly Kemsley told me that her father "volunteered to go along to help with the film project." Etherington probably had mixed motives. He had scientific data to record, but no doubt he was seeing in his mind's eye the sow and three cubs of earlier that season, lying dead on the floor of the wildlife lab in Banff. If the film could increase public awareness, perhaps fewer bears would wind up dead due to confrontations with humans.

At any rate, the two men were cleared to so, since one was a scientist doing work in the park for a sister agency, and the other a park contractor. Based on my experience with CWS, I think that, from a warden's point of view back then, Etherington would have been seen as being in control of the release operation. Some of my colleagues argued afterwards that a warden with a rifle should have been present. But Beverly Kemsley understood there was no warden available on the day in question, due to other work that had to be dealt with. Also, strange as it seems now, there was no clear policy on carrying firearms during bear-release operations at the time. It depended on the hazards of the particular situation and the help available, because managing a gun safely while working at close quarters with other people takes one person's total concentration. It was more a matter of personal discretion. In Etherington's case, guns and hunting were not a part of his life, and his boss maintained: "If it takes a gun to approach a bear, then it's not worth it. It's too dangerous for the bear and for the person."

In any case, pilot Jim Davies told me he had released bears before without a weapon being present. However, he had never before released one under the conditions that were about to unfold.

At 2:20 P.M. Davies reached the release point at the head of Totem Creek near the north boundary of the park, a rugged, inhospitable place for people that precluded human contact with the bear. Etherington and Schmalz apparently picked the release site, an open alpine basin, more for its photographic potential than safety, according to an investigation conducted by Chief Warden A. S. Anderson. Perhaps it would have been safe enough if they had stayed close to the helicopter. Davies set the bear down, then landed on a bench about ninety metres away and eighteen metres higher while Etherington rolled the bear out of the net. (Nowadays, the net is constructed so the bear can be released without pilot or crew leaving the machine.)

The two men set up their equipment about sixty metres from the bear and ninety metres from the helicopter.

Etherington tape-recorded his comments on the operation and filmed the bear with an eight-millimetre camera. Bill Schmalz likewise filmed events. By 3:00 P.M., the bear seemed to be aware of their presence, though it could not control its limbs and move away. From the bear's point of view, the men watching were aggressors who it wished to get away from. Nobody knows what goes through a bear's head, but one of the things going through this bear's brain were molecules of "angel dust," which is what Sernylan was known as when it made its way on to the street; it is a powerful hallucinogen in human beings. It is not clear just what effect, if any, the drug has on a bear's mind, but it was a safer, more humane drug to use on bears than Anectine.

At 4:45, the bear managed to get up and wander down the slope. The observers moved after it; now they were 118 metres from the helicopter and out of sight from it.

At the helicopter, Jim Davies checked his watch again, feeling uneasy. He had observed far more drugged bears than either of his passengers and he had never seen anyone pursuing a drugged bear for such a long period of time, and unarmed. As a civilian pilot, however, it was not up to Davies to question a professional like Wilf Etherington. As a wildlife photographer, Bill Schmalz was also assumed to be a good judge of animal behaviour.

Schmalz, on the other hand, was critical of Davies for being too noisy, leaving his PA system on to receive radio calls and announcing to them on the PA when he had to leave the area temporarily, while he and Etherington were "trying to hang low, trying to tune in to the bear." It seems the real problem here was a lack of walkie-talkies to communicate between helicopter and photographers.

At 5:00, Davies flew out over Totem Creek Pass to make radio contact with the warden dispatcher, as required. On the ground, Etherington noticed that the sound of the helicopter had agitated the bear, which pivoted around after the machine although it could not control its hindquarters. In hindsight, Schmalz thought that they should not have ignored this danger signal. At this time, the two men were about forty-six metres from the bear. Davies flew back in, and was surprised to see how close they had come. He flew low over the bear "to try and find out if it was still drugged," as he put it to me. The bear immediately charged after the helicopter, charged again when he made another pass, and showed "very good mobility," according to the investigator's report. Etherington actually filmed the bear chasing the helicopter.

After discussing the bear's condition, Schmalz and Etherington next moved up to within twenty-eight metres (ninety-two feet) of this unnaturally stressed bear that they had been filming and observing for four and a half hours, according to the report. However, Bill Schmalz told me this figure of ninety-two feet was "very misleading." Because of a rocky buttress between them and the bear, the bear could not come at them in a ninety-two-foot charge, but would have to go downslope some fifty yards (forty-five metres) then fifty yards upslope to get at them.

Warden Rick Langshaw, who knew Etherington, believes it was out of character for him to press the bear that closely. For his part, Schmalz thinks they talked it over before they decided to move up. "We wanted to get [film] the bear leaving the area." That was an important scene in the film.

Photographers of bears, it seems to me, are like war correspondents. It's as if their motto came from Robert Capa: "If your pictures aren't good enough, you aren't close enough." Some full-frame close-ups of bears' faces have been found in the cameras of photographers who were attacked by bears. Laszlo Retfalvi (who once taught Schmalz zoology and considers him to be a very good wildlife photographer) remembers a frame like that in Schmalz's film. Etherington was filming the bear himself with an eight-millimetre camera; perhaps it was partly the spell of the rangefinder that overcame this normally careful man's judgement of the risk.

On the slope above them, Davies, alarmed by what was going on, hurried down on foot to check on the photographers. He arrived just in time to see the bear, below him, break from cover in a shambling run to the right of the camera position. Schmalz and Etherington began to withdraw, but moving too slowly to suit Davies. Schmalz said they didn't see it as a real charge until the bear veered uphill and came towards them. Thinking back, he suggested that perhaps a down-draft of air had carried their scent to the animal, causing it to turn towards them and charge. Finally they started running uphill through a draw to the bench above, from where Davies watched.

Bill Schmalz, carrying his camera and tripod, made it up first and turned to the left with Etherington about ten feet behind him. The bear closed on Etherington. "Drop your pack!" yelled Davies, and Etherington complied instantly. The bear ignored the offer as Etherington made it up the draw and broke to his right, running more on the level now.

Warden Rick Langshaw, who would arrive on the scene after the attack, believed the bear went after Wilf because he happened to turn on the side of its one good eye. "Otherwise," he told me, "it might have just as easily chased the other guy." At any rate, the bear was focussed on Etherington and it followed him across the bench. Etherington turned, his hands outstretched towards the bear as if to ward it off, then ran back down the slope. The bear hesitated for a beat or two, as if reconsidering, then went down the slope after Etherington. Bill Schmalz ran back towards where Etherington had disappeared to try and assist him. He heard the hapless biologist shout "No" as the bear closed on him.

Davies had already turned to dash for the only weapon they had, which was the helicopter.

At his home in Banff in 1998, Davies stared pensively out over the Bow Valley, recalling the Totem Creek fiasco for me, an event that Etherington's daughter Beverly described, most accurately, as "a cascade of errors ending in tragedy."

"I didn't even bother to put the seat belt on," he told me, his face grim at the memory. "Normally you bring the engine up to flight-idle slowly, watching the temperature all the time. Then you wait a moment for the battery to recharge before you take off. When you do an emergency start you skip right through all that."

"That must have been dangerous."

"Well, the trouble is, if you bring it up too quickly, you can flood the engine and not start at all. Another twenty seconds would have made all the difference," he added, ruefully.

But it was twenty seconds he could not capture. And I couldn't help wondering what might have happened to Bill Schmalz if

Davies had stalled the engine. He lifted the Jet Ranger up and quickly slipped it over the bluff. Schmalz, about six metres from the bear and above it, was yelling and throwing rocks at it, trying to drive it away from Etherington. "I saw blood," he recalled. "I was in shock, kind of flipping out." Indeed, he was fortunate that the bear did not come after him.

Etherington had apparently fallen down at the bottom of the slope. But Laszlo Retfalvi suspects that the bear may have swatted Etherington on the head at this point and knocked him down, since his injuries included a broken neck. The blow would have stunned him or knocked him out. The bear delivered a lethal bite to Etherington's skull, according to Langshaw, who had time to look closely at the injury after the attack. He remembers very clearly the damage done and assured me, "Wilf would have died instantly."

Davies brought the ship in until he was practically on top of the bear, determined to drive it away from Etherington. The bear turned and went after this noisy enemy, going down through the krummholz for about 135 metres, on its hind legs at times, trying to reach up and swat the machine out of the sky.

"The bear was so angry at the helicopter," Schmalz told me. Schmalz then ran down to Etherington, dragged him off the slope onto flatter terrain to which Davies returned, landing beside him. "I couldn't hold the door back there and load Wilf by myself," Schmalz recalled. It was obvious that Etherington was dead. Davies kept his eye on the bear and saw it charging back up the slope. "Leave him! Get in, get in!" he yelled. Schmalz quickly eased Etherington's body back down and rolled into the machine, and Davies lifted it up. He turned downslope towards the bear, intercepted it, drove it far down the mountain again, away from Etherington. He flew back and hovered closely over Etherington's body for a moment, but there was no doubting that the man was dead. Then he flew out to the highway to radio for help and obtain more fuel.

Davies had flown many rescue missions by 1973 and had seen more than his share of human fatalities. But he knew this smiling man, Wilf Etherington. This death produced such a state of real shock that he had to spend a few minutes trying to calm his trembling body before he could fly back in again.

Monte Rose with Warden Rick Langshaw flew in with him, while Schmalz stayed behind to give the details to the RCMP. Etherington's body had not been disturbed. Langshaw jumped out with a rifle in hand to guard the body, deeply shocked at what he saw. Etherington had trained him in tranquilization procedures early that summer and he had come to know and like this kindly naturalist. Etherington still had his small tape recorder clutched in his hand.

Rose and Davies located the bear where Davies had left it. It had taken refuge in a thicket, but now it charged out and jumped up at the helicopter. Rose would not risk having this bear return to Lake Louise or any other place where it might encounter humans. "I didn't like killing animals," said Monte, recalling the incident. "But it was something you had to do at times. The old bear was probably trying to figure out what the hell had happened." Rose leaned out the open door with the rifle, put his sights on its heart and squeezed the trigger.

Wilfred Etherington was the head of a very close-knit family. "When he died," his daughter Beverly told me, "it was total devastation for us. We really lost our compass when we lost our father. . . . There isn't a day goes by when I don't think about him. At family gatherings, there is always that sadness because he isn't there.

"My mother used to love to go into the mountains with him. She doesn't like to go hiking there any more."

In his field notebook that summer, Wilf had recorded an incident in which a Calgary man was treed by a bear that he had come on suddenly. The man felt grizzly bears should not be allowed in national parks. Etherington dutifully recorded his statements. Underneath them he had pasted a stamp reading "Save Our Parks." On the bottom of the stamp he had pencilled in one word: "Amen."

Chief Warden A. S. Anderson, reporting on the Totem Creek

incident, listed a number of "minor contributing factors" that might have led to the charge, such as the fact the bear had been "handled" three times, that it was antagonized by the helicopter, which it may have associated with previous handlings, and possibly by the removal of a tooth for aging purposes (while it was tranquilized) and the two days confined in the live trap. He did mention that one "minor factor" was "the build-up of tolerance to – or rather, loss of natural intolerance of – people that this bear built up in past years, in a dump situation where numerous visitors come in close proximity. . . ." He concluded that the "major contributing factor" that resulted in the bear charging was the judgement shown by the two men involved in approaching the bear too closely. He pointed out that Etherington knew the bear's history and both men had seen the warning signs the bear displayed in charging at the helicopter.

His report concluded with a decision that in the future a warden armed with a rifle would be present when bears were released, or when it was necessary for any outside agencies to work in close proximity to bears. I can confirm that this was the policy followed afterwards.

Schmalz, though deeply shaken by the tragedy, carried on and completed the film for Parks Canada.

I believe both Schmalz and Etherington thought they were in control of the situation that day on Totem Creek, though in fact they had surrendered control to the bear by moving too close to that powerful animal when it was unnaturally stressed and fearful. A grizzly bear can outrun a horse over the short haul. It can run straight up a steep slope for three hundred metres, let alone for ninety, and this has always to be remembered by those who approach bears.

But the "cascade of errors" that killed Wilf Etherington began long before the Totem Creek bear was captured. One thing was missing from Anderson's report and it's the most obvious thing of all to me. So let me add it now as my unofficial, uninvited addendum after all these years, after all the bitter lessons yet to come. If garbage and human foodstuffs had been properly stored and disposed of in

Banff National Park prior to 1973, more grizzly bears would have lived out their lives without dying at the hands of their protectors. It seems possible that fewer people would have been injured by bears in that decade in Banff Park, and Wilf Etherington would not have made his tragic mistake and died in the jaws of a beast that he only wanted to help survive.

Yet when it came to garbage management, the handmaiden approach towards enforcement continued for many years after the Totem Creek tragedy. It would finally come to a head in 1979, a year after I resigned my position. That spring, Warden Eric Langshaw repeatedly warned Canadian Pacific Hotels and Banff Park management about a hazardous garbage-storage situation at Chateau Lake Louise. There were fourteen problem-bear incidents there by July 10. He wanted to lay charges; his supervisors wanted him to "wait and see" it the hotelier would co-operate with him. But Langshaw had seen firsthand what a grizzly bear could do to a human being. Aided by the RCMP, he was finally forced to shoot a garbage-habituated grizzly bear that had previously cornered Chateau staff. He then pressed charges, successfully, against CP Hotels, contrary to the instructions of the park superintendent, only to be charged with insubordination by the chief park warden. After a public outcry, abetted by an article I wrote for a national magazine, this threat was rescinded.

But the message given to the warden service was clear. As a former colleague would sum it up: "It just goes to show that if you would only wait and see, you'd never get into trouble with the administration."

In 1980, Parks Canada spent $800,000 on a garbage-management program that included shutting down the Banff Park landfill site and trucking all garbage out of the park for disposal. This proved to be a tremendous improvement in the long run, but in the short run, unfortunately, it resulted in some bears moving closer to the town to forage for calories. Despite improvements, the years of poor garbage control and "wait and see" enforcement climaxed that

September in the notorious Whiskey Creek maul-a-thon right on the edge of the townsite. Four people were beaten up by a large garbage-habituated grizzly that was guarding its food supply – garbage – from interlopers. One of them later died as a result of his injuries. One of the victims, a Swiss national, successfully sued Parks Canada for negligence and was awarded the sum of $112,000. After Whiskey Creek the real crackdown came, followed at long last by the installation of bear-proof garbage containers.

There are still some authorities in jurisdictions in western Canada who could save themselves some misery by heeding the hard lessons learned in Banff National Park. As I write this, bear-proof garbage containers are still not a fixture in many parts of grizzly country.

One more thing: there are many instances of people who have spent their careers "developing" wild lands into oblivion who then have wild mountains named after them. I think Parks Canada should honour Wilf Etherington's memory by urging the Canadian Permanent Committee on Geographical Names to put his name on a peak or a stream in the vicinity of Totem Creek. They were quick in 1973 to point out his one and only error, which he made while trying to help Parks Canada complete a high priority project: after all these years, it's not too late to honour his love of national parks, his dedication to wildlife preservation, and his gentle, generous spirit.

CHAPTER ELEVEN

A Horse Named Candy

Not many horses live to the age of forty; Candy, a sway-backed white mare of uncertain breed, was already twenty-two years of age when I first made her acquaintance. She was selling for only $400. The price was based on the price of horse meat in that year of 1982 – forty cents a pound, as I recall. Her owner, rancher John Sekella, had himself saved her once from the canners but now he had more horses than he needed. You might say that it was in her best interests to throw in her lot with the Marty family instead. Unless somebody bought her soon, she was headed for the abattoir.

It was a pleasant June morning in the high foothills of the Rocky Mountains, though snow still clung to the ledges of the Livingstone Range, which towers up from the valley floor a few kilometres west of our south Alberta home near Pincher Creek. I was half inclined to buy the old cow pony. I had ridden her a few days earlier, herding some cattle with my neighbours and not expecting much action: I got plenty. When it came to herding cows, the little horse could turn on a dime, and when we had ridden into the forest, she had tried to chase down a wandering moose – just for the sheer hell of it, it seemed. There was still life in that middle-aged nag, I reasoned; she might make a good horse for our boys to ride.

I was inspecting her feet, checking for thin horn and other defects. Clamping a front hoof between my knees, I cleaned out the dirt around the frog with a hoof pick. Candy, looking sleepy, leaned some of her 1,000 pounds of weight on me – a bad habit she had – and turned her head to sniff curiously at the back of my neck.

"Some people would say I was nuts to think of buying you, considering your age," I told her. (I am the kind of guy who talks to horses; I make no apologies for that.)

Candy snorted, apparently offended by such talk, and sniffed with interest down my back.

"So tell me, old mare. What's your advice? Are you worth four hundred bucks?"

Now here was a coincidence. There came a sudden tug at my hip where my wallet protruded from a back pocket. I glanced back over my shoulder and burst out laughing, dropping the hoof. There stood Candy with my billfold gripped in her front teeth. I chose to take it as a sign; the horse wanted me to assume title.

Candy dropped the wallet. "Alright," I said, grinning. "I'll talk to John."

Candy was a smallish horse, about thirteen hands high, stocky and undistinguished in a region noted for its taller, powerful quarter horses used in ranch work, but in that diminutive body there beat a mighty heart. She was named after her penchant for eating anything sweet, from jujubes to apples. Her origins were a mystery, but it was said that she had been foaled on the Blackfoot reservation. In fact she looked like a cayuse, an Indian horse descended from those brought to North America originally with the conquistadores, but she seemed to have a touch of the Morgan breed in her chunky body.

There was a bonus attached to buying Candy: she came with a partner, Freckles, a rangy, wall-eyed Appaloosa gelding that John said he would loan us because the horse needed some exercise, and because a horse is a herd animal; it will not stay with you long without another equine to keep it company.

Candy was the first of several horses we would purchase after buying the homestead of an old ranch once known as the PN Bar, after its brand. Myrna and I were new to horse ownership, but not to riding. I had spent many seasons in the saddle patrolling the mountain backcountry during my days as a federal park warden in the mountain national parks, and Myrna sometimes rode with me until our sons came along.

In 1978 I resigned my position to pursue a writing career, and the pace of life became more hectic in the urbanized setting of Canmore, Alberta, where we had settled. Canmore grew far too fast to suit us. When we moved to these isolated foothills, we expected our lives to slow down. But Myrna found herself driving sixty miles a day to a job in Pincher Creek, and I myself was often on the road pursuing interview subjects as a journalist. Life was going by too quickly, but we had to earn a living.

In the barn was an old Swiss bell, its origins unknown, which I had unearthed one day while digging a post hole. In the old days, our warden outfit had always included a bossy lead mare known as the bell mare – the leader of the herd, the one that the other horses would never leave. The Swiss bell reminded me of the days when Myrna patrolled with me at Tonquin Valley. I would hobble the horses and turn them out to graze, hoping they would not pull out on us and head for the barns in town. The mellow, brassy note of the bell, fading on the breeze, then growing near again, would lull us to sleep. I don't think Myrna or I have ever lived quite as fully from one minute to the next as we did in those horseback days in Jasper Park, when life unrolled at the speed of a horse's walk, and never went faster than a brief gallop over an alpine meadow.

The first thing I did after counting out the four hundred dollars in John Sekella's calloused hand was to hang the old bell around Candy's neck. That night its one note echoed over the hills above the house as we stood in the dark meadow together, listening; it was like being in the backcountry once more. "You smell like a horse again," said Myrna.

"Is that good?"

"That's very good."

Myrna and I wanted our boys, Paul (age ten) and Nathan (seven), to enjoy horses as we did. Of course, what is needed for an equestrian school is a very safe and reliable mount. Paul and Nathan were fearless little rascals who needed no urging. Most days the boys didn't bother waiting for my help in haltering the horses. They would lure them into the corral with a pail of oats, then, tugging mightily together, swing the pole gate shut. Now, Candy was a stubbornly independent cuss, at least until you got her saddled. As a rule, she did not encourage adults to approach her with a halter in their hands, sometimes shaking her head vigorously to indicate her disapproval. She approved of children, but loved to tease them by moving her head around while they tried to get the halter over her ears. Freckles, however, loathed all humans great and small and simply ran off when the kids approached him.

If the cagey old plugs would not allow themselves to be caught, there were other methods. The old log stable was gradually sinking into the ground; its roof was easy for boys to climb. Once on the roof, a boy waited for a horse to walk under him, then jumped onto its back with a triumphant whoop and grabbed a hand full of mane in lieu of a halter rope. This dangerous business went on for a while before I caught them at it. Meanwhile, they learned that this technique was not wise to try on Freckles. The first time Nathan jumped on the old gelding's back, he might as well have jumped onto a trampoline; with one buck, Freckles sent him flying into the dust. "Boys," I warned them, "you will not jump off that roof again!" and I explained why it was dangerous to both horse and rider. The boys were willing to compromise: they used the top bar of the corral as a mounting block instead.

Candy, however, hardly responded to their ambush except to

salute a kid's sudden arrival by breaking wind, loudly, before shuffling into a reluctant trot around the corral. If they fell off the horse at this point, it was because they were laughing too hard to hold on.

We became used to the sight of Candy trotting across the meadow in front of the house with two noisy kids on her back – who sometimes rode standing, like circus riders. When friends came to visit, the action picked up. On one occasion we were relaxing outside when Candy trotted into view. There were four kids on her back, two boys facing forward, two girls facing backwards and giggling. Another child, a small boy, clung around her neck like a monkey. A visiting poodle dog had her tail in its teeth and was being skidded across the damp meadow as if on water skis. A less patient horse might have kicked the poodle into oblivion. I heard Nathan shout "Yah – giddy-up!" Hampered by the monkey, Candy shambled into a half-hearted trot; the way led right through a shallow rainwater pond where the dog submerged and let go the tail. The monkey, startled at the spray of cold water, lost his grip with an indignant shout and a loud splash, followed by the rest of the crew. Candy stopped instantly to avoid stepping on her charges, who were soon embroiled in a mud-wrestling match right under her belly. Candy was the most fun babysitter the boys ever had.

Within a few months, the boys could ride with a nonchalant balance, bareback, and at the gallop. But where Candy was kind and forgiving with youngsters, Freckles was a stubborn and reluctant mount; he knew how to nurse a grudge.

One day a few years forward in time, a mink burrowed into the chicken pen and slaughtered a dozen of our hens. The bodies, partly incinerated, were piled in a barrel in the corral awaiting further cremation, when an adolescent Nathan came trotting by on Candy. Freckles was standing nearby, apparently communing with a cowbird at his feet. Nathan swears the horse had a sinister look in his eyes. As he rode past the barrel, Freckles jerked his head up, little Candy darted underneath, and Freckles clothes-lined Nathan across the chest with his big head, knocking the boy off Candy's back, right into the barrel of well-ripened chickens, seat first. Freckles and Candy watched with interest as the U-shaped Nathan struggled to free himself from his nauseating lodgement.

Freckles's role in the schooling was to teach us all not to take a horse for granted. One day he bolted while carrying Nathan, and after that I forbade the boys to take him on the trail. I made a serious error one day with Freckles when I allowed a visiting teenager, who I thought to be experienced, to ride him. Freckles started out calm enough, but a few minutes later, he took the bit in his teeth and took off, drumming the earth with his hooves. Jim was in trouble, unable to rein the horse in, but Paul shot after him in a flash, urging Candy forward with a speed I had never seen before. They went tearing over a narrow cattle trail along the slope of a 1,800-metre-high ridge that rises above our house. Up ahead there was a barbed wire cross fence: Freckles seemed crazy enough to run right into it. In the distance. I heard Paul's shouts: "Hang on, hang on to the horn!"

"Get in front of him!" I shouted. "Uphill – pass uphill!" I feared a terrible fall if he tried to turn the horse downhill at that speed. Paul could not hear me, but Candy knew what was required; she darted uphill where a deer trail joined the cattle path and passed Freckles without any direction from Paul. She shot down in front of the gelding again, causing him to suddenly slacken speed and then stop. Paul caught the reins and held the horse while I came running up on foot.

Freckles, looking sulky, stood staring obliquely over the valley, catching his breath; Jim's face was white as a ghost. Candy's blood was up, her eyes were bright with excitement; she loved a good hard run. She allowed me to bestow a grateful hug around her neck. But for her intelligence and speed, the outcome might have been far worse. Jim finished the ride on Candy's more tolerant back.

As the days grew short and autumn came on, I started putting up firewood for the winter. One day I was working – like a horse – dragging heavy logs through the snowy forest to the woodpile, when

I heard a merry-sounding whinny and saw Candy peering over the fence and watching me, her ears perked up. The horse was trying to tell me something, and I suddenly knew what it was. It had never occurred to me that this cow pony was drivable – trained to work as a draft horse that is – but a horse of her age might very well have had some experience that way.

I had noted some old harnesses hanging in the barn. Looking closer, I found a skid harness hanging there complete with collar and tugs to attach to a logging chain. I had used such rigging before as a park warden. "Well," I muttered to myself, "let's see what the old girl knows about this."

Candy was easy to catch for once. Sure enough, some previous owner had trained her to drive, for she stood patiently while I adjusted the straps to fit her frame, turning her head to watch my movements as if in supervision.

She waited, breath steaming in the cold air, while I chained her up to the first log. She gave her head a shake, eager to begin and stepped forward at a flick of the long reins, and pulled with a will, dragging the log easily along the snow-covered path to the woodpile. Soon she was dragging two logs at a time, and the work fairly flew along. At last there was only one log left, a puny thing that a boy could have dragged. I chained her up to it anyway, but to my astonishment, she balked, and would not drag it despite all my urging. The log was too small; it was beneath her dignity to haul a mere stick. When I unhooked her and picked one end of it up to haul it, she followed along behind me, snorting with satisfaction, prancing through the snow as if in a victory dance.

As the snow piled up around the house that winter, drifting snow closed the roads several times. But the stove crackled day and night with no shortage of fuel, thanks to Candy. Time had finally slowed down for our family, ranged around the fire with good books to read. We were living in an older era, the era of horsepower, while in the barn the horses, safe from the cold air outside, smelled the summer again in the hay we had put up for them.

We were always short of money in those days, but that winter the land provided for us. I shot a fat deer near Christmastime that provided us with enough venison to get by for a while. It was Candy, plunging through the drifts, who dragged it home for me on the end of a lariat rope well after dark. Northern lights danced over the pine-covered ridges. I huddled in the saddle, grateful for the warmth of the horse on my cold, wet knees. Breathing hard, she forged an arrow-straight path through the night. In a window far below us, the lights from our Christmas tree were like Japanese lanterns guiding us homeward through a world of snow.

As time passed, the boys grew into young men, until the day came when Myrna and I rode the trails alone as we had done in the early days of our marriage. Freckles had returned to John's ranch to look for fresh victims. Myrna rode a young brown mare named Tasha now, and Candy, who had once ruled Freckles every move in the paddock, was now subordinate to the bigger, more powerful female. Despite Tasha's bullying with tooth and even the odd kick to get priority over the forage, the two were inseparable friends.

As the 1980s came to a close, Candy's age was beginning to tell on her. She had injured one eye on a stick and gone partly blind in it; her hearing was gradually fading. Then on a day in 1991, she fell down while I was walking her on a safe, flat road. The will to snap those short little cannon bones forward was still as strong at thirty-two as it had been at twenty-two, but her career as a saddle horse was over.

"You'll probably want to ship her off to the plant," suggested our kindly neighbour, Steve Sekella, over coffee one day.

Myrna was aghast at the thought. "After all she's done for us? No way!"

Like Myrna, I could not stand the thought of Candy waiting in line at the door to the killing floor, humane as the final act there might be.

The winter of 1995 seemed particularly hard on Candy. Her teeth were sound, her appetite was excellent, but despite all the oats and hay I heaped on her, her ribs were showing by spring. Now we questioned our resolve to let her "reach her own conclusions."

"Let her have the summer," said Myrna sadly. "I don't think she's feeling weak. She still gallops after Tasha at times."

That summer was the wettest in years, bringing a once-in-a-century flood on the Oldman River on June 6. July saw water streaming everywhere and new springs erupting all over the place. Myrna stepped out on the deck on the morning of the twentieth to greet a very chilly dawn, a steaming cup of coffee in hand, as was her custom. Her brown mare was away, being romanced by a local stud horse. There was a strange patch of white at the far gate of the corral. Myrna hurried over and beheld a desperate sight: Candy was bogged down right up to her withers in a brand new sinkhole we had not seen before. The old mare greeted her with a weak whinny, unable to move anything but her ears. Hearing Myrna call my name I rushed out, wearing a velour bathrobe and rubber boots and nothing else. Candy groaned and tried to move her nostrils out of the muck, which threatened to suffocate her.

I floundered in to help her: my boots filled with freezing muck, my bathrobe turned into a sponge as I held the mare's head up. It would have been hilarious if it hadn't been so dangerous.

Quickly, Myrna collected some boards for me to kneel on to avoid sinking myself. I could feel Candy relax, letting me take some weight off her neck. "You were always good at that," I told her. "Don't worry, old girl, we'll get you out."

Then, while Myrna worked a halter around Candy's ears, I tried to shovel some muck away from the legs.

"Okay, Candy – c'mon girl!" Myrna pulled on the halter rope and Candy struggled furiously for a moment to move her legs, then sank back again, exhausted.

"It's no good, honey. Her legs are probably completely numb. Go call Steve and John. Ask Steve to bring his tractor!"

"Do you think she'll make it?"

"Absolutely. She's got a heart like a stove." I kept my misgivings to myself, yet I was encouraged by the mare's steady heartbeat. She had been in bad fixes before, and her humans had always got her out of them.

I was blue with cold and trembling like a leaf as we waited. Soon Myrna relieved me and I had a chance to get some clothes on. The tractor rumbled into the yard. John drove in next in his pickup. Steve took one look, and quickly backed into position, then threw me a rope end. "Work it around under her tail, and under her brisket. We'll have to pull her out sideways."

The tractor rumbled forward and the watery grave made an ugly, sucking noise as the white horse, covered in mud, came sliding free. She made an anguished groan, the like I had never heard from a horse before, then struggled to stand, but could not get her feet under her. We propped her neck up on some hay bales while she lay there, then we started drying her with rags and rubbing her stiffened joints.

John shook his head as he watched, and offered to put the horse out of her misery and save me the grief. "She'll never get up again," he declared. "Her joints are all frozen up. She's probably been in half the night." Steve agreed with the prognosis, but Candy just then took a bite from the hay bale with the corner of her whiskered mouth and began chewing with real appetite.

"She's not done yet," I said, cheered. "I'm going to keep rubbing her legs and try and get her up," I told them. "But I sure do thank you guys for the help."

Grinning at my stubbornness, my neighbours left; Myrna went off to work in town, leaving me alone with the old mare. Responding to my massaging, or probably because she was offended by the familiarity, Candy tried several times to get up, to no avail. Northward, the clouds of a thunderstorm hove into sight; it was now or never. Candy's main problem lay in her exhausted neck muscles. I tied a bowline sling in a thick rope, put the sling around her neck, and shouting encouragement, hauled upward on it with all my might. With her neck supported, Candy suddenly struggled upright and stood on wobbling legs in the high brome grass. I got an arm around her neck and held on hard, determined to keep her eight hundred pounds upright by brute force. "Whoa now, old girl, easy." I said soothingly. Her neck drooped over my shoulder as I strained to hold her up; then I heard the sound of her jaws tearing at the grass and began laughing uncontrollably. She was using me as a leaning post again, so she could get at the fresh green hay behind me. In a few minutes she could walk on her own.

I hurried in and telephoned Myrna. "I knew you'd get her up," she said, relieved. "It's not her time to go, not yet."

Candy put on some weight that summer, but not enough to see her through the winter. Though we had saved her from the bog, we could not save her from the risk of falling and breaking bones on the icy slopes of our property. What if it should happen while we were both away? By December 22, it was clear that we had to make the decision we had dreaded making, and put our old friend down.

"The boys will be home by Christmas Eve," said Myrna. "Let's give them a chance to say goodbye to her."

Christmas Eve came, and with it extra rations of oats, mixed with molasses, for the horses. The boys were saddened to see how scrawny their old pal had become. "I don't think she should continue like this," said Paul firmly.

Nathan nodded in agreement. "She can't keep warm without some fat on her," he said huskily.

For the countryman, the birth and death of livestock is part of his way of life, but I dreaded having to pull the trigger that would end Candy's life. Yet that moment was about to arrive, and Candy would make her death as easy for me as she had made her life useful to our family.

On Christmas morning we were up early, as usual, getting a Christmas breakfast together before opening our gifts. Then I felt Myrna's hand on my shoulder. "Candy's down again. She's on a patch of ice."

"Oh no." I hurried out, and found Tasha standing over her fallen companion, nuzzling at her neck. Candy was conscious and alert, but made no effort to rise. In her eyes I read a message, and it was one of complete acceptance. The mare was thirty-seven, and this was to be the end.

We huddled around the fallen warrior, trying to comfort ourselves as much as anything. Finally the boys led Tasha out of sight; Myrna's mare was obviously upset and nervous; she knew that something terrible was afoot.

Some might think it takes a pretty hard-hearted man to kill an animal he professes to care about; they would be wrong. I thought of two riders I knew who had horses badly injured far out in the bush, who had nothing to dispatch them with but an axe in one case and a knife in the other. "You have it easy," I told myself. "All she asks is that you do it right." Moving quickly, I put the small calibre weapon on the correct spot on the mare's forehead, wished her Godspeed, and pulled the trigger. Her death was instantaneous.

We stood around our old friend's body, and it seemed each of us had a story to tell, the ones I have told above, about what she had meant to us. That was her memorial. We covered the carcass with a tarpaulin, and went back inside. John had promised to come by with his tractor and carry the old mare off to a distant pasture she had loved, where her energy would go back into the earth, and into the golden eagles and coyotes that share this place with us. The opening of presents would be delayed for a while.

All this seemed fitting enough. But what we had not counted on was the grief that Tasha suffered at the loss of her stable-mate.

"Dad, take a look at this," said Paul, staring out the window. The brown mare had pulled the tarpaulin off Candy with her teeth, and now pushed vigorously at her with her muzzle, as if to urge her to get up. She circled the small form at the gallop, whinnying loudly and shaking her head. It was more than I could bear to watch. I went out and covered Candy up again. Tasha, who always came up to me to have her ears scratched when I appeared, dashed away from me today, as if in reproach. The next time I looked outside, the brown mare had pulled the tarpaulin off again; now she was lying down alongside the body, completely immobile, as if she had no interest in living any more. I learned something that day, that horses are capable of mourning their dead, just like us humans.

Around noon, Tasha got up as John arrived with his tractor. He scooped the white mare up in the bucket to carry her off. Whinnying as if her heart was broken, Tasha followed the tractor down to the cattleguard and watched it go down the road and out of sight.

But as I stood beside her, trying to comfort her trembling body, I saw a small form approaching. News travels fast in the country. It was Steve, and he was leading a white mare, name of Cindy. Except for a humorous brown freckle on her buttock, she was a dead ringer for Candy. "I thought that mare of Myrna's would be pretty lonely with Candy gone," drawled Steve. "So if you want to keep her for awhile, well you're welcome."

"Merry Christmas, Steve."

"Well, backatcha."

"You better come in for some wassail."

"You betcha."

The two horses sniffed noses, squealed out greetings, and in a minute were galloping around the barn. But later that day I saw them down at the fence, staring down the road as if waiting for something to return.

Later that day also we exchanged our Christmas presents. The first one I opened was a carving, sent by my brother-in-law. It was done in the calcified white burl of a pine tree, and it was a perfect rendering of a tiny white horse at full gallop, her mane flowing in the wind. It was Candy, of course, caught in a moment of pure joy, the essence of what she offered us in the end; an emotion which makes our eyes light up whenever her name is mentioned in these hills she loved.

CHAPTER TWELVE

Whence Is Courage?

What is our innocence,
what is our guilt? All are
    naked, none is safe. And whence
is courage: the unanswered question,
the resolute doubt, –
dumbly calling, deafly listening – that
in misfortune, even death,
    encourages others
    and in its defeat, stirs

the soul to be strong? . . .
           – Marianne Moore, from "What Are Years?"
           The Complete Poems of Marianne Moore, 1982

 Spring comes to the East Slope and before the aspen buds leaf out, returning red-winged blackbirds warble in a song fest, bounce off the windows and scrap with each other from tree to tree. And while the sun beats its brassy hoop over the mountain and the grass shoots up; while moose troop through the yard like commuters from their endless willow winnowing, and spring avalanches roar down Centre Peak, I sit inside a tiny wooden shack I call the Wheelhouse staring for hours at pages of manuscript. A yellow-bellied sapsucker – now there's a name to conjure with! How many poltroons have we met in our time who could answer to that description? – comes, in a series of halting swoops to roust me out of this wintery den. Myrna named him Tintin after his manic habit of pounding on the steel cap of the garage chimney with his bill. So poring over my research notes, I nearly jumped out of my chair when he suddenly hammered on the metal chimney cap of the Wheelhouse: BONG BONG – BING-BONG BONG. It's a challenge – come out and fight like a knothead.

Everything in creation calls me outside, but a fundamental paradox of my life is that I sit indoors and write about the outdoors. That goes back to 1978, when I quit the warden service to become a full-time writer. There were good reasons for leaving the outfit and for leaving Canmore, where we had bought our first home, before waves of absentee investors settled on the little town like blowflies and puffed it up with greed-toxins – but that's an old cavil I've pecked away at elsewhere.

I think it was Joseph Heller who warned in an interview once: "Don't ever quit your job on a matter of principle. You will probably regret it later." The advice came too late to help me and I don't believe it anyway. But the trouble is, you never really leave that old warden service way of life – in your head, that is – so you may as well stay in harness and keep drawing the pay.

The wardens of my era were notorious for spending a lifetime in the outfit, and then dying within a year or two of retirement, as if nothing outside of that roving commission could console their days. I was too young to succumb to that tradition when I quit, but for example when I go riding on my neighbour's ranch, I find myself jumping down to throw deadfalls off the path. I find myself jotting down the species of game and birds I encounter every day. And when the spring bear-hunters stop by to ask if I've seen any black bear in the area – well, they wish they hadn't. "Why don't you just buy a hog at auction, put it in a pen, and shoot it," I suggest. "That's about how hard it is to kill a poor little black bear."

"Christamighty. You'd think he raised the goddamn bears from pups to hear him talk!" I heard one complain as he got back in behind the wheel of his 4x4.

Anyway, switchback to 1978 and I've plunged full-time into the writing game: writing articles, travelling to interview people or to read from my works – the so-called literary life. After a year of this, the sound of my own voice started to nauseate me. And I thought my hind end was going to graft onto the oak of my typing chair. In the outfit, a shift patrolling the high-visitor-abuse area might be numbingly boring. Then the radio crackled and you'd be going full-out to help with an emergency, sometimes a life-and-death situation. It took a long time for the leftover adrenalin to leave my system.

Meanwhile I had the strangest recurring dream: I dreamed the warden headquarters was burning down, that my old comrades were locked inside, chained to computer monitors, and it was up to me to break the doors open and get them out.

I remember Myrna turning to me one night, taking my hand in hers and saying, "Honey, maybe you should see somebody . . ."

It was in the wake of one of these episodes, late July 1979, that I heard that Neil Colgan had died while on patrol at Douglas Lake, out where I had patrolled with him only one year previously. He had died on the lakeshore, all alone.

I couldn't believe it. I thought of all the years some of us had worked along the northeast boundary and of the close calls we'd had. I should have bought it out there myself several times. (My sometime partner, John Wackerle, came mighty close one day when he got hung up in a stirrup bar and was dragged down a mountain-side.) But not this kid spending his first summer out there.

I have the pictures of that long-ago patrol, spent with the Marvel Lake Kid and Bill Banting in the last days of my wandering commission. There is Neil on horseback and old Bill, sitting his horse out on that rocky platform in the eye of the wind. They hang on the wall of my study up in the Wheelhouse, but at this stage of my life – "A quiet madman, never far from tears," as poet Irving Layton says it best – I can't bear to look at them too often. Perhaps this feeling, too, will pass.

I wondered about the Kid at the time, travelling alone in strange country, where there was so much grizzly sign. But bears are not a problem to a warden on a good horse. It was but a rite of passage – until his luck went bad. What happened to Neil is what happens to all of us eventually. It happened to Bill, who would survive a terrific fight with cancer only to die in a fall down his front stairs out in Maple Ridge, B.C.

But the death of a young person is always harder to accept. I saw a bit of my younger self in Neil, a part of myself I never wanted to lose touch with. Neil was an all-round outdoorsman, a climber and a skier. He was really excited about getting on with the warden service. He planned to earn his professional guide's licence and hoped to work in the public-safety function eventually.

I don't think I've ever seen as many beautiful young women in tears as I saw at Neil's memorial in Banff. His friend Danny Verrall said Neil had many love interests. His attitude seemed to be "If you can't be with the one you love, love the one you're with." But there was one young lady, name of Laura, who Neil was quite serious about in the last year of his life.

In that last year he had travelled from the Saint Elias Mountains to Bolivia and many places in between. "You've done more, seen more and experienced more in a year," he wrote in his journal, "than most people do in a lifetime, Colgan – do you realize how fortunate you are?"

That was one month before he died.

I thought of Neil's death now and then as the years rolled on, as my own boys turned into teenagers. He had remained forever young, untouched by the passage of time; unmoved by the endless compromises the living make, trying to outwit a fate they can't foresee.

One evening, a zig-zag forward in time, I was reminiscing about Neil with Perry Jacobsen (later chief park warden of Banff National Park) at a pub in Canmore. "When we found him," Perry said," he looked just like he was asleep. He had composed his limbs before he died."

"In what way?" I'd asked.

"Well, he was lying there on his back, his hands folded on his chest."

I had stared at Jacobsen, experiencing a shock of recognition. In *Men for the Mountains*, I had described the death of an old-time warden who was fatally injured by a grizzly bear. I had written there: "Knowing that help would never reach him in time, Goodair had composed himself to die. When they found him, his hands were folded over his chest and his legs were lying out in front of him. He had tried to make the spectacle of his death as easy on his friends as he could, imposing on his last remains the stamp of the courageous soul that had passed out of them."

Listening to Jacobsen's account, I recalled that Neil had read this book of mine; he had complimented me on it the first time I met him. Had he remembered this passage, even acted upon it?

Maybe – but more likely his way of heading west was in accord with the creed of the young romantic that he was. An entry in his journal in June of 1979 reads

Muria – the man who skied Everest was more concerned about failure than death. A 20th century
   Samurai.
   Life is not life without honor
   To lose one's honor is to lose one's life.

It sounds a bit Byronic at first blush – but those who are honest with themselves may recognize a hard kernel of truth. Neil savoured his life fully; it was precious to him. But faced with death, he did the best he could to get that right, too.

In 1988, I hit another rough patch in the freelancer's rocky road to financial ruin. Myrna's term as an adult-education assistant was done, writing assignments had dried up temporarily and now I had to make up for lost income. I hit the pike to try and find a cash job for a while, dropping off resumés by the score but receiving no reply. I had three strikes against me, given the political agendas in favour then, and now. I was male, I was white, and I was over forty. My options were even more limited by my employment experience.

I was then in an uneasy truce with Parks Canada, which had hired me in 1984 to write the park history for the 1985 National Parks Centennial. But that would cut no ice with anyone in the personnel office. I dropped off the brag sheet anyway. Fortunately for me, there were still people on staff in Banff who remembered what a shitty stick I had been handed in 1978.

On a Friday afternoon in late May I was staring at the minus signs in my bank-book when Myrna called me to the phone. It was Keith Everts, then assistant chief warden in Banff Park. "Marty, I have a proposal for you. How would you like to take a couple of horses – and go back to work exactly where you left off ten years ago?"

I was electrified. "Holy shit! When do I start?"

"Monday morning at oh-eight-hundred."

"You lucked out," Keith told me later. "We'd hired everybody that was on the eligibility list, but we still had one opening for a warden patrolman. You are more than qualified for that, so we didn't need to hold another competition."

Of course there was a catch: I had to take a law-enforcement course and an updated course in mountain rescue before I could ride off into the sunset.

So it was I came back to suckle at the wizened old dugs of the great Über-Bear (a.k.a. Parks Canada) one more time. I was determined this time to suckle warily – she was famous in Ottawa for eating her own young – or rolling over on them suddenly, leaving them feeling crushed.

After signing back on at the Kremlin, helped through the red tape by Everts, I drove down to the park compound and found my way to stores. It was eerie. Ted the storesman was still standing behind the wire cage where I'd left him ten years earlier after turning in my .308 carbine and other equipment. He welcomed me back – I hadn't realized Ted could smile before. "Do you want your old uniform?" he said. "It's probably still hung up here somewhere."

I blinked at him for a beat. Had he actually been expecting me to come back all these years? "Uh, you know, Ted, I think I'd prefer a newer one, if it's all the same to you."

"No problem. Head down to Monod's later and they will fit you with climbing boots. Give them this form."

A bit dazed, I walked back into the warden office to find the locker room. Out front they had my name on a mailbox already and there was a letter in it addressed to me. I stopped to open it: a reporter from the *Crag and Canyon* wanted to interview me about my return to the fold. I crumpled it up and threw it away. Loose lips sink ships, I told myself. And recognized a motto heard during my old sea-cadet days aboard HMCS *Assiniboine*, when we'd cruised off Taiwan during the Cuban missile crisis of 1962.

Standing in the warden's meeting room later in a brand new green uniform I looked up at the rogue's gallery of the retired and the dead and saw my signed photograph, made in 1973. I felt like a ghost from the past. A friendly hand slapped me on the back; it was Scott Ward, my old partner. He is a dedicated cyclist and a runner; he hadn't aged a day. "You must feel like you are in some kind of weird time warp," he said cheerfully, summing the situation up. "How long has it been?"

"Ten years, Scotty."

He shook his head. "Unbelievable, isn't it? Welcome back!"

The warden common room was different now. Most of the faces seemed like newcomers to me – but in fact some had been in Banff for many years. There were more women in uniform than there used to be. So much for *Men for the Mountains*, I thought to myself. If I wrote that book today, I'd have to call it *Persons for the Peaks*. The room, once boisterous with male joshing and profanity, was now more like a library, full of serious-faced people, thinking before they bespoke themselves. One wore white gloves – he was handling some colour slides, to be fair. Nobody smoked in there, and that was one of the biggest changes of all.

Chastened, I drove down to the fire hall and signed in for the basic law-enforcement course.

The lesson plans filled a tome some three inches thick, and covered such topics as powers of arrest, collecting evidence, and inter-viewing subjects. It ended with conducting prosecutions in court. It was a far cry from the primitive training of the 1970s and there was a new emphasis on self-defence and the use of force. "There's an attitude problem nowadays," explained our instructor. "These people will tell you to do something that is physically impossible." We practised breaking from choke holds, searching suspects and "proning" them out. "Don't put your hand down the front of a guy's pants," warned the instructor. "Some bikers carry knives in there with the blades pointing up." I was wrestling full-timers a few years younger than me, and new recruits, some of them half my age. A bearded warden, Tom Davidson, had a glint in his eyes and steel bands for wrists. The women also seemed to like mixing it up. At the baseball game we got up after work, Warden Cyndi Smith from Jasper pitched underhand so fast that it fanned sweat off my nose.

I could see I was in a new era.

I promised myself I would be diplomatic out there lest some biker felt compelled to kick my middle-aged butt. The wardens were not yet carrying pepper spray and billy clubs – that would come a few years later. But we did rehearse taking down suspects and stop-ping cars while pointing shotguns at them – coached by a fatherly detective – symptoms of the Brave New World to come.

One of our instructors, a homicide cop, showed us pictures of men who had accidently hanged themselves in elaborate masochistic rituals. I was wondering what that had to do with checking for fishing licences but decided the brand-new me needed to have a brand-new attitude – at least during office hours. So at lunch I bought a bright button that said YES and pinned it on my lapel, and wore a smile on my face to go with it, which caused the Mavens of the Meeting Room to frown ever more deeply.

At the end of the law-enforcement course they asked for questions and suggestions. A few ideas came to mind but the words died when I felt the cold muzzle of the Great Über-Bear, that bureaucratic kobold, snuffling at my neck, checking for a live sense of proportion.

"C'mon, people. Let's hear your comments," urged the instructor.

Oh no you don't, I thought, smiling ever more broadly. Thirteen dollars an hour, I said to myself. A family counting on you. Paycheque every two weeks first time since 1978. Just keep that thought in mind.

But one of the young women spoke right up, like a character out of a *Police Academy* movie: "I was just wondering," she trilled, "do you think it would be possible for us to learn how to shoot these guns before we point them at people? Because, frankly, I hardly know which end does what."

I bit down on my tongue to suppress a hysterical giggle of agreement. It takes a woman to cut through the macho bluster and point out the obvious absurdity. The instructor fixed a cold eye on her and made a brief note on his pad. "No worries. We'll schedule some firearm training at some point."

"Thank you." She turned to me, as the old veteran, inviting me to acknowledge the obvious. I wished I could have afforded the luxury, I really do. Instead I smiled encouragingly and nodded down at the YES button on my lapel, causing her to eyebrow-raise her disappointment in me.

I shared a Pan Abode cabin at the Castle Mountain camp with a young seasonal named George. Every day I got up at 5 A.M. and ran uphill to Smith Lake and every night I cycled on the 1A highway and after two weeks I had managed to get down to a thirty-six-inch waist and 228 pounds, which was at least the beginning of a beginning.

One evening I found an earnest-looking George modelling a shapeless warden Stetson and frowning into the mirror. "This is the only outfit I know that gives you a bad hat and then gives you shit for wearing it," he complained.

I got the kettle going, showed him how to steam it and reshape it.

George was a kayaker. He said some of the kayakers were parks people. They knew about my return. They said I was never any good as a warden – couldn't ski, couldn't ride a horse, etc., etc.

I thought of some of the spoiled horses I had taken on in years gone by – horses spoiled by city-boy recruits who didn't like horses – horses that nobody else would take out in the bush. "Who are these people, George? Do any of them wear white gloves, by the way?"

"I'd rather not say. But I put in a good word for you."

"Thanks, George," I said. "But you see that's what I get for making fun of myself in print for the edification of the humourless. As Monte Rose would say, piss on 'em if they can't take a joke."

I cracked us both a beer. "I mean, in 'my day,' as you insist on calling it, I never noticed anybody following me over Shale Pass with a plastic bathtub strapped to his butt."

George laughed nervously. Things were not going that well in his life just then, either.

Came the mountain rescue course and a ray of light. Tim Auger was in command, flashing smile and dark brown hair intact, ageless and full of sky-eyed humour as in days of yore. The first time I had climbed with Tim was on Grassi Ridge at Lake O'Hara, twenty-one years earlier. A big fat rock was kicked down from somebody on Bernie Schiesser's rope above us. It landed on the foot of Calgarian Peter Spear, splitting his boot and foot open and causing him terrific agony. His foot turned into a sprinkler and it took some doing just to get the bleeding stopped. In his matter-of-fact way, Tim had set up an improvised lowering system, pointing out its features to me as he went along like the born teacher he was and is. Tim got Spear strapped on my back in the "split-rope carry," as it's called. Tim lowered us down one pitch, then belayed us down for several hundred feet, until the angle eased and I could carry Spear without a belay. Banff climber Gordon Rathbone was also on the route that day, looking down in disbelief. He described it at a party in Tim's honour in 1996 as "Two scrawny teenagers wearing bicycle helmets – because they couldn't afford the real ones – lowering their poor adult victim down a cliff." Actually, all I had was a construction worker's hardhat tied on with a bit of thong. That was in 1967. That autumn, after a night watching Sputnik whirling by over the Opabin Plateau, Tim led me up Mount Hungabee, where lightning smites the mighty down – a climb that was the highlight of my life back then. In 1969, I was offered but had to decline a chance to return to O'Hara. The chief warden asked me if I knew any climbers who would be suitable for the job. "Hell yes," I replied. "You already have the guy on your trail crew – his name is Tim Auger and they don't come any better."

The chief warden looked into it and then promoted the Vancouver lad to summer warden; he's been with the service ever since. By 1988, Tim Auger was known as one of Canada's foremost mountain rescue experts.

My self-confidence, after years spent staring at a typewriter, was lagging as the course began, but given instructors like Auger, Marc Ledwidge, and Diane Volkers, I gritted my teeth and went at it. Auger had inspired me twenty-one years ago to get the lead out – and now he was at it again, the Cheshire cat grinning down at me once more. Putting on a climbing harness is like putting on war paint – there's a kind of commitment to bravado implied there. I stepped up to the rock, started trying to put a move or two together without looking like an idiot. But then, like sun breaking through cloud, I experienced that sudden shot of physical joy to be back at the great old game. The muscles of that young man, though dormant, were still there, still willing to extend themselves from past to present. I found myself swarming upwards like a newt; sat on top watching my bruised fingers remembering how to set up a rappel brake or tie a knot. After the first day I wondered – why did I ever quit doing this? The answers didn't seem so obvious any more.

There's nothing like being put in a group of younger people to make you push yourself. I remember that a thirty-ish beginner, terribly worried about his progress, turned to me for advice. He may never know how happy I was to have the answer he needed. The smile went to my eyes, turned real: I tossed away the YES badge. Nobody got the joke anyway.

Slinging under the helicopter was the final test at the end of the short course. From a highway pull-off near Vermilion Lakes, we would sling up onto the face of Mount Edith, climb the peak, lower off down the east face and descend to the road. I stepped into the old Peter Pan harness one more time, my hands trembling slightly, needing a hand from Scott Ward to sort out the straps. I had been entrusted to fly in with Mary C. I believe it was the first time on the sling for her. I felt the old knot of doom tightening in my guts as the engine worked itself into a frenzy. Gone was the Jet Ranger and Jim Davies's familiar face; he had retired in 1986. The pilot, Howard Massecar, was flying a French-made A-Star that day.

Up went the big bird and we lifted off the ground as if launched from a trampoline: Mary started giggling wildly. We swayed together in our harness cheek to cheek, so to speak, swinging over the river, then bounced up and down with the helicopter in runaway elevators of choppy thermals, as the machine ascended, following along a ridge line. I plucked at the sling rope; it hummed like a bass viol. Jesus, I've got to get this weight off me, I thought. I caught myself adjusting the straps in mid-air – old routines coming back. I glanced at this merry young woman, thinking, if Myrna were here now, she'd be laughing just like that. She wouldn't make herself crazy worrying about stuff she couldn't control. She'd have a blast.

"Sure fun, eh?" I shouted into Mary's helmet at one point.

"Isn't it great!" she yelled, grinning, waiting for me to continue the encomiums.

Oh, just peachy, I thought to myself. Just then Howard, who was angling up along the treed ridge of the mountain, giving us some good close-ups of Clark's nutcrackers, did a 360 to the left, out where it all dropped away to a big wah-hoo, gaining altitude, sending us around in a wild swing that made Mary's eyes pop open wide as a china doll's. At the same time a vicious paw of cross-wind swatted us into a spin.

My stomach flew up into my throat. The town of Banff whirled past like a midway in the distance. Suddenly, watching Mary's expression, I felt the feckless laughter of youth bubbling to the surface and thought, Goddamn! It is fun, if you stop worrying and just go with the power.

There was Tim Auger on the ledge, a group of trainees above him in a splash of pumpkin-coloured anoraks. And now I felt more in control of events, pointing out the O-ring 'biner, saying, "Mary, when your feet touch, grab for the rock and hang on. Just watch your balance. We'll unhook you."

She nodded and our boots hit the mountain where Tim waited.

Sitting on the summit of the peak later, eating lunch in a brief deluge of flying graupel after following Scott Ward up a series of bluffs and rotten ledges, Tim Auger said it was good to have me back. Scott agreed. And if those repositories of skill and knowledge that kept the service operating gave me their approval, then it mattered nought to me what the Great Über-Bear was plotting.

I knew her minions were onto me. A former Banff manager from the old days, a buckeroo of the swivel chair who had rolled on to greater glories, had phoned Keith Everts to give him hell for hiring me back. It was the first indicator that the slippery sonofabitch had ever given that he hated my guts. I knew he would be watching if I tried to sneak past the dozing Über-Bear for a second reincarnation.

A few days later I was back at the park barn for the first time in years. Here was the hidden soul of the outfit, this cavvy of spirits waiting to go roving in the name of mischief. Tossing manes, flashing teeth, flying hooves, and farts of defiance. They put the fear of Jehovah into many an urban recruit, but not your reporter, who was owned by several of these creatures back home.

The park barn was shady and redolent of horse flesh, sweated leather, and neat's-foot oil. A colt named Whiskey looked up from his hay to study me; a fine-boned face, liquid eye, and quick ear. A horse with lots of mind. His haunches were trim and well muscled, showing the quarter-horse blood line; his hooves looked pliant and neat, but not too small to float on soft ground.

For the summer I had, on the other hand, drawn Mabel, a wither-less, high-strung mare, and her gelding sidekick Craig, a pack horse to the manner born, though these horses are all trained to ride or pack. Horses should be allowed to earn a name with cachet and not be saddled with boring monikers. I thought of Sailor, Bootlegger, Banjo, Whack, and many others. These two were tall horses, a thorough-bred–quarter-horse line in their mix, a matched set of blacks.

Nathan, the contract farrier, was pounding on some shoes, watched by the barn boss, Johnny Nylund, who nodded a greeting as I came in. The shoer spoke of some cowboy customer he didn't like: "He wears the shit on the inside of his boots."

I started loading packboxes for the ride into the Stony Creek District. Johnny came over, ten years older, still feisty, tipped his brim up and frowned up at me. "Where did you get that goddamn hat?"

"It came with my uniform."

Johnny turned his head and spat at the idea. "I never thought I'd see you back here, Sid. I thought you were going to get rich writing books."

"Johnny, I never said I would get rich." Johnny went back to lead out the colt.

Ahead of me were miles of grizzly country, country of the heart; Neil Colgan country. My thoughts were on those at home who I wouldn't see for ten days. As I strapped the carbine scabbard under the stirrup leather I stopped, assailed by sudden doubts.

Is this really only about wages? This obsession taking you away from your family like it did before?

Be honest!

I tightened Mabel's cinch, thinking, Alright, I admit, there's some selfishness in it.

I left this place in a matter of hours back in 1978. I cut off this life and these mountains like a man cutting a live fruit tree down with an axe. I turned my back on what a young man cared about and believed in. I hurt myself somewhere deep.

But you can't be that young man ever again.

Ha! Don't I know it. But that was the happier me she married and deserves. That was the me that connects with my own kids. And he is there inside me, still wondering what the hell happened. Funny how many old clichés ring true. "The boy is father to the man." I want to let him say goodbye, or Christ I don't know. To say hello again, whatever it takes. I want the two of us to be one; I want to be somebody I used to admire.

Nylund helped me pile the boxes on. It had been a long time since I'd thrown a diamond hitch over a pack-horse load. He managed to show me a trick I had forgotten, without mentioning it.

"You take it easy out there. You're not as young as you used to be."

"Johnny, this may come as a surprise to you. But you aren't exactly a teenager yourself."

"Ha. You got that right."

Mabel had a big lip on. She'd thought I was just another kayaker she could asshole until I caught her up short, stepped up, and crawled her frame.

Johnny handed me Craig's lead rope. "Johnny, if you ride my way, bring the whiskey. Git up!"

"Ha! Check that cinch after a mile or so," he called after me.

We jogged around the back of the Buffalo Paddock, shaking the kinks out, and headed up the trail. The saddle they had given me was a good old antique Great Western but it didn't fit me worth a damn. So that hadn't changed. The stirrup leathers were uneven – I'd have to punch a few new holes or I'd wreck my knees.

Half an hour later, after taking to the bush at times to dodge motorhomes on the Minnewanka Road, we were moving through the Bankhead meadows and came to the trail that led up to the old warden residence. I swallowed hard, picturing a tall, long-haired young woman walking down the trail towards me with a little boy named Paul in a knitted cap, their hands full of illegal wildflowers under the big wedge of Cascade Mountain. I threatened to arrest these ghosts. To sentence them to a life of being loved by me to the death. She would be in her garden now at home, or hanging the new washing out on the line. The boys, slow to get up, putting on fresh clothes that smelled of aspen woods and sunlight. How could I ever leave her when I carried the taste of her in my mouth, the scent of her, the memory of her body along my bones with me, and I thought of the two of us riding double, riding bareback and mostly naked in the dappled forest on a snuffy gelding long ago. I remembered how her milk would dampen my bare chest like a blessing when she was first nursing the baby. How she said even when you are talking about nursing with other women the milk will start to flow by itself. I called her the Dairy Queen and she cuffed me a good one.

Up the lane of trees we went, three kilometres travelled, and Mabel almost resigned to the idea of twelve more to go. Craig in the drag still experimenting with the halter rope, applying more tension on my arm, like a patient nurse on the bone ward. I took a dally around the saddle horn and cranked him up a notch or two. And where our old warden home had been was now only a square of grass. They'd moved away the house where Lion, our golden retriever, used to retrieve the toddler, Paul, from the approach of black and grizzly bears; where I had worked on the manuscript of *Men for the Mountains*. The Über-Bear of progress had licked away the memory of us, of wardens Jim Robertson, Ernie Stenton, and their families before. *The memories of small-timers*, sniffed the Über-Bear. *The dedication of the misguided.*

"Horseman, pass by," sayeth W. B. Yeats.

The Über-Bear stopped at the gate into wilderness, whining its resentment; thwarted. A thing weaned on a paper-shredder, fat with secrets like boils that needed lancing, could not go where the parking lots ended and life stepped out into the open.

I headed up the Cascade road – even that would soon change, but for the better. In a few days, they would start pulling the gravelled cart road out so no more vehicles would drive this country. The old road, raised into a hiking tread, would last forever, its right of way grown in with pine saplings and fireweed, given time.

So we took the long road leading through low hills past beaver ponds. The laughter of ghostly children still lingered where the trout were rising. They rode with me. They argued with their mother for the truck keys four hours south of there. Bear-bells like prayer bells jingled as we greeted backpackers along the way and gave information and pep talks on bears and ornery cow moose. Craig farted in warning when kids tried to get too familiar. I checked travel permits and fishing permits and answered questions. There was a lot of bear sign up ahead and the trail was closed at Stony Creek until I could check the sign and declare it safe again.

And we rode on, into the backcountry. How glad I was to be travelling alone! Gord Irwin, backcountry area manager, had worried about that. But he had bears and trail-rider outfits elsewhere in the district and had decided he must split his two patrollers up. Mike Comeau, the other guy, had worked years as an outfitter's guide and was self-reliant also. Irwin said, I'm sure people in the office here will be glad to take a trip or two with you. One of the careful, career-conscious crew summed it up for everyone that summer, booting up his 'puter, shaking his head sympathetically at such a risky notion.

He said, "Sorry, Gord. Can't touch it."

How proud I was to be one of the Untouchables! I was insufferable about it, really.

The sun burned down and made my head sweat under the felt Stetson. It was ten years ago, it was ten days ago, the last time I was here. We clip-clopped across the Cascade River bridge, and kept on going.

I thought of the young man who knocked at our door for advice on high water one spring. How I warned him carefully, explaining about runoff; urging him not to attempt river fords when travelling alone like that. How he didn't listen.

Who knows what voice he was hearing, but whatever it was, was important to him. His body had been white as the stones on the gravel bar. The river took everything he had. I remember you, I said aloud to the emerald serpent glinting between the pines. I still grieve for your lousy luck, poor lad of summer's lost.

The ranges were waiting, the Vermilion and the Palliser were drawing us into them; the clouds rushed up the valley to gather at the end and wait our arrival at Stony Creek, wetting the dust in a brief shower. Down we went to the well-kept barn later on that afternoon; the old frame cabin, newly painted. Hay in the hay-shed well stocked by Nylund, for the taking out of the road would change this back a hundred years to a pack-train economy; a chance to turn back the clock, restore the wilderness. Now that's what I call progress.

I unpacked at the house, my knees only a little stiff from the fit of the saddle, kicked the horses out in the pasture with enough hay, waited until they had rolled safely to scratch their backs, then went and said hello to the old frame shack once more.

I opened the wooden shutters, studded with nails to ward off grizzly bears, scarred by their talons regardless. Here was the headquarters, opening to my key again, my voice booming hollowly once more in the empty room, rattling the chimney pipe. The sun shouldered in past me like a hunting dog and Silence fled into the meadow. The district map on the wall shone in the beams of daylight, conning all the directions. From here we had a world to keep in order, to the Dormer, Panther, and Red Deer Rivers then west within a few miles of fateful Douglas Lake to the head of the Cascade in Flint's Park. There was Badger Pass and Johnston Creek after that – or there was Forty Mile Summit and Mystic Cabin. Every horizon beckoned with mountains and streams flowing out from paradise.

Water purled over the mossy cement of the spring's edge where I filled the coffee pot and then drank deep of memory; there were thirty head of elk in the pasture, staring down the horses with haughty, long-necked looks. The new calves would soon be dropping. I hoped they would move upslope and off the hiking trails in their moody, half-angry post-partum days. The horses leaned over the rails, staring at me, ears pricked up until I caught them at it, then turned back to their feed.

This was what I wanted to do, and it would be late in the season, snow piling up already in Dormer Pass, when I forded the Dormer River for the last time that year and took the shortcut trail to Barrier Cabin on the Panther River. I had brought red wine, fit for the occasion. A bit of steak to fry in the evening cool over hot coals, half cooked already from riding in the saddlebags on the horse's warm sides.

With the horses put up and the stove going, I gathered some fresh shaggy-mane mushrooms, the last of the year from the corral. I don't believe I had pointed out those constant fruits of horse pastures to Neil before.

In a hot black pan, with a little Danish butter (the canned product) they were soon sauteing with fresh garlic I'd carried along with me, and some crushed peppercorns. A fitting garnish for Alberta beef. "There's lots here to go around," I said aloud. "If anybody wanted it," remembering the steak Neil had cooked for me so long ago.

I poured two glasses and proposed a toast – "to the mountains."

A month earlier, while on days off, Johnny Nylund and Scott Ward had ridden up to the Sandhills cabin, about eleven kilometres west of Scotch Camp, to buy Neil's ghost a drink. John had issued Neil the horse, Gunner, who allegedly kicked him – old Gunner, after all, was never tried and convicted. (On the other hand, Neil obviously hadn't kicked himself.) Neil took out Gunner, having brought in his first pack horse sored up and needing to convalesce. We frowned on saddle sores, symptomatic of young riders who could go and go but were not watching their horse flesh going. Sores left white hairs to rebuke a rider for years afterwards.

Gunner was mostly a pack horse, known to act squirrelly in the presence of biting flies. But Neil was riding him that fateful day, regardless. "He probably got tired of beatin' on Beggar," Nylund had surmised: this was apparently a lazy saddle horse. (Some wardens were slow to appreciate the use of spurs.) "So if the kid is there, he'll probably step pretty heavy on me."

It was good, I felt, to swap these animals from one task to another; it kept them tractable. I guess Nylund and Ward drank Neil's rum for him that night. His peripatetic spirit had a lot of other places to haunt, and only the mice ran over Nylund in his sleep. But I had come to Barrier, the last place I had seen Neil Colgan a decade ago, to buy him a drink for old times sake.

As full darkness fell, I lit the Coleman lantern to bring the room back into view. But the place seemed hostile to the intense glow, and there was no room for a ghost to feel at home. I didn't want to visit with this false sun. So I killed the lamp and lit a candle instead, and sat down at the table to do what you can't do after work when on patrol with other people, which is to reach, focussed by the solitude of the mountains, into the greater solitude within yourself, and to write.

I found it hard to talk to a spirit, but I thought he would read over my shoulder anyway, and maybe he could use a laugh about someone we both knew, rather than my gloomy old mug reflected from the windows. The memory had been tickling me all day and I needed to put it down:

Neil – you can guess who this is about.

Warden X. was disconsolate when I first patrolled with him here, over the break-up of his first relationship. He was given to brooding silences when awake and conversations in his sleep. Her name was always on his lips as he fiddled with his meals and laughed aloud for the nonce. He began to waste away right before my eyes, poor man.

I tempted him, Neil, with beef Bourguignonne, or with chorizo and Myrna's cornbread redolent with green chilies and other delicacies, but to no avail. He wondered, anorexically, if there was still Kraft Dinner in the cupboard. This was at Scotch Camp, by the way, where you have more kitchen space for your culinary elan. A cook like you would appreciate that my sympathy for X. waned like the moon.

It happened that a pack rat sussed out an access hole and left his stinking piss stains up and down the cupboards. We set traps for him, but he sprung them and made an unholy racket at night trying to drag them off to his nest as trophies.

One night as X. slept across the way, moaning in distress at a nightmare featuring his former pelvic affiliate, the pack rat slithered in through a loose chink, rattled along that big purlin in the back, then paused thoughtfully, eyeing my wristwatch down below him, glinting in the starlight on a chair. He'd brought a rusty bottle cap along to trade for anything shiny, gripped in his teeth. But he was thinking about how good and valuable a thing is pack-rat piss, thick as molasses, a musky love-medicine for skunks; an elixir well-worth leaving just on its own account in exchange for stolen silverware, say, or wristwatches – anything a feller might pack off to the den under the tack-shed, there to ponder it nestled on a bed of dried horseshit, deer bones, bits of barbed wire, and sundry pages copped from *Playboy* magazines. Why waste a perfectly sound bottle cap on these unappreciative bipeds? No, piss is your man every time. Slap it on a burn for an ointment and there you are; spread it on your toast; use it to tack on a horseshoe. By Jiminy, you could tar a roof with it, and it makes a wondrous smelling salts! Gosh, it must have a hundred uses.

Thus inspired, having turned his worst vice into a virtue, he lifted his plumed tail and voided a carefully measured tot of it down onto my blankets – like a Ralph Klein Tory offering a pious word of fiscal wisdom to a welfare case – and awaited my sighs of gratitude. But for some reason this trickle of treasure gave me the fear of the Black Death falling onto my face as my eyes sproinged open in alarm.

It was then I decided, as a resource-conservation officer, to collect this interesting rodent, *Neotoma cinerea*, for science, and donate him to the national museum. Reaching into my pile of plunder stacked nearby, I drew my trusty Webley .38 and tracked Mr. P. Rat with the radar light until I got a clear shot.

Farewell, you spawn of Satan.

It happened that his lifeless form fell on X., just as he leapt up screaming in terror from the echo of the thundering report.

Did I mention that I prefer travelling alone?

X. might have easily taken umbrage but he chose to see things in a positive light. He said now he would at least have something to worry about other than What's-Her-Name. He said golly I'm hungry what time is it I think I'll get up and fry me up a mess of huevos rancheros.

Later he credited my shock therapy with helping him to forget whoever that was he was connected to before and now he is happily married to a wonderful woman who is worth remembering.

The night wind stirred in the chimney, a soul coming, or going? And only the coyote down on the river flat was laughing.

Have I dismissed myself, Neil? You know I've always been more of a rum drinker, so I hope you like this South American wine. Here's the thing. When I think now about my dream of saving my cohorts from a burning building, I realize your face was not among them.

Isn't it funny how we look back with 20/20 vision and see how everything was connected? If I had put my YES badge on for a few months back in 1978, the Über-Bear would probably have dozed off and forgotten what a bad boy I had been, criticizing the director of national parks from coast to coast. Most likely I would have wound up right back here in the bush, and you would have been given another assignment.

There. Now I've told you what's been bothering me all this time and you can tell me that I'm full of shit. That nobody knows his fate. And who would want to? That you can't change your own unlucky stars or anybody else's.

Here's to you, kid. It sure as hell can be dangerous travelling alone. My wife thinks I'm crazy to come out here by myself, and she's right. I am crazy, but I was crazy at home in a different kind of way. She said if you die out there don't you come crawling around back here expecting me to pick up the pieces.

I guess you realized too late, Neil, that you should have left a note in the cabin on your whereabouts. And if you hadn't been bawled out a couple of times before for missing scheduled radio calls, Vroom would have probably got out here a bit faster on Thursday, July 26, 1979. Maybe he could have called in the helicopter rather than driving all the way to Scotch and then riding nine miles to Sandhills looking for you. It was his day off; perhaps he was thinking: *Colgan, the free spirit, is at it again. Not only not calling in, but he's outside the district. What the hell is he doing at Sandhills, anyway? Should I call the chopper? If I do that, somebody will notice and the Kid will get into trouble. Guess I'll have to go out there on my own and chew him out and hope the chief warden doesn't notice.*

Bill Vroom is gone now, so it's hard to know just what he was thinking; we can only speculate, based on what was known at the time.

The procedure on radio calls was pretty slack in the old days, not the way it is now. I have to call in the morning and tell them where I'm going, call in at night to tell them I'm still alive. If we miss two calls in a row, the chopper is sent out at great expense to find us. They implemented the disciplined method after your accident, but there still isn't enough manpower to send wardens out in pairs on every patrol.

Not that any of this would have made a difference, since you probably died within one or two hours after your horse kicked you – or ran you down and stepped on you – on Wednesday, July 25. They said even if somebody had been with you, had galloped down to the cabin and radioed for the chopper, it still would have been too late.

They found your saddle lying on the Douglas Lake trail where Gunner had bucked it off after the accident. You had spread your slicker over it in a square shape to make a beacon. It worked: Lance Cooper spotted it from the helicopter when they searched the area early on Friday morning.

When Warden Perry Jacobsen, a skilled horseman, examined Neil Colgan's saddle, he found the rigging was in good condition. He believed that Neil must have gotten off to adjust his blankets and saddle, and slacked off both cinches to do it. It was a hot day; the flies were bad and this makes a horse restless and irritable. The horse likely kicked him as he went around behind it. Perhaps he slipped and stumbled, startling the horse and causing it to fire at him. Bill Vroom felt the horse might have pulled its halter shank free, started bucking and spinning, got the saddle under its belly, and run right over Colgan as he tried to keep it from running off.

There are too many variables, too many things that might have caused it. Being kicked or knocked down is something that has happened before to many horsemen, myself included. But the blow in this case was powerful and to the vitals, rupturing the right kidney. Internal bleeding must have been severe. Bill Vroom, who also saw Neil's body, claimed he could see the outline of the hoof on Neil's back.

The horse quickly bucked the loose saddle off, and headed back to Sandhills. When Jacobsen approached Gunner in the pasture, the veteran horse was wild and flighty, "as if he had been in a wreck," as he put it.

That Wednesday, in the agonizing state Neil was in, he was not going to waste time writing an explanation in his notebook of what went wrong.

Neil crept painfully along as far as he could on the back trail –
about a kilometre, where he stopped and built a small signal fire.
Eventually, unable to move farther and knowing he would soon lose
consciousness, Neil had carefully extinguished the flames. He
worked his way down close to the lakeshore, knowing that death
was very near. Perhaps he had hoped to find a clearing there, visible
from the air. He slumped down at last among the spruce trees on
the lakeshore. The shadows were closing in as he took one last look
at the mountains where he loved to be. At the end, he was thinking
about his family. So he wrote a note to try and console them and
buttoned it to his field jacket where the searchers would find it early
Friday morning.

Then he lay down and died in an old-fashioned and lonely way,
but in a courageous manner that was true to his nature, with his
boots on. The note, written like a verse, read:

> If i die out here
> i'm glad it's here
> and not on some highway
> Mom and Dad you did well
> And thank you
> And i love you more than you'll ever know
>   neil

CHAPTER THIRTEEN

Putting Out the Cows

"The two-legged bear has become a force equal to glaciation or continental drift, or vulcanism. We have to change quickly. One on one, four-legged bears can whip us, but as a species they don't have a chance."

– Charles Jonkel, bear biologist

Charlie Russell was raised in bear country right on the boundary of Waterton National Park. At age twenty, he travelled widely as a cameraman with his father, Andy, filming bears in the mountain wilderness of Alberta, British Columbia, Yukon, and Alaska to make a documentary film about grizzly bears and grizzly country. He is not a biologist, but like a bear biologist, he has been studying their habits at close range for a very long time, reading their body language, examining the food they eat, crawling into their dens (empty dens so far) to learn more about their long hibernation. At the time I am writing about, he was still running some cattle on the family ranch. He was working as a guide in British Columbia's Khutzeymateen Grizzly Bear

Sanctuary in the summers, and was about to embark on a project that would result in his book on the kermode bear, the white bear of the rainforest.*

Charlie thinks like a bear, and over the years, as his thick black hair has taken on a silver tinge, he has even begun to resemble a silvertip grizzly in a peculiar kind of way. It is there in his pawing gestures as he talks about wildlife and wild country. It is in the growl of his voice when he starts talking about bear hunters. In his presence, I have approached grizzly bears more closely, and with more confidence than I ever did when I worked as a bear policeman with a tranquilizer gun or a twelve-gauge shotgun in my hands. Under his tutelage, I have stood in a B.C. salmon stream while a three-hundred-pound black bear caught salmon fifteen feet away. I watched as a white kermode bear – which is a colour morph of *Ursus americanus* (the American black bear), not an albino – shouldered up beside Charlie and stared into the water when Charlie splashed his hand in the stream like a salmon.

We have hiked up on the lee slopes of these Alberta mountains and crawled into abandoned grizzly-bear dens dug into the hardscrabble on old avalanche paths. And in the rainforest of the Khutzeymateen, we watched an adult grizzly foraging on eelgrass thirty feet away. Charlie showed Myrna and I their beds, which they made on cliffside aeries, created by the roots of huge cedars, liedowns that looked more like goat hideouts then bear beds.

But kids, don't try this at home. I strongly recommend against approaching bears this closely to anyone who is not a trained researcher. Most dangerous, I believe, are bears that have been exposed to humans, particularly in national parks or near other settlements. Yet in dealing with true wilderness bears, Charlie has embarked on experiments whose results fly in the face of the old theory, the theory that says that bears are naturally afraid of people and that bears are

---

* Charles Russell, *Spirit Bear: Encounters with the White Bear of the Western Rainforest.* Key Porter Books, Toronto. 1994.

always dangerous to people. Charlie has found bears, not previously exposed to people or to human food and garbage, that are not only not afraid of us, but that manifest a curiosity towards us that I would have to describe, from what I have seen of it in the field, as non-threatening in most cases, and in one case, as friendly.

Charlie has already come under a lot of criticism for the free-lance experiments he has been conducting. The idea that a wild bear might be friendly to human beings is very controversial – to say the least.

My own experience with bears makes me tend to err on the side of caution, while wishing Charlie well with his ground-breaking studies. I have dealt with trapped bears so enraged (or fearful) that they would have torn me to pieces if they could have reached me. I used to sometimes wonder what would happen if I met up with just such a relocated bear in the backcountry who remembered me from the other movie. But I have met with bears, both black and grizzly, who have given me the trail, then stood off a ways watching me pass. And I sometimes wonder if they had something to tell me, other than hello and goodbye. But all this is far too esoteric for human society as a whole. That society is severely divorced from its old intimacy with beasts, and capable of meeting with bears close up only through the cathode-ray tube or the silicon chip. Until there is some macro-scale shift in our sensibilities, I urge extreme caution, for the sake of the bears, if nothing else.

Charlie will still laugh at jokes about bears, but I think he is just being polite. My favourite one is about the fisherman who is treed by a grizzly. The grizzly stands up and shakes the tree as hard as it can, but the fisherman refuses to fall out. After a while, the bear suddenly turns and disappears into the forest. The fisherman waits to make sure Bruin is gone, but just as he is starting down the tree, the bear comes back, carrying a live beaver in its jaws.

"You know," Charlie growled, "maybe the bear just wanted to get acquainted."

My father gave me his old truck after my own finally gave up the ghost. "Don't worry about the temperature gauge," he said. "If it reads 'hot,' just pull over to the side and let it idle until the needle goes down."

The truck ran like a top from Aspen Valley all the way down to the Russell Ranch. It didn't boil over until Myrna and I pulled up in front of Charlie's workshop.

"It's the thermostat," I said, hopefully. Myrna's eyes tend to glaze over when I start talking car trouble. She went inside to visit with Sandi, Charlie's wife at that time. Charlie's face showed doubt, and on a mug like his, doubt shows formidably. "Always look a gift truck in the radiator," he muttered.

A couple of hours later, after replacing the thermostat as well as removing and testing the radiator (which we reinstalled with hay-wire in lieu of rusted-off brackets), the genie in the temperature gauge was dancing on the "normal" setting and I allowed myself a small smile of triumph as Charlie, ear cocked suspiciously to one side, stood scowling down at the engine.

There was a bang and a hissing noise. Charlie grinned and pointed at the problem. The oil filter had exploded! Oil streamed out like black blood all over the manifold. I had never seen such a thing in all my life. I gave Charlie a phony smile.

"Defective filter," I told him cheerfully. "Happens all the time."

Charlie looked at me hopefully, as if waiting for the punchline. "Bullshit," he said. Charlie tends to emphasize his points with a sort of fierce trembling of the chin, which reminds me of the old political warhorse John Diefenbaker. He is soft-spoken as a rule, except when he starts talking provincial wildlife policy. "This is serious," he said, "and also very w-weird."

I turned off the motor. Charlie went into his shop – which was not easy – and started rummaging around among the spare engines and boxes of rusted tractor parts. He lifted his three-wheeler up with one hand, peered under it enquiringly like a bear looking for a beetle under a stump, and dropped it again with a crash. He crawled under the wing of his cracked-up ultralight aircraft and I heard a muffled cry of triumph. Out came a greasy paw, an orange oil filter gripped in it.

"Try that."

I went back out, smeared the gasket with a flourish of oil, joined male to female ends and spun the oil filter home with a skill born of long experience in the used-car business. I topped up the oil again.

Charlie started the engine. Little flecks of orange paint suddenly stood up like guard hairs on the end of the filter. I stared at the filter with disbelief. It was swelling up like a balloon. "Turn it off," I yelled.

Charlie complied. "We'll fix it tomorrow," he promised. "Right now we have other problems."

"We do?" I asked, mystified.

Charlie nodded. "We have to put out some cows. But that's not the real problem. The real problem is my truck. It is stuck in a couple of feet of mud." He gestured vaguely at the nearby Rockies that shoot up in great water-stained walls right out of his west pastures. "Over that way," he said. "Needs the tractor to pull it out. It has a lot of weight on it."

"Uh huh. What kinda weight is that?"

"The cows."

I scratched my head. "How long have they been there?"

"Several days."

I gaped at him.

"They were dead," he explained.

"I see. So, what would we be putting them out for?"

"For the bears."

I blinked at him. "Say what?"

"For the bears."

Of course. Why didn't I think of that; so obvious.

Charlie never does things simply, however, even when putting out dead cows for bears. He had loaned the tractor battery to a neighbour who then started thinking about it as his own. But being a think-ahead-type guy himself, Charlie had parked the tractor on

an incline. All I had to do, he pantomimed, pawing the air descrip-
tively, was push the tractor down the hill. He would then pop the
clutch and start it.

I had to use a fence post as a pry bar to try and move the tractor.
It was a John Deere, but it felt like a John Elephante. I was glad I'd
enrolled in a Charles Atlas body-building course as a boy. After
some herniaeical (hernia causing) straining, I managed to get the
great beast and its large jockey rolling. It rumbled down the slope
and started with an outraged roar. The brakes didn't work, of course.
Charlie lowered the bucket of the front-end loader to the ground
and stopped with a jerk.

It being a warm May day, the women decided to accompany us.
Sandi stood up beside Charlie, and Myrna and I rode in the steel
bucket of the front-end loader, having been issued two worn red-
velvet cushions from the sofa for padding.

The tractor growled up the hill below Hawk's Nest Cabin where
author Andy Russell wrote some of his famous works. The cabin was
originally a hunting lodge built by Charlie's maternal grandfather,
Bert Rigall, a guide, outfitter, and naturalist. From the front veran-
dah, there is a view that takes in the prairies toward Cardston, the
Milk River Ridge, Chief Mountain, and the mountains and lakes at
the entrance to Waterton Lakes National Park. Standing on that
porch one time, Charlie had swept his arm around the wind-blasted
horizon and said, "It's really hard to live in this country, isn't it?
Look at it – there's nobody there." He had trembled with sheer
delight. "Isn't that w-wonderful?"

In fact there are people there: Charlie's rancher neighbours, most
of whom have cleverly placed their ranch houses in valley bottoms
to escape the fury of the Chinook wind, but the urban refugees are
beginning to move in.

The Russell kids, four sons and one daughter, were raised on
wild game. Every autumn when the aspen trees have turned to gold,
Andy Russell (he is now in his eighties) climbs up to the porch of
Hawk's Nest with his favourite deer rifle. He sits on the porch with

his German binoculars and waits for a mule-deer buck or a white tail to step out in the meadow. When the wind and the deer are in alignment, he will pick it off at ranges of 350 to 400 yards. Venison in the autumn is a kind of tonic to the countryman's soul. Someday they will do a venison study and find why this is so; then they will lock us all up as a hazard to seed munchers.

This day Charlie turned off at the ranch house below the cabin. We took an old trail down through an aspen grove, sliding sideways in the mud, the big wheels up to their hubs in slushy snow. I smelled new buds and old wet poplar leaves; I smelled the mountain perfume of young pines. I smelled tractor exhaust. In a forest pond, a chorus of ecstatic little frogs sang the praises of ice cubes and slime.

Then we came to Willow Creek, chocolate coloured with runoff. We dipped sharply down into the creek, got partway up the opposite bank, and we were stuck. Charlie said afterwards that he knew he was in trouble when the bucket went down too far and a bit of water ran over the top. The clay in that creek would be great for making pots. It filled in the tire treads and chains with a slick blue gesso. The big rear wheels were half submerged.

Ah, mud, wonderful, fertile muck. Beloved of ten-year-old kids, and despised by their mothers. Home to frogs and tiger salamanders, smacking and squelching its happy welcome to warm mammal feet, legs, and thighs. Forerunner of spring, welcome mat to rain, swallower of every living or mechanical beast that tests its placid depths.

Three things are required to get a two-wheel-drive tractor out of a mudhole. Chains, hip waders, and an eight-foot-long railroad tie, as shall be revealed. Fortunately, the nearest railroad tie was only a mile away, back at the ranch. There is no end of uses for surplus railroad ties on a ranch. "We'll drag it here with my three-wheeler," said Charlie. "After we fix the three-wheeler."

It was my turn to look doubtful. I'd rather shoot a three-wheeler than fix it any day.

We hiked back to the workshop and began overhauling the

three-wheeler, which was in need of some major adjustments. I
recall a welding torch coming into play at one point.

That day in late May felt like July under the bright sun. Later
that afternoon, dressed in hip waders, I found myself standing up to
my waist in slimy goo, doing a slow mudhole boogie to keep my
feet from getting hopelessly mired. You simply grasp the wader with
both hands at frequent intervals and pull upward with herniaeical
(hernia-friendly) effort until the foot is free. While slowly sinking
into the goo, you wrap a logging chain around both ends of the
railroad tie, then you wrestle the hundred-pound tie down under
the icewater in front of the rear tires. You grope around and find the
logging chain down there, and fasten it to the wheel hubs.

It would be too easy to provide hooks on both ends of the chain.
It is more challenging, while up to your armpits in the water, to use
haywire to secure the chain, and slippery fencing pliers to tighten
the wire. Gloves, of course, are out of the question: this is Alberta,
where men are men and women know we are silly.

All this time the engine was running, because there was no battery
to start it up again should it be stopped. The front-end loader, its
teeth biting into the ground, kept the machine from rolling backwards and crushing us.

Once set in motion, the big wheels turn slowly around until the
tie is rolled underneath and then behind them, lifting them partly
clear of the mudhole. All you have to do now is unchain the tie,
which is under a foot or so of sucking gumbo, hook one end of the
chain on a wheel, and spin the wheel to winch the tie to the surface.
Then simply reset the tie as many times as it takes to crawl out of
the mud. You could cross the Okefenokee Swamp with this technique, given world enough and time. But a philosophical attitude is
mandatory for this exercise. Humour also helps. "Charlie, why did
the Mellowrooney cross the road?"

"I'll bite," growled the bear.

"He didn't. He just said he did."

The bear laughed. By this time, the women had departed for

saner activities "back there." Ahead of us somewhere "over there" was the battered green four-wheel-drive pickup, sunk to the hubs under a ton of dead bovinity.

A few words on why one would put out dead cows for bears.

Over the years Charlie, along with some other enlightened souls in Alberta and Montana, had become increasingly fed up with the way wildlife, grizzly bears in particular, was managed in these parts. It is a concern I share. It is obvious to me, having been involved in the bear-management process once myself, that our current approaches need a second look.

There are supposed to be around 225 grizzlies in Glacier National Park, Montana, whose boundary lies a few kilometres south of the Russell place, but that figure may represent bears that are counted more than once. Waterton park wardens estimated that twenty individual grizzlies frequent the Canadian park, part of Waterton-Glacier International Peace Park. The number of black bears was anybody's guess. As I write this, there has been no budget available to study bear populations in Waterton for many years. Both species ignore all boundaries and wander freely.

Every spring, after waking from the annual hibernation, grizzly bears wander eastward out of the mountains of Waterton-Glacier International Peace Park looking for carrion on the adjacent prairies. Before Napikwan came with his cattle, bears were sure to find rich meals of winter-killed buffalo, elk, bighorn sheep, moose, and deer. This annual migration is an opportunistic habit, evolved to ensure the bears find a rich supply of energy at a time when they are gaunt after the winter's hibernation.

With the end of the buffalo and the advent of ranching, the carcasses of winter-killed cattle can become a drawing card for bears. That is where they get into trouble, because bears get impatient waiting for cows to die, and on occasion, some bears will kill cattle, particularly calves and yearlings. Particular bears can become accomplished cattle killers, especially on yearlings, which are unwary and can be run down or crippled by being stampeded into a tree. There is also a human tendency to blame bears for killing cattle that they have actually merely claimed as carrion. At one time, the ranchers had an incentive to blame bears for cattle loss because they received compensation from the provincial government: 80 percent compensation for confirmed bear kills, 50 percent for probable, and 30 percent for missing cows. This has since been discontinued.

Grizzly bears are protected as an endangered species in the U.S.A. In Canada they are subject to limited hunting seasons each year on provincial lands. But Montana's protected bears are sort of like the American movie industry: they don't recognize international boundaries. Unlike American films, American bears are not popular with Alberta ranchers. The place where they can get into the most trouble is Poll Haven, an eighty-square-kilometre tract of private and Crown-owned grazing land, much of it forested, abutting the International Boundary and Waterton Park. Formerly, these lands were part of Waterton National Park. Between 1972 and 1990, six grizzlies are known to have been killed illegally in Poll Haven and eight were destroyed by provincial wildlife officers. Some grizzlies were also relocated or destroyed in Waterton Park during the same era. An Alberta bear biologist, Brian Horesji, examined the situation. He maintained that at least seventy-seven grizzly bears from the ecosystem that includes Canadian and American lands had been killed or relocated on Canadian soil during that period. At the time, Alberta Wildlife Management Unit 300, centred on Poll Haven, led the entire province in problem-bear kills.

Horesji maintained that Glacier Park's estimated population of 225 bears was far too high because it was the American bears that were mainly dying at Poll Haven. Horesji had a solution to the problem in 1988. He wanted the government to eliminate cattle grazing on Crown pasture at Poll Haven, buy up one hundred sections of private land around Waterton at a cost of fifty million dollars, and create a grizzly-bear refuge. That idea went nowhere with the Alberta government. Instead, the forestry minister, Don Sparrow, suggested a fall grizzly hunt might be the answer to the problem.

At the time, Charlie was fed up with the slaughter of grizzlies and the arbitrary trapping and tranquilizing and dumping of bears into habitat chosen by the officials. Nobody knows how many bears starve to death in these moves, or are injured in turf wars with resident bears. Charlie knew that a Montana government biologist had embarked on a controversial experiment to deal with the spring bear problem. With the co-operation of local ranchers, the biologist began collecting carcasses in April and distributing them in Montana Wildlife Management Areas that held prime grizzly habitat.

By May 15 each year, the carcasses were the centre of bear-feeding activity. Grizzly-bear management specialist Mike Madel would later tell me that since 1988, there has been an 80 percent reduction in bear-human conflicts.

Charlie went down to Montana to see how things were done there and came back full of enthusiasm. His plan was more simple and more local. He would drag the springtime carcasses close to the Waterton Park boundary, which runs along his ranch, instead of watching the bears wandering far afield looking for them and coming to grief as a result. Once they had fattened up on the carrion, they would wander back into the mountains and start looking for green stuff and berries. A grizzly bear's diet is 80 percent plant material. Charlie was putting out the cows, hoping to save a few bears for the future that way.

Once out of the mud, the tractor snorted and puffed into high gear as we rolled slowly across the soggy meadows and through the wet aspen groves towards the mountains. The sun was hot, and its rays, I've noticed these last few years, have at these altitudes a kind of sizzle to them that is forebodingly different from earlier days I recall. ("You're getting a nice pre-cancerous glow there," is the way Myrna likes to sum up a sunburn at the fag end of the twentieth century, as she hands me the sun block. It makes me long for the good old days of the intact ozone layer.) But some black clouds off to the north were whipping up a big chill for later. Two sombre-looking moose watched us clank by for a moment and then stuck their heads back under water to discuss the bizarre sight with the muskrats. Charlie's son Anthony caught up to us on the three-wheeler, spooking up squadrons of Canada geese, which lifted from the creek, and a herd of deer from the bushes. At the next mudhole I swore I could feel the warmth of spring in the water slipping in over the tops of my waders.

Few things are heavier than a dead cow, or smugger. Smugger than an OPEC sheik, smugger than a Liberal party bagman suffocated in a pork barrel – just about the smuggest thing on earth. Not going to be eaten; you fed us all that grain and hay for nothing. Now all we have to do is lie here grinning and stinking until we fall back into the fertile muck and turn into something beautiful and free, like a golden eagle, or a grizzly bear.

Charlie thought one of us would have to walk home when the tractor sank to the hubs while trying to pull the pickup truck with the two dead cows on it. "We should have dragged that railroad tie behind us," he said.

"No need," I said eyeing a nearby stand of aspen trees. I was starting to get into the spirit of this bizarre occasion. "I'd be willing to bet there's a chainsaw underneath those dead cows."

Charlie glowered at me reflectively. "I think you're right. I forgot all about it."

His face brightened. He picked up a handy aspen log. Holding his nose, he pried upward on a dead cow, then reached in with one hand. "Ha!" He wrapped one paw around the handle and tugged at the thing, making the dead cows jiggle, and pulled it out, a battered Homelite. "Now how did you know it was under there?" he asked wonderingly as he unscrewed the gas cap and sniffed at the tank.

"It was there the last time I looked," I said, "And that was only a year ago."

"Got gas in it too. Good thing I didn't clean the box out."

"Yes." I said dryly. "You have outwitted yourself once again."

Even with a few aspen trees lashed on to our tires, it became obvious that the truck was not about to move. We compromised; we hooked a logging chain around the hocks of a dead cow instead, and dragged it off onto the ground. Then we were off at a good clip, the cow sliding along behind. We dragged them across the valley and left them on the edge of a big clearing where there was good escape cover, and where one bear could see another one coming, so it could get out of the way in case of aggression.

Then the sun blinked out, and a hard, cold wind with some snow in its teeth pelted me on my bare arms. I felt goosebumps standing up on my exposed skin as I stood beside Charlie, hanging on. I felt silly for leaving my jacket in the truck. In a few minutes, a cold spring norther enveloped us and the temperature plummeted like a stone (I learned later) from 16°C to 0°C with a severe wind-chill. We splashed across the swamp and detoured down Willow Creek to the main road. Sleet veered down and stung our faces like flying sand. We had several miles to go and my teeth were hammering as snow coated the tractor, melted on my head and ran down the back of my T-shirt.

Charlie had on a thin pair of coveralls. "How ya doing?" he asked, with his old mountain-guide-concerned-about-client voice.

"Excellent. I'm simply exhilarated."

We pulled out on the main road, with several miles to go to get back to the ranch. After ten minutes or so, a car pulled up alongside. It was Anthony's mother, Margaret, ex-wife number one. Charlie dropped the bucket and stopped us in a blaze of sparks. I hopped down to speak with Margaret. She was going up to Hawk's Nest for dinner with Charlie's sister-in-law, Valerie. "Jump in," she said.

"Maybe Charlie would like to park it and ride with us," I suggested as I got in and closed the door. "Do you think . . ."

Margaret pulled away, smiling. The windshield wipers were going strong and the heater was divine. I watched the tractor recede in the rearview mirror. "So how is Myrna doing?" she asked brightly. Margaret has a lovely smile; she beams at you.

The truck looked very forlorn as I ran by it into the house.

Inside, the mountain women had built a roaring fire; there was wassail, there was elk roast. And eventually, there was Charlie, his ruddy face lit up with delight. Knowing the cows were put out and the bears would soon be fed. "What a wonderful use for a dead cow," he said. "I don't know why we never thought of it before. God knows I've seen enough bears on enough dead cows before to realize it: just move the dead cows closer to the bears."

I called up Charlie a few days later. "How are things going with the bears?"

"Good. They have found the cows and they are really enjoying them."

"They? How many is that?"

"We've counted what looks like eight individuals. They have been having a wonderful time. They bed down in the timber and come down to feed every once in a while. They are very relaxed. Very little conflict."

"Eight bears. Eight grizzly bears?"

"Yes. Everybody is very happy. The cows are nice and ripe now, and the bears are having fun rolling in them. What have you been up to?"

"I've been putting out the seed."

"Seed? How so?"

"For the chickadees. In the bird feeder. How's my truck doing?"

"Great. It hasn't moved an inch. We're thinking of using it for a planter, you know, for flowers. Just until you come and get it."

"Uh huh. Charlie, just promise me one thing."

"Yes?"

"Promise me you won't use it as a feeder. For the bears."

"Don't worry."

But I did; I still do.

CHAPTER FOURTEEN

Rum Is No Burden

It has taken me half a lifetime to fully understand what those seasons at Lake O'Hara in Yoho National Park meant to me. At first they seemed to represent a thwarted aspiration – to be a mountain guide, to live in the mountains, trailing the guide's glory. Bernie Schiesser offered me the chance to follow that trade, offering to pay the fees for me to take the guide's test in 1970 if I would guide for him that summer at Lake O'Hara.

It was the greatest compliment he could give – but I declined, electing to sign on again with the warden service instead. Yet it was at Lake O'Hara that my true life, a completely different kind of life from what I had imagined for myself, began: it was there I first strove to open myself to the world, when time slowed down to the pace of a heartbeat, and I let the mountains live inside me as much as I lived within them. When the moon rides over Centre Peak, old voices come back to my memory. I must speak for those souls now, and for the mountains that they loved.

It was two decades ago that I last saw Lawrence Grassi, and that September, as the aspens turned to gold, I remembered the last words he'd said to me: "I give you some advice: Don't grow old; don't live as long as I have."

That was a year before he died, at the age of eighty-nine.

I had laughed uneasily. "Better to grow old than to die too young," I said.

"But if you get oldt," countered Lawrence, "and you die slowly, that isn't so good." A confirmed bachelor, Lawrence lived a reclusive life in a tumbledown miner's cabin on the edge of Canmore. Kids on dirt bikes roared through his yard at night, terrorizing him. He was alone and ailing. He had climbed countless mountains in his life, but "now," he said sardonically, "I can hardly walk onna da level."

His last advice to me was a sort of curse, I see now, not that he intended it to be. In fact he could scarcely see, through the cataracts that clouded his old eyes, how young I still was then, as he sat among the mountaineering books he could no longer read in that dusty, low-ceilinged shack heated by a coal stove, where I could not stand upright without hitting my head.

As time went on, I fought off a tendency to turn reclusive myself, steered back to reality by the urging of my gregarious mate to try and maintain old ties. Faced with a right-wing political juggernaut in Alberta, where only writers with pro-conservative views can earn an income by commenting on environmental and social issues, I found myself isolated and alone, unwilling to join the cheering section when Calgary made a national spectacle of itself by blowing up the only hospital in its downtown core – in a time of acute hospital bed shortages; not willing to join the line dancers while the seismic lines snake over the mountainsides.

My political iconoclasm built some walls between myself and some old confreres of the peaks. Rick Kunelius, long-time warden-service cohort of those days, resigned in the early nineties and became an apologist for commerce in the park.

Little does he realize, I told myself, that is where the Über-Bear makes her bed. For his part, Rick believes that wild animals are smarter than we think they are, and able to adapt to some of our intrusions. Ranger Rick and I made a few horseback trips together since then, but we tended to skirt around our differing viewpoints on conservation.

Bernie Schiesser and I had always diverged politically. Though he moved past Objectivism and began to study spiritualism, his path has tended to the right, and I wandered off into backwoods social-ism – or was that nihilism, mixed with pantheism, washed down with mysticism? Bernie has long referred to national parks as "national prisons." He is a pilot, and he took to slugging it out in the newspapers with Parks Canada on its decision to shut down the Banff airport. He was also irked when the Banff park-warden service initiated a controversial "controlled burn" program in the park, to reduce the dangerous fuel load and open up the canopy to increase the browse for ungulates like elk and deer.

Several controlled burns got out of control – now they call them "prescribed burns." As a sometime logger, Bernie felt it was ridicu-lous to burn up valuable timber, which could provide revenue for Parks Canada and work for loggers. After the wardens burned up some old-growth stands in my old patrol area on the Panther River, in a province where old growth is rapidly diminishing, I began to wonder if he didn't have a point. As a historian, however, I remem-ber how long it took the Feds to phase out the old timber limits in the parks. I can understand why park lovers have a fear and loathing of logging: their own provincial governments have set such shoddy standards in the past.

The endless controversy about the commercialization of the Bow Valley and its cost to park values and to wildlife, flaring up again and again in the national media, took on the overtones of a funeral dirge over the years. Meanwhile, we had our own wars to wage with the Earth Eaters in southwestern Alberta. Old co-conspirators in Banff told me, "You're lucky you got out when you did," but luck had nothing to do with it.

In 1996, *Canadian Geographic* sent me out with the Eastern

Slopes Grizzly Bear Study Team to find out how the bear was faring in the Banff Park of the nineties. The experience reminded me that when you leave Banff's 320 kilometres of roads behind you, there are 1,500 kilometres of hiking and riding trails and thousands of square kilometres of wild backcountry ahead of you. It is vitally important to remember, though, that 37 percent of Banff's 6,641 square kilometres consists of rock and ice where few wild things can make a living.

The bear news was not so good. Bear habitat was increasingly fragmented. Female grizzlies refused to use wildlife underpasses to cross the fenced-in sections of the Trans-Canada Highway. There were fears the population would become inbred and die out. (The fences had been installed, reluctantly but inevitably, to try and reduce the constant killing of park wildlife on the road I had dubbed the Meatmaker back in 1978.) On the plus side, bear-proof garbage containers were commonplace (after 1981) in the park and garbage was trucked to Calgary landfills for disposal starting in 1980.

Incidents requiring trapping and tranquilizing became less and less frequent after the mid-eighties, and nowadays these procedures are done only as a last resort.

Bear "overpasses" have been built at great cost to try and convince bears to go over if they won't go underneath. But where Bill Vroom believed 110 grizzlies roamed, the scientists today have pegged the number uncertainly at 55 to 80. Grizzly bears are slow breeders and the population, threatened by the loss of females during the bear wars that only wound down in the early eighties, has yet to recover.

Black bears are thought to number about 50 to 60 in Banff Park. To put that into perspective, in the summer of 1964, the town warden, Jim Robertson, dealt with 150 black bears in Banff townsite alone.

At the same time as bear populations are in decline, the population of Alberta, and of Calgary in particular, is rapidly increasing. Premier Klein and Mayor Duerr, still inspired by the nineteenth-century bigger-is-better shibboleth as the twenty-first century comes on like a jackhammer, are thrilled by the oncoming population explosion. The frequency of bear maulings is up, because more and more people are roaming through bear habitat. This is bad news for both species. Obviously, even 55 grizzly bears cannot make a living in Banff Park alone.

It is becoming more and more urgent that we abandon the outpost-resource-management mindset in western Canada. That mindset is a luxury best left for the diversion of idiots. The idea that we can manage national parklands and wildlife as if they were magically separate from surrounding lands and wildlife is patent bunkum, but politicians are very slow to act upon this old news. At the same time, industry's notion that you can bulldoze, drill, graze, clear-cut, and mine right up to the park boundary is equally irrational and goes against the public interest in supporting wildlife and wild lands, not to mention protecting the watershed for the potable water of the entire region, which is hardly ever mentioned by anyone these days.

Writers on the outdoors and other artists who love the land must continually strive to change public perception, until we finally come to view all land, not just parkland, as a sacred trust. The reason for this is, of course, painfully simple: God ain't makin' any more of it. Here endeth the lesson.

In the spring of 1998, I heard some news from old friends in Banff that shocked me. Bill Vroom was dead. The courageous cowboy-mountaineer, who had stuck his neck out a mile on a number of occasions to rescue others, had been afflicted with a serious illness and had suffered a mind-crippling depression. He had taken his own life, despite all the efforts of his wife, Maureen, to keep him in the land of the living.

Who will rescue the rescuer, so far away?

There were more than two hundred people at Bill's memorial. They shared a lot of warm memories and affectionate tributes, and some laughter at the stories told about him. Like the time a large rock came down a mountainside when he was climbing without his helmet on. The helmet was in his pack and got smacked by the rock. "Good thing I didn't have it on my head," he'd said.

There were many familiar faces, showing the marks of the years, in that hall. Among them were Rick Kunelius and Bernie Schiesser. Bernie had been a neighbour of Bill's. The slim young man had become a slim older man, still with the same disarming grin. We didn't talk park issues on this occasion: we talked about Lake O'Hara. "We should go back there," he suggested. "Have a walk around."

This notion coming from my old mountain teacher surprised and pleased me. I hadn't been back to Lake O'Hara since 1980, though I had never stopped seeing its circle of mountains in my mind's eye. And there was Kunelius, he of the wicked black moustache, the pariah of the boys in green these days, known as Ranger Rick to some and Parson Rick to others. Kunelius had branched out into the marrying business and conducted nuptial celebrations in outdoor settings. He was in demand. He had been climbing mountains every weekend to keep fit.

Slouching there in middle-aged sedentary decline, I thought of something Keith Everts told me: "If you want to get fit, you've got to go up." I remembered those words of his again, sitting on the deck among the falling leaves after Bill Vroom's memorial with an old song playing itself in my memory, about how time keeps on rushing us into the future. I told Myrna that if I kept on choosing my friends on the basis of their politics, I would soon find myself with nobody to talk to but her. She handed me the telephone. "Call those guys," she said. "Go have some fun, for Pete's sake."

I dialed Ranger Rick's number. "Let's go up Abbot's Pass, stay at the hut, and then climb Mount Victoria. Just for old time's sake."

"Sidley, that's a fabulous idea. I'll phone Schiesser, see if he wants to go with us."

Are you a male and muddled mountaineer-in-waiting, looking for a taste of youthful adventure, and do you need, for some reason, to feel even more humbled by life than you already are? Well, rest assured you can find even greater humiliation by merely lumbering into an outdoor equipment store to buy yourself a climbing harness.

Be prepared for skepticism in the eyes of the clerk, who appears to be about fourteen years old but has an amazing knowledge of climbing gear, and also the body of a professional gymnast. By the time she was twelve, she probably mastered some aid climbs harder than anything you could imagine. Who, in 1963, could have imagined sport climbing and an amazing creature like this? To her, on the other hand, you too are a freak of nature. She circles your carcass like a coyote dancing around a bull moose, while you fight your way into a harness designed for the Sugar Plum Fairy.

He looks like that Burl Ives guy Grandpa always admired, thinks this budding Lynn Hill. But she is a good sport behind that brilliant white grin: she disappears into a storeroom and emerges with a dusty box containing an extra large harness. It is purple. It's the only one they have. And you've always been a khaki and heather-green type guy, just on the cusp of actual camo in your most radical moments. You glare at it. It is trimmed with neon-yellow flashes to frighten the prudent clear of your fall line. The logo emblazoned upon it shouts ROCK EMPIRE. That's okay – you can black that out with a felt-tip pen. You're not buying this to go to a ZZ Top concert. It is a space-age creation, very high tech. If there were work horses on Mars, this is probably what they would dress them in.

I bought a few slings, passed on the helmet that wouldn't fit my head, threw in a few 'biners to rattle for old times' sake, and slunk out of the place, blushing, like a man leaving a sex shop.

I drove up to Banff, where I slalomed my way between squadrons of identical white rental cars driven by Japanese and German tourists. Direct tourism expenditures in Banff Park totalled $750 million a year in the mid-nineties. That's the engine driving development here. But the Über-Bear now charges you seventy

dollars a year for an annual park-entry pass just the same. I headed
for Eleanor's House, the bed-and-breakfast mansion run by Ranger
Rick and his spouse, Eleanor. Rick was already busy packing in
front of the garage as I got out to join him. We had brought an
impossible amount of junk to pack, and after struggling a bit, an
old warden-service curse flew to my lips unbidden – "Backpack,
daypack, stuffsack – *tabernac'*!"

"If we're thinking of things to cut out," I added, "we've both got
a mickey of rum. We could leave one behind."

"Rum is no burden!" cried Ranger Rick. "Bring it along, for the
love of God!"

I knew he was right. It's true that progress has been made in this
item of mountain medicine, for the Lambs Rum Co. now produces
it in lightweight plastic bottles, to the delight of backpackers – or it
would be a delight except that, among the nouveau cadre of the
shining path, few are those who know of its virtues. But consider
our Canadian heritage: how was it that generations of voyageurs,
pursuing the mighty beaver across this mighty land, could shoot the
rapids without a fibre of Kevlar under their chilblained buttocks,
climb the Athabasca Pass sans polypro booties, with only moccasins
on their feet, face down grizzly bears without a can of pepper spray
to hand, and endure blizzards and drenching rain sans the techno-
alchemy of Gore-Tex, wrapped only in a wool capot made from a
Hudson's Bay blanket?

It was because their nerves were anaesthetized by rum. "Har
Gaston! Lent me that belt-knife un moment s'il vous plaît. I just haf
to trim a few of dese dead toe off . . ."

Long before Canadians of every ethnic stripe were welded
together by jumper cables stretching from coast to frozen coast, we
were united by the love of glorious overproof rum, which is like
nitro to kickstart the frozen engine of the heart. Casks of the finest
Jamaica, jealously guarded by thrifty Scottish trolls like governor Sir
George Simpson, were cannily measured out when the going got
tough and the tough got thoroughly pissed off. Rum would wash

down yet another nauseating bolus of pemmican; inspire men to tote that barge, lift that bale, and strike up another chorus of that incredibly boring tune "Alouette, Gentille Alouette."

I took a look at the instant pasta meals Kunelius had planned, and tossed the rum back into my pack. It was going to be needed, and besides it was a hell of a lot cheaper than buying a Gore-Tex jacket. It's true the sun was pouring down like honey on our lady of the harbour, but on the phone, a cautious Schiesser, who is otherwise a veritable Dale Carnegie of optimism, sounded like the Leonard Cohen of weather gloom. This is a guide thing. A storm was predicted: the weather looked pretty variable. But we could start out at least, and see what happened.

The clouds looked threatening as we drove west in my venerable Multi but we kept on going and soon we were aboard the aging Lake O'Hara bus, on our way to Shangri-La once more.

As we rattled up the road to a chorus of grinding gears, Schiesser spoke enthusiastically of his plans for setting up a mountain lodge west of Golden, B.C. He sounded like he was still twenty-nine years old. But Parson Rick confided he was thinking of retiring from the stressful marrying business.

"If you're retiring, sell me your suit." I said. "After I slog up Victoria, it will probably fit."

"Thinking of going into the marrying biz?" asked Rick.

"Anything is better than freelance writing, chum. Look, there's Cathedral Mountain, where you tried to kill Peter Poole." They laughed at my glum expression.

"I always thought that would be fun," said Kunelius, ignoring my jibe. He had produced a guidebook on park wildlife.

"It has its moments," I confessed. "But over the long haul, it's probably easier to hire on driving fence posts with your forehead. Depending on how thick your skull is, you could probably retire after driving in one post. But with writing, it goes on until your brain fails or you drop dead." Disbelieving laughter greeted this rant.

"They say it's a calling, but I think it's more of an addiction." I was half in earnest. I thought of a friend who started down the writing path with me. His poems are in all the important anthologies. Scholars have written theses on how brilliant he is. Now he lives in a halfway house, permanently medicated; his reward for a life devoted to poverty and literary excellence. A slave to beauty if there ever was one. And I shivered at that shadow.

Bernie glanced out the window and said the weather looked variable.

Tim Auger had warned us off attempting the ice of Abbot Pass from Lake Louise. I was disturbed to hear how the old twilight zone had become far too dangerous in the past thirty years due simply to glacial recession. The ice grows thin, and buckles more easily passing over underlying features in the bedrock. Peter Fuhrmann had told me that instead of one bergschrund, there were now about twenty. "It's been a no-go for the last five years."

He had climbed up the Lefroy Couloir and marked out the old Swiss-guide's alternate route from Lake Louise via the plateau that stretched across Lefroy and up to the ice near the hut. Just follow the yellow band, he said, as if it were the Yellow Brick Road and not a monstrous scree wallow edged by precipices. We said to hell with it. We'd settle for the old slog up the rock pile from Lake Oesa.

The bus let us off at Sargent's Point, into air redolent with sun-warmed spruce sap and mossy lake-edge. I walked slowly down to the water in front of the cabin, where I had stood so many times before watching mountaineers at play high up on the surrounding peaks. The mountains greeted me once more in their spellbound circle. They had put on their autumn necklace of golden larches that stretches around the valleys at the timberline. The light up there among them was the light of Van Gogh's *Sunflowers*. There was the familiar roof line of the lodge, and the small cabins among the trees along the shore. Woodsmoke and laughter over yonder. And the clink of martini glasses later. Smiling, we shouldered the backpacks with the usual cracks about who had the heaviest one, and set off, crossing the footbridge over the brook below the cabin, quickly settling on a pace, without discussing it, that worked for all three of us. We would maintain it all the way to the hut.

To the south, Hungabee, the old shape-changer, leaned back against the sky up there at 3,490 metres and basked in the noon-hour light. Bernie claims he has seen several UFOs over Hungabee in his years guiding at O'Hara. "It's a very spiritual place, O'Hara," he said mysteriously. I traced the route to the summit with my eyes, remembering the undercut gullies near the top, some with running water in them. Remembered how Tim Auger finally overcame one of them and I followed him up on the sloping holds, the slippery facets of black rock near the summit like black glass underfoot: Tim calls it "chip shale." On the tiny summit itself we lounged on either side of the cairn and passed the tobacco offering – two boys smoking their peace pipes with the Chieftain in the clouds. We were blessed.

In those days, Tim recalled, the peak was only climbed success-fully about once every two years.

I thought of how Don Vockeroth had watched Ernest Feuz lead a party to its summit a couple of years before us. Vockeroth had stood on the shore and watched Ernest, seventy-six years old, lead-ing on this challenging peak he had first climbed in 1936, when he traversed the massif with Miss Georgia Englehard. He met with the old boy later as he returned to the lodge. Don checked his watch and said "Ernest, do you realize that you completed the climb in the exact same time you did in '36?"

Ernest, leaning on his long ice axe, smiled up at the tall young guide. "Well you see, Donnie, that's the whole point. Once you find a pace that works for you, it will work for your whole life." That was a year or so before Ernest died, aged seventy-seven. His older brother Edward lasted to the age of ninety-six.

We passed the Huber-Wiwaxy trailhead, where I had last seen Edward Feuz at Lake O'Hara back in the sixties. He had stopped to admire the catch of trout on my fish chain. He was leading several elderly women who turned off and headed up the trail. Up to that

point, I had never seen a group of silver-haired grandmas, glowing
with health, marching up a mountain in lock step like a squad of
mountain troops.

"Good morning Mr. Feuz," I'd greeted him. "Off for a morning
constitutional?"

"Oh ve will do a bit more than that," rasped the old man, his
eyes twinkling. "Ve go up *Wiwaxy* and have a little *picnic.*"

I smiled at this yarn, thinking it hard to credit. There was no
trail to that summit, and it was a seven-hundred-metre scramble
from the lake, and very steep. "These girls," he said, motioning with
his ice axe, "haf been climbing with me since they vas *kids.* They got
some good vine, some good cheese and sausage. Ve will have a grand
time on ze *peak.*"

I grinned at the memory of that as I followed along behind Rick.

For I recalled how later that day, scraping a boat on the jetty, I'd
heard rocks rattling down and glassed the peak, expecting to see
mountain goats.

There were goats alright: the old goat, sending me smoke signals
with his pipe and the aged nannies gathered around him, admiring
the view from the col. There must be close to three hundred years
of living among those four old coots up there, I'd thought, and I
shook my head, amazed. And damned if one of them didn't have
enough wind left over, after reaching the summit a bit later, to start
yodelling, probably after imbibing a litre or so of French wine. By
God, I thought, this mountain climbing has got to be a healthy
sport. And sexy too.

This day with Rick and Bernie, I felt like a teenager by compar-
ison to Edward's example. But the scree slope above Oesa was worse
than ever – more loose boulders ready to flip over on your ankles,
less loose shale but enough small stuff to get inside your boots. We
trudged our way to the top by early afternoon. Clouds bellied and
swirled through the pass and a cold wind was blowing up from the
Death Trap. We found the hut with surprises in store. Young Danny
Verrall, hut coordinator for the Alpine Club, had added something

to it that summer that it had lacked for seventy-six years: a front deck, a place where you could sit in the sun, or tie on your climbing ropes. The stone had been repointed all around and the shingles were in great shape. The infamous outhouse was gone, replaced by a massive new meta-crapper mounted on a platform. You ascended regally upwards to gain this throne room in the clouds above the hut. Underneath was an enclosed holding area with barrels to collect waste, which were hauled out by helicopter when full, but muscled out first by whoever happened to be at the hut, according to the hut rules. Sort of the opposite of winning a lottery. Gone forever (I hope) are the days when you might arrive at the hut to find that a pack rat had transported the contents of the outhouse, one turd at a time, and stashed them thoughtfully in a huge pile in the attic for recycling through the long winter nights. Under the deck was a massive firewood supply, flown in by chopper when the throne room was serviced. What luxury!

In the hut we found George Field and his assistant, who were public-safety leaders for Kananaskis country, with two young park rangers who were there on training exercises. A couple of overnight backpackers were getting ready to leave. The Canadian Alpine Club had done wonders with the interior also.

The spacious attic held a raised sleeping platform covered in foamies. The kitchen counters were clad with galvanized metal to prevent fires. A modern wood heater graced the common room. The walls were insulated and painted white for brightness, and most startling was a solar-powered radio-phone connecting with the Lake Louise wardens. The days of abuse and neglect and running like hell for miles to get help for accident victims were over. The old guides would have been very pleased.

Field and company, being dead keen, soon roped up on the deck and cramponed off to practise crevasse rescues on the ice below Lefroy. Ranger Rick and I went outside and abused our health with a couple of quality Dutch cigars while Schiesser entertained the backpackers with mountain lore. The way up Lefroy (3,436 metres) was blue ice studded with fallen rock. Impossible that Arnie Shives and I had glissaded down two-thirds of that west-face route in a matter of minutes. I had never seen that big ramp in such poor condition for climbing. Most parties that season had been turned back by rock fall. Now I knew what Grassi meant when he told me I was lucky to have such an easy time on Lefroy.

What a storied place it was, that old pile. That night, after a lovely dinner of Rick's specialty – satay-flavoured pasta-glue – we got out the rum, which loosens the tongues of memory. Peter Fuhrmann features in many anecdotes about the place, he was such a frequent visitor. The three of us had heard a number of his stories over the years. I remembered one from Grassi's day: a party of climbers had an accident below the hut; one of them was killed in a crevasse fall. His friends managed to haul his body out of the hole. They dragged him up to the hut and laid him out in a sleeping bag on the floor. Then they hurried down the Lake O'Hara side to contact the rescue team. (Grassi had told me it took a party of eight wardens, travelling sans helicopter, to retrieve the body.)

Fuhrmann and his friend Bob Geber, a fellow mountain guide, arrived at the hut later that evening, unaware of the accident. They assumed the sleeping rooms must be full and this guy on the floor had no other place to bed down. They couldn't avoid making some noise, preparing supper. Fuhrmann thought the guy was probably lying there awake. There was soup left over and rather than throw it away, Fuhrmann bent down to ask the still figure if he would like some. That's when he discovered the sleeper was not breathing and they had been dining with a dead man.

The wind whistled over the roof of the hut and somebody put another log in the stove. Schiesser went outside to check the weather. He said it looked variable and would probably continue variable tomorrow.

Field's crew had been kept awake the previous night by something running through the hut and knocking stuff off the shelves. There was no telltale urine or crap that would vouchsafe a pack rat in residence. "Place is probably haunted," suggested one of the rangers, half jokingly. I went on relentlessly with my ripping yarns, like ancient mariners will.

Recalling how in the olden days, the strangest people used to wander up the ice and follow the tracks of climbers, not having a clue where they were headed. I intercepted a few of them who were dressed only in hiking shorts and running shoes, and convinced them to turn around. Fuhrmann had told me how he was here one cold night when he was startled by a sudden loud knocking on the door. He threw it open. There stood an odd sight: a man clad in a dark business suit, his beard full of frost, who enquired in a plummy English accent: "I say, is it too late to get a cup of tea in this place?"

Kunelius recharged our glasses, and we rambled on.

Once Fuhrmann had taken a client up the North Peak of Victoria via the pass. They descended through the Death Trap, noticing some strange tracks in the snow as they went. They stopped at the Plain of Six Glaciers teahouse. Peter had told me, "There were two little girls there, about fourteen years of age. Just dressed in shorts and tennis shoes, and little tops. They said, 'Where did you come from today?'"

"We climbed the North Peak of Victoria," said Peter. "How about you?"

"Oh, we went up to the other teahouse and then came back here," came the reply. "We had tea up there and they didn't even charge us for it."

They had come tripping up through the Death Trap, those two little lambs, following Fuhrmann's tracks in the snow until they got to the hut. Somebody was at the hut when they arrived, brewing up some tea, and offered them a cup – standard mountain hospitality. So they thought it must be a second teahouse.

Field et al. grinned at these fables. Field was old enough to believe them but the young rangers, I think, found it hard to credit that somebody could wander up that mini-Khumbu ice fall wearing halter tops and running shoes.

You had to be there, I guess. It never occurred to me back then that the route would be become nigh-on impassable in my own lifetime.

Before we went to bed, Rick and I improvised a ghost trap, using the mop pail with a piece of wire across the top, the wire piercing an empty can which revolved on the wire if touched, the outside of said can baited with peanut butter, which ghosts are fond of. It is easy for a ghost to digest, and they have no allergies in the other world. A piece of kindling leaned against the pail for an access ramp.

That night, we rolled into our sleeping bags not knowing what chances the morning would bring. A certain somebody was snoring, and though I had earplugs, they were not heavy-duty enough. A couple of hours crawled by while I tossed back and forth, wishing I had brought along a mallet and a large cork – or perhaps some spare strips of Velcro. I had just drifted off when something ran by my head with amazing speed and tore down the ladder into the common room. Whatever it was felt as heavy as a sheep running by my face like that.

There came a noise from the kitchen down below, like a boxer working out on a speed bag with both fists. This was our poltergeist spinning the can on the wire at high speed. The noise was followed by a loud crash that made some sleepers startle with whines and snorts of protest. The noise continued, as the ghost beat hell out of the bucket, then bounded in and out of the cooking pots under the counters. I heard it rattle across the floor and go scratching up the wall then through the panel overhead, back and forth several times at warp speed. Then came a sudden and complete silence. A poltergeist gets hungry at night at these altitudes and often needs a midnight snack, I told myself. The stertorous sleeper waited craftily for five minutes. Just as I was drifting off, he struck: KK-CHAK-K-K!!

I put my head-lamp on and crept down the ladder. The mop pail, complete with mop, had been knocked over and rolled across the floor. A few pots had been overturned. I tidied things up, noting the poltergeist had left no telltale scat behind after cleaning up the peanut butter.

I put on some footgear and my anorak, went outside, and lit up another cigar. It was cold and breezy. A few snowflakes drifted down in my head-lamp beam, and snirt (snow mixed with dirt) was blowing up from Lake Oesa.

The waning moon duelled with the clouds, and the ice on Lefroy gleamed wickedly in the changeable light. I switched off the lamp and, lit only by the cigar end, floated up behind the hut like a sprite myself as I stared down into the Death Trap, to the terrible shadows where the moonlight does not go. It looked bottomless, a drain where all life is funnelled down through ice into the furnace under the crust, like something imagined by Dante as the entrance to the final pit. Implacable, it denied my memory of those traverses I once made. Above me, the ridge of Victoria walked the gigantic sky, awash in stars, opposing all desire to ascend. This cold and restless night made me wish I was home in bed with the queen of my domestic bliss. There is something relentlessly Nietzschean about this pursuit of mountains. It was he who wrote: "The secret of the greatest fruitfulness and the greatest enjoyment of existence is: to live dangerously." I have never seriously disbelieved that, though on the other hand, Al Purdy, a poet whom I valued above Nietzsche, once said to me (this was in my younger days), "Unlike you, I no longer think of myself in heroic terms." I had been shocked at the comment, not because I actually thought that way, but because I had somehow given him that impression. On that note of sobering remembrance, I butted out the cigar and wandered back to bed.

In the morning, our indefatigable cook, Rick, presented us with hot porridge-glue and hot chocolate to fortify us for the climb. Schiesser and I scoffed this swill down, praising its viscosity and caloric potency.

The attack of the alpine poltergeist was discussed. There were three camps on this. One: Pack rat. Two: Pine marten delivered by air mail in sling-load of firewood. Three: Paranormal hell-kitty. I paid lip service to number two but secretly plumped for number three. "You should have filled the bucket half full with water," I told Kunelius, "like you do trapping mice."

"Why? Does it need to have a bath?"

While we digressed over the afreet, canny George Field had his team suited up to sneak up the route ahead of us. But age before beauty is the rule. We donned our boots and jackets and went outside to rope up. There was a bit of fresh snow higher up, and the clouds were in retreat. Bernie stared up towards the ridge, his nose wrinkling, smelling the air.

"Probably some verglas up there," he said. "But the sun will melt it."

We set off on shortened rope, carrying a few coils in hand, ice axes strapped on the packs. Up the old highway bestrewn with cairns, then switchbacking over to the southeast ridge, where I stuck myself on top of a pinnacle for a long moment like a crow goosed by a fence picket, staring down the abyss to Lake Oesa. Below me also was the roof of the hut – a helicopter view. If I fell off here it would be right through the roof of the crapper.

Field et al. are close to hand, determined to eat my lunch, and I flounder upwards, trying not to kill anybody with dislodged stones. The ridge requires snippy traverses from one face, to the other, to round buttresses, while other mini-walls are attacked directly. I've always liked this puttering and pottering up a mountain's nose, but Schiesser keeps gazing longingly out onto the southeast face, causing me to eyebrow-raise my worry. "Can you believe this," he says. "That whole thing was always covered with snow and ice at one time, now the rocks are completely exposed. When you think of it," he added, grinning and blinking his eyes at the wonder of it all, "it would be just like doing a brand new ascent out there."

Oh oh, I think. Don't say it. Surely caution must prevail, after all these years. But of course it doesn't, because although the mountain is changing, Bernie is the same old Zarathustra of the adrenalin rush that he always was. I can almost parrot the words right along with him as I stare glumly down at the quartzite rubble at our feet: *Why don't we wander up . . .* "Why don't we wander up that face and see how it goes?" he suggests. "It looks a bit more interesting than this."

"Okay," says Rick, brightly.

Oy veh, say I to myself, though I am not even Jewish. But that terrain out there has an Old Testament kind of look to it and "okay" won't come to my lips.

"Whaddaya think, Sid?"

"Oh yes, it looks very interesting."

So we traversed eastward across a down-sloping bit of a ledge, coated with verglas, right under the path of an isolated patch of ice that has not yet got the news that its days are done, leaving Field et al. staring after us, wondering what's up.

I know what you're thinking, George. If one of those three old bastards buys a rock hit out there – Jeez, that would be awful, but – what an opportunity to practise emergency first aid and evacuation with improvised rope stretcher!

And of course I didn't really have a clue what Mr. Field was thinking. But, sure enough, here he came anyway, his charges close behind, abandoning the ridge for more interesting quarry.

Meanwhile, last to cross a shallow gully below the ice, I smelled something coming down from above before I heard its telltale rattle, shouted "Rock!" and dodged behind a boulder that was only half as big as me. A blur of something big whiffled by and hit with a crash just below us. Across the gulley, Bernie coolly watched it come down, before stepping to one side. "We should stay closer together," he suggested, politely.

Bernie moved up the cliffs as Rick hauled in rope, and I stepped quickly across the slippery slope to join him. After a while, Bernie got fed up with the loose rocks in the gullies, sighted a direct line up a series of buttresses bottomed by ledges, the steepest rock he could find, and we started climbing up from one belay to the next, still on the short rope, constantly on guard against kicking down loose rock, kicking some down anyway. Field and company turned up-mountain, content to parallel us and avoid our cast-offs. Soon they had their own cannonade booming down.

What a junk pile! I watched stones leap out and bounce all the way down to the entrance of the Death Trap, to the ice humpbacked and slashed by crevasses. Once, this route was covered with snow underlain with ice, marked only by the tips of those buttresses. Now it was naked.

With an eerie tremor that shook me head-to-toe I realized this was where the Mexicans had fallen, though the last trace of them had melted from these rocks and washed down to the glacier long ago. Only once did my knees betray me, jackhammering on some slippery toeholds, as I pictured the climbers flying down towards me, tangled in the ropes.

I thought, I'm going to come off, but I can stop myself on the ledge. But the rope went tight as one foot let go. Rick peered down at me under his helmet brim, the rope belayed around his shoulder, serious but vaguely amused. I remembered that look from when we lowered him off the top of Mount Yamnuska on the cable, to pick up a stranded couple from the Red Shirt Route, so many moons ago. "Stay with us, Sidney," he urged. Up above I could see Bernie staring down. I was twenty-one when I first went climbing with Bernie, and he was twenty-nine but one of those guys who always looked older than his age.

He looks good up there, but he looks different and I realize it's because he is sixty-one years old. He said he has climbed this mountain over twenty-five times. And today, on a whim, he has decided to pioneer a new variation. I swarm up past Rick's boots and stand up again. Yes; one frame of time at a time would be timely.

At last we traversed left up to the ridge, and after less than two hours of climbing, sometimes on pleasing pitches but mostly not, we were sitting on top of South Peak, gulping down water and admiring a view all the way west to the Goodsir Towers. It was a view of endless, higher mountains to keep our little hike in perspective. There was lots more out there for us to do, should the urge strike us again.

We wandered on and descended to the Sickle after lunch. There was the Centre Peak of Victoria perhaps another hour away. The Great Divide fell down the ice to the green water of Lake Louise, fell down through a portal in the rock to the robin's-egg-blue water of O'Hara. I could see a place at the far end of the Sickle where Walter Perren used to perch and urge his troops, "Stand up, boys, you won't hit your heads."

We pondered the Sickle for a few moments, staring towards Centre Peak in the distance. I was still savouring the taste of South Peak. Bernie was happy to go, or to stay. None of us felt a biting urge to continue. "One of the things I like about being grown up," I said, "is not feeling the need any more to prove anything. Besides, I already know I can climb Centre Peak."

"Been there, done that," said Rick.

"Which doesn't mean we won't feel like climbing Centre Peak next time," I added.

Bernie grinned his agreement. We climbed up to a sun trap between the topmost edge of the glacier and the ridge and settled down on the rocks to rest and soak up the heat, lazy as lizards and content at 3,310 metres above the sea.

"What a privilege it is to be here," said Bernie, fervently, speaking for all of us; it was a kind of prayer.

I know the mountain doesn't love us, but we can love it, anyway. That's what we do. That's the best thing we do, the only thing that we are here for. The thing that redeems us. The thing we have to keep striving for.

It was early in the evening, the coolness softening my sun-chafed face, when I dropped my pack at the log cabin called Le Relais, a combination teahouse and information hut across from the warden's cabin. Rick said he would have the beer chilled in the creek when I joined them up at the Alpine Club meadows. I walked over to see the lodge once more, strolled around the path that I had once helped to maintain with wheelbarrow loads of gravel, stood on the jetty that I had helped to build with stones hauled by barrow from a rock slide. A faded legend was painted on a boulder there.

"RCSCC Undaunted," the name of my old cadet corps. I wondered if it meant anything now to anyone but myself. Austin Ford had sold his interests here many years ago.

I wandered back up to the lodge, to the main door. But a sign there said day visitors were welcome from 9:30 A.M. to 3:00 P.M. A young guy was working around the grounds with a rake and gave me a suspicious look. I remember looking at "daytimers" like that myself before Grassi showed me how little you can learn about somebody based on appearance. I had been glad to work at the lodge those long-ago summers and I was glad to not work there again. I was glad I looked like a guy who wouldn't pay hundreds of dollars for a place to lay his head even if he could afford to. So I strolled back over to where my soul felt welcome, at Sargent's Point.

The warden cabin was locked up. Allan Knowles, the summer warden for twenty-one summers, was off that summer on sick leave. He was over sixty-five years old, and his hard-working feet had finally given out on him.

I remembered watching the cabin builders working on this place; the fit of the logs was a testament to an old Canadian craft. I pictured again the smaller, original version of that cabin, to me every bit as fitting to the scene. When they first gave me the key to Grassi's cabin on Sargent's Point I took up residence at the foot of the sublime, and I have dwelt there ever since.

Most mornings I would walk barefoot a few yards down the path to this pool on Cataract Brook, below the log footbridge of the lakeshore trail. I had the magic wand of the fly rod to hand. I would wade carefully in past the willow boughs to where the cutthroat waited to see which fly I would drift down over the riffle to the pool just before dawn. I couldn't believe they were paying me to live in paradise, and I wondered which god put the taste of new fir needles and willow buds into the mists of morning, here at the foot of Grassi Ridge.

So now take these hot boots off, whitened and scarred by the screes of Abbot Pass and Mount Victoria, the cast-off detritus of old ocean floors.

And wade in, wade in gratefully again, going out to greet the fishes one more time, the melt of a glacier shouting the blood alive in your tired feet. And now I am fully in mid-stream, at least I hope I am, with half a lifetime left me, I pray.

While yellow willow leaves drift by, faces float up to greet me in the glimmering water: faces young and old; faces of the dead and of the living – an epiphany in every countenance, held in the pool of memory. For they go out beyond me; they live in more than one man's mountains and are at home in people I know and in people I may never meet, limned by the light they have bestowed. And there is my own face last of all.

Nor am I more the weathered Narcissus than that white-bearded goat on Wiwaxy's ledges, staring down from its mountain into the looking-glass water, watching itself growing older. It doesn't know that it will die someday, or if it likes what it sees.

But I know.

And I do.

A Simplified Glossary of Mountaineering Terms

Arête   A narrow ridge between cirques.

Belay   To stop a falling climber by means of friction, applied by the belayer's braking hand and body, to the climbing rope passed around the belayer's hips. See also *Carabiner*.

Bergschrund   A large lateral crevasse that forms near where a glacier joins the headwall of its cirque.

Bowline hitch or *bowline knot*   A knot, of nautical origin, attaching a climber to one end of the climbing rope; a tie-in method used in pioneering days. The knot itself is still used to tie into a climbing harness.

Buttress   A towerlike projection abutting a mountain face.

Cagoule   A sheet of waterproof material, complete with hood, that fits over a person carrying a pack.

Carabiner   A snap link made of metal alloy, clipped to pitons or other climbing aids; the climbing rope is threaded through it to gain mechanical advantage for the belayer should the leader fall. Some people use it to hook tow ropes to foundered Jeeps. Do not climb with these people.

Cirque   A concavity in a mountain face, ground out by a glacier and exposed over time as the glacier retreats.

Crampons   A set of metal spikes strapped or clipped to climbing boots to grip on ice.

Crevasse   A hole in a glacier surface, sometimes very deep, formed by the down-slope movement of the ice mass over time. May be covered wholly or in part by snow forming a snow-bridge, which can break under a climber's weight.

Col   A low point between peaks, sometimes forming a pass between valleys.

Cornice   A large windrow of snow that forms on the lee side of a mountain ridge, overhanging the face of the mountain.

Cosmic humour See examples under *Cornice, Crevasse, Couloir, Scree,* and *Talus*

Couloir   A gully in a mountainside, which may contain running water or ice. It forms a natural conduit for climbers going up and for rocks and snow on their way down.

Direttissima The direct line up a mountain face. "Dire" is the operative syllable of this Italian word.

Direct aid   The old definition: tension or pull upon the rope, applied by the belayer, to help move the leader upward when the rope is threaded through carabiners placed above the level of the leader's waist.

Face   An expanse of mountain side of a particular aspect, such as north face, east face, etc.

Graupel	A kind of sleet, composed of small but very hard granules of ice.
Headwall	That part of a glacial cirque that is ice-free and rises above the glacier.
Kruppelholz	This German word means "crippled wood" and refers to dwarf trees, their growth retarded by climatic factors so that they tend to grow along the ground rather than vertically.
Leader protection	Pitons, slings, or more modern aids placed in rock or ice by the leader as he ascends, the rope being clipped to them by means of carabiners, to give the belayer mechanical advantage in arresting a fall.
Lowering station	A belay position from which a climber can lower a person with the rope.
Objective hazards	Hazards offered by the mountain as a supplement to the "subjective hazards" people carry in their heads. See *Cosmic humour,* above.
Packboard	A frame of metal or wood complete with shoulder straps, used by people to haul loads that should be hauled by mules.
Pitch	A portion of a climb, its length dictated by the belay stances (positions) available and the length of the rope available.
Piton	A metal spike driven into rock or ice with a piton hammer and fitted with an eye to take a carabiner. Makes a musical "ping" when driven into a safe crack in the rock and also when pulled out of a bad crack during a fall.
Prusik knot	A sliding knot formed in a loop of thin (i.e. 7 mm.) climbing rope (the prusik sling) when wrapped around a thicker climbing rope (i.e. 9 mm. or 11 mm.). It grips the climbing rope when weight is

placed on it, and can be slid up or down the rope when weight is removed. *Prusiking* means ascending the rope using prusik slings as stirrups for the feet.

Rappel,   To lower oneself by a controlled slide down a
rappelling   climbing rope, cleverly stopping before the end of the rope is reached. The phrase "he rapped down the cliff" has nothing to do with rap music.

Standard route   On mountains, usually the line of first ascent and descent; often it is the easiest or most obvious line, or "natural line."

Scree   Rock fragments loosely piled at the bottom of a mountain face, often forming a steep slope. Invites the unwary to run or slide (glissade) down it at great speed, only to painfully trip over a hidden rock band or go whoops over a surprise cliff. Forms a fan-shaped deposit at the bottom of couloirs and on the inside of climbing boots.

Split-rope   Used to evacuate an injured climber by means of a
carry   rescue seat, improvised out of climbing rope and protected by a belayer. Invented by Anonymous, who also invented the packboard.

Slings   Come in various lengths, and are made of nylon webbing or thinner climbing rope. The various uses include prusiking (now replaced by jumaring, but never mind), connecting a carabiner to a piton or other aid, and forming improvised chest harnesses or rappel seats. Also handy for tying a boot sole back on when one has been struck by lightning and forgotten to pack a sewing machine.

Talus   A deposit of larger fallen rock accumulating at the base of a scree slope. A good place to look for mountain-goat skulls.